Mission Possible
A Daily Devotional

Mission Possible
A Daily
Devotional

✝ ✝ ✝

365 Days of Inspiration for
Pursuing Your God-Given Purpose

TIM TEBOW
with A. J. Gregory

WATERBROOK

Introduction

D o you struggle with anxiety about your purpose? Are you trying to extract the meaning behind life's unavoidable responsibilities and visions of a greater future that you're striving hard to manifest? Do you ask yourself questions like these?

- *Is there more to life than _____?*
- *What difference can I make?*
- *I'm bored at work. I need to do something that is truly fulfilling, but what?*

If so (and I think we all struggle with this at some point), there's good news: The purpose of your life is a lot simpler than you may imagine. Ultimately, for believers of Jesus Christ, it is to know God and make Him known. And through that fundamental directive, we love and serve Him and others.

Maybe you've picked up this book ready to launch a new year with ambitious goals, maybe some nervous anticipation. Or maybe it's spring and you're looking to refresh your morning quiet time. Or maybe it's a "random" time of year but you know it's time to make real, positive change. No matter when or how, you're holding this book in your hand right now because you want to make your life count! And I'm so glad to be here with you for the next 365 days.

Whatever your time with God looks like, I want you to approach these special moments with intention and expectation. Yes, God has a purpose for you. And yes, He wants to use you within His great plan for humanity. Take your time ingesting these words. Don't rush—I know very well the temptation to do so. Give yourself a chance to gain some spiritual training by hearing God speak to your heart.

A mission-possible life is marked with adventure and sealed with significance. There are moments of immense joy. But a mission-possible life can also feel like sprinting through knee-high mud.

You're going to get sore. You'll get tired. You will have to learn to depend on God for resources, energy, and courage. You will feel depleted at times. But through it all, you'll also reignite a greater purpose in every day that will leave you with more meaning and fulfillment than you have ever known.

This devotional revolves around what a mission-possible life means and what it takes to live it. You'll learn truths like the fact that *surrender* is not a dirty word. You'll get an in-depth look into the character of God. You'll better appreciate the rewards of sacrifice, and so much more.

You'll also have a chance to hear from some special people in my life, people we've served through the Tim Tebow Foundation (TTF) who have graciously offered to share words of comfort, hope, and challenge through their perspective of living mission possible.

In addition to multiple themed devotionals, twice a month you'll read through a prayer I have written for you that is taken from a mix of different passages in Scripture. To get the most out of the prayer, look up these verses in the translation of your choice and spend time meditating on them.

What I call mission essentials also appear approximately quarterly. These devotionals target timeless truths to keep you encouraged, anchored, and focused on God as you continue to live mission possible.

Be sure to keep a prayer journal or notebook handy so that at the end of each devotional, you can jot down answers to the reflection questions and any thoughts you may have. Or consider doing this in the margins of the devotional, if you prefer.

I believe that as you learn more about God and yourself, your life will spark great changes. Let's start making each day count, together.

Mission Possible
A Daily Devotional

A Prayer for Newness

+

Dear God,

Thank You for being the Maker of all things new. As a believer who trusts in Jesus, I affirm that the old has gone and the new is here. I am a new creation. Today is a new day.

Help me to make the right decisions and say goodbye to the former things, like bad habits, addictions, and negative attitudes. Help me in each day to become more aware of whose I am. Teach me to reflect Your image and not mimic the patterns of this world. Transform my mind so I will grow in Your wisdom and discernment and discover what Your plan is for my life.

When I get overwhelmed by doubt or insecurity, remind me that in You I am a masterpiece—that even before I was in my mother's womb, You created me to do good works in Your name. I pray those things come to pass in their right time.

As I begin to grow and learn through these devotionals, open my spiritual eyes and ears to recognize the hope of Your calling and to value what's most important. Thank You for leading and guiding me.

In Jesus's name I pray. Amen.

Based on: 2 Corinthians 5:17; Isaiah 43:18–19; Romans 12:2; Ephesians 2:10; 1:18

The Greatest Trade

✝

If anyone is in Christ, this person is a new creation;
the old things passed away; behold, new things have come.

2 Corinthians 5:17

In 1975, in what is arguably one of the worst trades in sports history, the Milwaukee Bucks traded Kareem Abdul-Jabbar to the Los Angeles Lakers. The Bucks got four players in return, none matching the caliber of talent Abdul-Jabbar possessed. He would go on to make history with the Lakers, winning five championship titles and a record *six* MVPs. This story makes me grateful for being on the receiving end of the greatest trade in the history of the world: God exchanging the sin of humanity for the righteousness of Christ.

Because of His trade, we go from old to new. From dead to alive. Darkness to light. Bondage to freedom. Separation to united with Christ. Lost to found. In debt to paid for. We don't have to earn or work for salvation. We definitely don't deserve it. Jesus paid the price for us. It cost Him everything. It was also His mission.

When we accept Jesus, we are viewed as righteous. We are made right with God, and we experience the joy of a new, purpose-filled life. So live out of that joy. Celebrate this new life you have because you have been traded to the greatest team of all: the family of God.

How does being reminded
that you are part of the greatest trade of all
encourage you to live out your purpose?

You Are a Divine Work of Art

+

We are His workmanship, created in Christ Jesus for good works,
which God prepared beforehand so that we would walk in them.

Ephesians 2:10

Many people spend their lives wondering if they're normal (or wanting to be), hoping to fit in. Maybe you've experienced this. Maybe, to feel a sense of belonging, you wore the same brands or listened to the same music as everyone else. It's funny how hard we try to be something we're not.

Trying to fit in is a solid strategy for living an average life. But God didn't call you to be average. He didn't make you the same as everyone else. When the apostle Paul called us God's workmanship, he used the Greek word *poiema*, which means "making," in the biggest, most creative sense of the word. A good translation might be "the works of God as creator."[1] Some translations use "masterpiece" instead of "workmanship." You are a divine work of art.

You are one of one, created in love, for love, and by Love.

When you start to embrace and even celebrate how God made you, you can begin to do extraordinary things. When you accept your divine image and see yourself as God sees you, the stress and anxiety of comparison will fade away. Be free to be who God says you are. You matter too much to God to be just like everyone else.

What does it mean to be an image bearer of God?
How does that make you see other people as valuable?

God Is Looking for You

+

The eyes of the Lord roam throughout the earth, so that
He may strongly support those whose heart is completely His.

2 Chronicles 16:9

God longs to help you create and live a mission-possible life. But we all must realize it is *only* through Him that this is possible.

It's important to understand the context of the above passage. The words were spoken by the seer Hanani to King Asa of Judah, the southern kingdom of Israel. King Asa had once relied on God for deliverance from a formidable enemy. God had come through and proved His faithfulness. For the next thirty-five years, King Asa enjoyed a peaceful reign. However, when Baasha, the king of the northern kingdom of Israel, threatened to invade Judah, King Asa's dependence on God shattered. Instead of seeking divine help as he had done in the past, King Asa sought the aid of a foreign country. He was admonished by Hanani, who reminded him that God looks for loyalty and devotion—for men and women who wholeheartedly seek Him.

It seems much easier at times to depend on self-sufficiency rather than an invisible God. Yet God is searching for you. He is looking for the heart that longs for Him—that desires to know, depend on, and be committed to Him. As His eyes roam the earth, will they land on you?

What is holding you back from being all in
and letting God help you live mission possible?

Aim for Significance

✝

*What good will it do a person if he gains the whole world,
but forfeits his soul?*

Matthew 16:26

I believe that one of the greatest tragedies would be to reach the end of one's life and look back and say, "I was successful in things that did not matter." I want you to be successful, but more than anything, I want you to be *significant*. And when you live for Jesus and you love people, you're going to have a life of eternal significance, no matter how insignificant your life looks on the outside.

I like to think of success in material ways, but significance is harder for us to grasp. Success is focused on self—for example, becoming an entrepreneur, reaching certain milestones, or just excelling in one's occupation. Significance has an outward reach; when we strive for eternal significance, we become compelled to share and give back. When we succeed, we influence our own lives; when we are significant, we influence others.

To transcend from individual success to lasting significance, you must find a need and use your gifts to meet it.

What have you been given? Are you using your gifts to influence what really matters?

To be truly successful, aim for significance.

***How can you shift your idea of success into a more
meaningful way of making your life count?***

Willingness Is What Is Required

+

If you are willing and obedient,
You will eat the best of the land.

Isaiah 1:19

A mission-possible life is not about our ability; it's about being willing. When Moses was *eighty years old,* he was still working as a shepherd for his father-in-law. We're not sure what his retirement plan was at that point, but it sure doesn't seem like the career plan a man who had been raised in a royal court would appreciate. However, everything changed when God spoke to him through a burning bush. Moses received instructions to return to Egypt, the place from which he had fled forty years earlier, and lead the nation of Israel out of captivity. Moses hardly seemed the man for the job. He told God this by listing five excuses why God must have gotten His wires crossed:

1. "I don't have the ability" (see Exodus 3:11).
2. "I don't know enough" (see verse 13).
3. "What if the people don't believe me?" (see 4:1).
4. "I'm the worst speaker ever!" (see verse 10).
5. "Send someone else" (see verse 13).

But God didn't let the reluctant man's bevy of excuses keep the mission from moving forward. The stage was set, and Moses was already part of the scene. Despite Moses's perceived lack of abilities and skills, God was waiting for him to offer his willingness. Eventually, Moses relented and carried out an incredible rescue mission.

A mission-possible life is not about feeling ready; it's about being willing.

***What excuses hold you back from being willing
to step forward and live mission possible?***

Choose to Discover

+

Taste and see that the LORD is good;
How blessed is the man who takes refuge in Him!

Psalm 34:8

One of my favorite things to do is visit and share hope with inmates imprisoned on death row. I enjoy it because I want to have a heart for loving people the world has forgotten. I don't visit these people to get something from them. There's nothing they can do for me. I am there simply to tell them I love them and, more important, that *God* loves them.

I believe the greatest form of love is to choose the best interests of other people and act on their behalf. That's exactly what Jesus did for you and me and the rest of humankind. He loves us without limits, without reserve, without measure.

God desires a relationship with you. Not just one where you show up at the same building once a week or say a rote prayer before you wolf down a meal. He wants you to know Him. He wants you to talk to Him. He offers a relationship with you that will never be severed. The ancient king David, who experienced his share of highs and lows, wrote a beautiful psalm persuading us to "taste and see that the LORD is good." Don't just take his word for it (or mine). Commit to pursuing God for the next year through meditating on these devotionals. Seek Him. Discover for yourself what it's like to know the God of the universe's unconditional love.

***Write down the steps you will take this day,
week, month, and year to discover God's presence.***

His Plans > Our Plans

+

A person's steps are directed by the LORD.
How then can anyone understand their own way?

Proverbs 20:24, NIV

Guest devo by Lori Skidmore
Relationship to TTF: parent of special-needs child
who attended Night to Shine

I had it all planned out:

1. Get my master's degree ✓
2. Marry the love of my life ✓
3. Have my perfectly healthy first child ✓
4. Five years later, have my perfectly healthy second child—
   but wait!

There was a rare disorder accompanied by so many unknowns for our sweet Turner. He is nonverbal, with too many limitations to count. From the beginning, my anxiety set in: *Will he be okay?* How I wanted our sweet baby to be able to do all the things a parent prays for their child! But because of his limitations, I questioned that, with much guilt and worry.

And it has been hard. But it has also been a blessing. Turner shows me that Jesus lives in him, and he shows those around him His love. The first time I saw this was when Turner made his way into a crowded room and found a woman who was hurting due to her husband's diagnosis of terminal cancer. Turner wrapped his sweet, pudgy arms around her as if to say, "Jesus is with you!" He has done this in countless situations.

My change of plans became a life full of Jesus showing His love through a little boy who many would say has little to give the world. If Turner can reach the hurting, what can God do with *your* life?

Spend time thanking God today
that His plans are better than we can know.

The Grand Purpose

+

"Love the Lord your God with all your heart, and with all
your soul, and with all your mind, and with all your strength." . . .
"Love your neighbor as yourself." There is no other
commandment greater than these.

Mark 12:30–31

The dictionary defines *purpose* as "the reason for which something exists or is done, made, used, etc."[2] *Purpose* is a word that
is often thrown around in Christian churches, but when it comes to
defining what our purpose is as human beings on earth, the answer
can be confusing. Does it have to do with a vocation? Is it related to
an inborn skill? Or is it a dream that has been burned into our hearts
ever since we can remember?

One thing is certain: You were created for a reason. You are not
here by accident. It is by design that the Creator of the universe designed you exactly as you are. He created you in His image, with
love, in love, and by Love.

I believe the number one reason we're on the earth is to know our
Maker, the person of God. How can we do that? By taking to heart
and putting into action the words of Jesus—to love God with all our
heart and to love our neighbor.

Finding your purpose starts with knowing God through His Son,
Jesus Christ. It's also about loving your neighbor. Who is your
neighbor? Everyone you come in contact with! So, before your mental and spiritual wheels start churning and searching for your individual purpose, begin to live out your macro purpose.

How can you love God and others well this week?

What Is a Mission-Possible Life?

✝

*May the God of peace ... equip you in every good thing
to do His will, working in us that which is pleasing
in His sight, through Jesus Christ.*
Hebrews 13:20–21

Living a mission-possible life means carrying out the good works that God has already prepared for you. We are each on a mission to make a difference and ensure that our lives count—a mission to help the hurting and reach the last, the lost, and the least of humanity. This looks different for everyone. It might take you into the darkness of a rescue mission for those who are being human trafficked. It might keep you in your own neighborhood, breathing life and spirit into your children or your neighbors.

When you are mission driven, you use your ability together with God's empowerment to help, serve, guide, teach, pray, and lead others in innumerable ways, each as unique as a person's DNA. In fact, helping, serving, guiding, teaching, praying, and leading others are perfect examples of what mission possible looks like lived out!

Here's a surprise for you: One's mission is not really as mysterious as it's made out to be. It's more available to you than you ever imagined. You don't have to go on a mission trip around the world or start a church.

Has God ever pricked your heart to take a step in a particular direction to meet a need? Doing that is the essence of mission-possible living! So keep taking steps to do good things for the kingdom. Left. Right. Repeat. Onward!

***What is something you feel
God pricking your heart to do?***

How Does a Mission-Possible Life Happen?

✝

I am the vine, you are the branches; the one who remains
in Me, and I in him bears much fruit, for apart
from Me you can do nothing.

John 15:5

You can live a mission-possible life today because of what Jesus did on the cross more than two thousand years ago. This kind of life is possible only because of the sacrifice He made and the power given to Him to trample death. When you live mission possible, you live a life that counts because of what God has done, and is still doing, through you.

The anchor of the gospel rests in the truth that we cannot save ourselves by our pedigrees, good works, or impressive career histories. We receive the gift of salvation through what Jesus has done for us on the cross. When we make the decision to trust Him with our lives, we are automatically seated at the table of the humanly impossible. It's not about what we can do; it's about what God can do through us.

To sum it up, a mission-possible life happens when you do three key things:

1. Know the person of God.
2. Trust the plan of God.
3. Live out the purpose that God has for your life.

These three keys are essential to moving beyond living a success-possible or happy life and finding your true significance. If you want to make your life count, start living these out today.

***How can you begin to grow
in your knowledge of God today?***

The Great Question

✛

Who, then, is this,
that even the wind and the sea obey Him?

Mark 4:41

In Mark 4, Jesus finished teaching a crowd, then He gathered His disciples to go over to the other side of the lake. "A great windstorm arose" (verse 37, ESV) that frightened the disciples who were on the boat. The disciples then woke a sleeping Jesus, and He proceeded to rebuke the winds and the seas. As the storm ceased, "there was a great calm" (verse 39, ESV). Instead of breathing a sigh of relief, the disciples "were filled with great fear" (verse 41, ESV). Why were they so afraid?

Note the interesting sequence of events: a great storm, a great calm, and great fear. Now here comes one of the greatest questions ever: "Who, then, is this, that even the wind and the sea obey Him?" (verse 41).

That is the question the disciples had to ask for themselves more than two thousand years ago, and it's one we must ask ourselves today.

If you haven't accepted Jesus as your Savior, you can say a prayer in your own words or use the following one:

Dear Jesus, I believe that You died on the cross and rose from the dead. I know that I am a sinner. Please come into my heart and forgive me of my sin. Thank You for forgiving me and trading the old for the new, the darkness for the light. Thank You for saving me. Thank You for giving me a home in heaven, where I will go and live with You forever one day. In Jesus's name. Amen.

Welcome to the fam!

The Great Response

✝

Go home to your people and report to them what great things
the Lord has done for you, and how He had mercy on you.

Mark 5:19

I n Mark 5, the Bible tells the story of a man who was demon possessed. He lived in a cave in the mountain, cutting himself with
stones. One day he saw Jesus from afar and ran toward Him. Jesus
healed the man, casting out the demons from him and sending
them into a herd of pigs that ran off a cliff, fell into the sea, then
drowned (see verse 13). When it was time for Jesus to get back into
the boat and return to the other side of the lake, the man who had
been freed from the demons begged Jesus "that he might accompany Him" (verse 18). Now, that's what I call a great response!

Though the man wanted to stay with Jesus, Jesus had a different
mission in mind for him. Jesus asked him to go home and tell the
people there what Jesus had done for him. The man said yes, and he
had an amazing impact.

God might have a different mission than what you have in mind,
but whatever it is, say yes. Go and make your life count. That is the
great response to the great question of who Jesus is.

**If you would like to commit to making your life count,
go ahead and tell Him right now:**

*Dear Jesus, I believe I can live a mission-possible life be-
cause Your mission was accomplished. Remind me that
because You have overcome the world, I can do whatever
You have called me to do. Thank You that I get to live mission possible. Amen.*

As You Go

+

As you go, preach, saying,
"The kingdom of heaven has come near."

Matthew 10:7

In the tenth chapter of Matthew, Jesus gave His twelve disciples authority to heal and cast out evil, as well as instructions on how to preach the good news. "Preach," He told them, "as you go." I love that phrase.

As you go.

Do you know what that means? To do it while living your daily life. Mission-possible living is defined in the same sense. We live out the purpose that God has for our lives by helping, serving, guiding, teaching, praying, and leading others whenever and wherever we are.

Do it as you straighten the living room for the eightieth time and raise your children. Do it as your purchases are being rung up at a convenience store. Do it as you style for a magazine photo shoot. Do it on the trading floor. Wherever you are, be the light Jesus has been to you.

The more we realize that God can use us whenever and in whatever situation, even if something seems meaninglessly rote to us, the more the idea of living mission possible will come alive to us.

When in the middle of an ordinary day
have you believed that God can make a difference
in someone else's life through you?

Trust in God and His Plan

✝

Trust in the LORD with all your heart
And do not lean on your own understanding.

Proverbs 3:5

There have been times when I haven't been the happiest I knew I could be because I wanted my situation to be different. However, I've learned that God can use me in whatever situation I'm in, even if I'm not thrilled about it.

The Bible is replete with heroes who were in situations they didn't like but were able to live mission possible because they chose to trust in God, who then used them greatly. I think of Daniel in the lions' den. I think of Joseph, sold by his own brothers and thrown into prison due to a false accusation. I think of Paul, enduring multiple shipwrecks, beatings, and imprisonments. I can't imagine any of them being excited amid any of those circumstances. (See Daniel 6; Genesis 37; 39; and 2 Corinthians 11:23–27 if you want to read those accounts.)

Yet here's the kicker: They trusted God. They said yes to the person of God, and they said yes to the plan of God because they knew His character and it was trustworthy. We can trust God because He gave His best when He gave His Son for us.

God has a great plan for your life. It may not be where you want to be in this moment, but always remember that He can use you right now, this very moment. Mission possible is where you are now, not just where you're going later.

What is one area in which you struggle
when it comes to trust? Spend a few moments in
special prayer today asking God for help in that very area.

Take the Pressure Off

✝

Oh, Lord God! Behold, You Yourself have made the heavens and
the earth by Your great power and by Your outstretched arm!
Nothing is too difficult for You.

Jeremiah 32:17

Though we at the Tim Tebow Foundation had been serving in
anti-human-trafficking efforts for seven years, in 2020 I thought
about going public with our efforts. I started asking people I trusted
what they thought. Most were hesitant. I admit, I didn't have the answers, nor did I have a ten-step plan, but I couldn't shake the feeling
that God was calling me in that direction. The more I learned about
human trafficking, the more overwhelming the problem seemed.
Have you ever felt a similar way?

Maybe your heart pulls toward food-insecure families or those in
rural communities who lack education. It might seem impossible to
end those struggles, and, frankly, you probably *can't* do it in your
strength and power alone. But here's a truth that can hopefully take
some pressure off: Our mission is not to end all evil or lack. If it
were, we would have every right to feel overwhelmed by not having
the power to end every pain and hurt in the world. Our mission is to
honor God as we make a difference wherever and however we can.
The outcome, the result, the stories—we don't have control over
those things.

Remember, living a mission-possible life is not about resting in
your own confidence; it's about growing your confidence in God.

***What is something God is prompting you to believe in
or do more for to live a mission-possible life?***

A Prayer of Surrender

✝

Thank You, Lord, for creating me with intention. Search my heart so that I may live pure before You. Shape my desires, my motives, and my intentions to seek after You. Remind me that this life is meant for something greater than achieving success, gaining wealth, or accumulating likes. Forgive me when my focus falters and my dependence on You wanes. I submit to Your will, God, knowing that You have planned for me a future worth having, filled with sustaining and everlasting hope. Remind me to trust that in submitting to Your will, I receive Your instruction and Your counsel and that Your eyes and hands will be upon me.

I pray each day to know You more, to know the power that raised You from the dead, and to know how You suffered because You loved me, chose me, and designed for me a life that counts. I'm so grateful for Your promise that when I seek You, I will find You.

I surrender my desires to You, trusting that You will straighten my path. I trust You because You gave Your best for me: Your only Son. Show me Your will that I might walk in Your purpose for my life, just as Jesus carried out not His own will but Yours.

In Jesus's name I pray. Amen.

Based on: Psalm 139; Proverbs 8:17; Philippians 3:10; Proverbs 23:18; Psalm 32:8; Proverbs 3:5–6; 1 John 5:3

Your Mindset Matters

✛

*Whatever is true, whatever is honorable, whatever is right,
whatever is pure, whatever is lovely, whatever is commendable, if
there is any excellence and if anything worthy of praise,
think about these things.*

Philippians 4:8

In July 2020, researchers at Queen's University in Canada discovered that the average human brain has more than six thousand unique thoughts every single day.[3]

Ranging from the weather outside to work meetings to feeding the dog to feeding the kids, that's a lot of thoughts! With our minds constantly racing from one thing to the next, we often forget how fascinating it is to *think*.

Thoughts can be the most private and powerful parts of our human nature. But thoughts can also be very destructive. They are often negative. We must take back control of what goes in and out of our heads (see 2 Corinthians 10:5)!

In Philippians, the apostle Paul is very clear in describing the things we should be thinking about: *whatever* is true, honorable, right, pure, lovely, commendable, excellent, and praiseworthy. In living a mission-possible life, developing a healthy, growth-and-grace-oriented mindset is crucial. *Mindset* is just a fancy word for a particular way of thinking. It's your beliefs plus convictions plus attitude that drive the way you think, feel, and act. Your mindset matters because it is foundational for true change.

***Now that you're thinking about what you think about
(ha!), identify things in your life that are true,
honorable, right, and so on.***

A Mission M.I.N.D.S.E.T.

✛

The mind set on the flesh is death,
but the mind set on the Spirit is life and peace.

Romans 8:6

I love the word *mission*: "a task or job that someone is given to do."[4]
Whether you realize it or not, you have a mission. What's interesting about our English word *mission* is that it comes from a sixteenth-century Latin word meaning "to send."[5] See, I believe God has sent you here for a reason. As I will say multiple times throughout this devotional, Jesus clearly lays out what we are sent here to do: to love Him and love others (see Matthew 22:37–39).

But have you ever noticed that He specifically commands us to love Him with all our *minds*? How often are we engaging with God in our heads?

Trust me, I understand there are many voices competing for our attention. But when we give in to negativity, lose focus, hit snooze, think we're entitled, and stop growing, our mission is in jeopardy!

Everything we do starts between the ears, in our minds, with our thoughts. Therefore, to be successful on our God-given mission, we've got to have the right mindset—one that will allow us to stay locked in on the task at hand.

So, I've come up with the acronym M.I.N.D.S.E.T.—a set of mental attitudes that I will share over the next few days to help you start and sustain a mission-possible life:

M—Maker
I—Interruptible
N—Now
D—Different
S—Suffer
E—Excellence
T—To the End

What do you think about most throughout your day?

Know Your (M)aker

✛

Come, let's worship and bow down,
Let's kneel before the LORD our Maker.
For He is our God,
And we are the people of His pasture
and the sheep of His hand.

Psalm 95:6–7

A mission <u>M</u>.I.N.D.S.E.T. starts by knowing your *Maker*. Think about it. Almost everything you interact with daily has been built, made, or designed. Your cell phone, your car, the highways you drive on, the building you work in, your laptop, your house, the clothes you wear, and so on. All those things were created with a specific intention and function.

Just like a painting has an artist and a skyscraper has an architect, it makes sense that the universe has a Designer. The stars in the sky. The crawling creatures on the ground. The colorful schools of fish in the coral reefs. All things—"both in the heavens and on earth, visible and invisible"—have been created by God and for God (Colossians 1:16).

But our Creator didn't just *make* everything and take a step back. No, He wants to know you and use you to demonstrate His love. You don't have a real mission without knowing your *Maker*. You don't have true purpose without knowing your *Maker*. You're not going to have eternal impact without knowing your *Maker*. Our *Maker* is who gives us these things. Even though we're called to a mission, that mission is not about us. It's for Him, it's with Him, and it's through Him. Why? Because He *made* us. A mission mindset is a God-first mindset. Period. It starts by first recognizing where our mission came from and who it is for.

How have you experienced your Maker in your life?

Be (I)nterruptible

+

The mind of a person plans his way,
But the LORD directs his steps.

Proverbs 16:9

H ave you ever planned or scheduled something and it didn't go the way you intended? How did you react? Were you angry? Anxious? I'll be the first to say that I can get a little annoyed when things don't go as planned. But the reality is that plans change. *The market takes a turn. You don't receive the scholarship you wanted. A storm cloud pops up out of nowhere.*

When does anything really go 100 percent according to plan? Hardly ever. I believe that most of the time, there's probably going to be a change in your plans. Why? Because God tends to interrupt our lives.

The *I* in M.I.N.D.S.E.T. stands for *Interruptible.* Be interruptible.

Part of having a mission mindset is saying, "God, I'm okay when You interrupt my plans." It's a mindset that not only accepts change but also welcomes it. It's tuning in to the voice of God and being willing to move wherever, whenever, and for whomever. Although it might not be according to your plan, it might be according to God's.

Does the Lord direct your steps? Do you give Him access to re-arranging your calendar? When things get out of order, do you ask, "Okay, God, what are You up to here?"

Next time there's a hiccup in your day, instead of getting frustrated (like I have so many times), look around and see how you can make the most of the situation.

As you go about your day, ask God to open your eyes and make you more aware of people's needs around you.

Act (N)ow

✝

Since his days are determined,
The number of his months is with You;
And You have set his limits so that he cannot pass.

Job 14:5

Imagine you're down by six points with two minutes left in the fourth quarter of the Super Bowl. If your team scores and kicks the extra point, you'll be a world champion! The only problem is you're on your opponent's twenty-yard line and time is running out. If you're the coach, what offensive scheme will you run to give your team the best chance at winning the game?

The two-minute drill, of course!

The two-minute drill is a hurry-up type of offense. This means you're trying to run plays as quickly as possible, taking advantage of every second on the clock. If there's ever a time to play with urgency, it's *now*!

Life is a two-minute drill of sorts. We don't know exactly how much time we have left (see James 4:14); therefore, it is necessary to make the most of each day.

You might be thinking, *Yeah, but, Timmy, I'm not in my two-minute drill. I'm young and healthy.* To that I say, help someone who is! I'm talking about the hurting, the abused, the abandoned, the trafficked, the forgotten, the hopeless, those who don't know Jesus—all those around the world who need us to act on their behalf! We can't live on our timelines; we must live on theirs!

The N in M.I.N.D.S.E.T. stands for *Now*. Don't wait. If there is something aligned with your mission that demands your attention, do it *now*!

**What have you been putting off
that you know you need to get done?**

Be (D)ifferent

✝

Noah was a righteous man, blameless in his generation.
Noah walked with God.

Genesis 6:9

The *D* in M.I.N.<u>D</u>.S.E.T. stands for *Different*. In Genesis 6, we get an inside look at the world after it had been cursed by God because of Adam and Eve's original sin. The author of Genesis tells us that as humanity populated the earth, human wickedness was widespread and every thought in the human mind was evil *all* the time (see verse 5).

However, there was one person who stood out among his peers. His name was Noah. He was different from the rest of the world. He "found favor in the eyes of the LORD" (verse 8). And because of this, God showed mercy on humankind and saved Noah's family from a global flood (see 7:23).

I think that way too many times, we want to live and act like everybody else. That's the opposite of a mission mindset. A mission mindset understands that to make a difference, you must *be different*. It doesn't care about being popular or liked. It sets aside what's "normal" and thinks of ways to stand out and stand up for God and people.

Now, let me be clear: I'm not saying to be different for the sake of being different. I'm saying that when God calls you to do something that may be against the grain, be willing to do it. Just like Noah, when you're willing to be a little bit different for God's glory, watch how He can use you.

What makes you, your company, or your habits
different from others?

Be Willing to (S)uffer

+

After you have suffered for a little while, the God of all grace, who
called you to His eternal glory in Christ, will Himself perfect,
confirm, strengthen, and establish you.

1 Peter 5:10

One of my favorite words in the English language is *passion*.
Today, *passion* refers to all sorts of things, including sex, emotions, and hobbies. The word's origin, however, is vastly different.
Our English word *passion* comes from the twelfth-century Latin
root word *pati*, which means "to suffer."[6] This Latin word was used
to describe the death of Jesus on the cross.

In biblical Greek, we see the same thing. The root verb for passion, *paschō*, means "to be afflicted" or "to undergo sufferings," in
either a good or bad sense.[7] See, passion is not so much about getting hyped or professing our love. At its core, true passion is our
willingness to suffer!

So, when you say you're passionate about something, what
you're really saying is that you care so deeply about it that you're
willing to suffer for it. This brings a whole new meaning to the word,
doesn't it?

A mission mindset embraces suffering. I'm not saying to be masochistic, but it's a mentality with which you're willing to make sacrifices, push through pain, and fight for what truly matters because
the mission is worth it. The S in M.I.N.D.S.E.T. is simple. It stands for
Suffer.

***What do you care so much about
that you're willing to suffer for it?***

Pursue (E)xcellence

✝

Whether you eat or drink, or whatever you do,
do all things for the glory of God.
1 Corinthians 10:31

In 1956, twenty-seven-year-old Martin Luther King, Jr., gave a speech at a church in Montgomery, Alabama, in which he addressed the challenge of achieving *excellence* in all we do. I love what he said:

> Whatever your life's work is, do it well. . . . If it falls your lot to be a street sweeper, sweep streets like Michelangelo painted pictures, like Shakespeare wrote poetry, like Beethoven composed music; sweep streets so well that all the host of Heaven and earth will have to pause and say, "Here lived a great street sweeper, who swept his job well."[8]

Now, I get that King was speaking with special purpose here: to help an oppressed group of people live beyond the unjust prejudice and bigotry that they were experiencing. But I am so inspired by these words that I want to learn from them too. Achieving excellence is a challenge, but I believe it should always be our aim. That's why the *E* in M.I.N.D.S.E.T. stands for *Excellence*. Pursue it!

Roughly nineteen hundred years before MLK preached this, Paul penned something similar in his letter to the church in Colossae. He instructed them to do all things for the glory of God (see Colossians 3:17). I'm not sure if we can ever achieve excellence (since it's a relative standard), but I do believe that when we pursue it for God, He will not waste our effort.

How can you strive for excellence
in the places God has you?

(T)o the End

✝

Having loved His own who were in the world,
He loved them to the end.

John 13:1

The *T* in M.I.N.D.S.E.T. stands for *To the end*. One of my favorite verses in the Bible is John 13:1. Here, Jesus finds Himself in a room in Jerusalem with His closest friends days before His arrest and crucifixion. In the twelve chapters leading up to this, John details Jesus's profound and polarizing ministry: His miracles, His teachings, and the religious controversy He caused. But here, at the beginning of chapter thirteen, John writes something that puts fuel in my fire:

> Before the Feast of the Passover, Jesus, knowing that His hour had come that He would depart from this world to the Father, *having loved His own who were in the world, He loved them to the end.*

Not when everything was going good. Not when He gained popularity or a certain level of income. No. Jesus loved . . . *to the end*. The Greek word for "the end" is *telos*. It means completion. Reaching the end goal.[9] Mission accomplished.

How did Jesus love? Until His mission was accomplished!

There were so many times Jesus could have said, "Hey, I'm out. I'm done." But no. He stuck with it. He went to the cross to save the world. That's *telos*. That's a mission mindset—that no matter what happens in life, you move forward in faith to do what's necessary to complete the task God has called you to. Whatever your mission is, when God calls you to do something, do it *to the end*.

What is God asking you to complete "to the end"?

Until Practice Becomes Reflex

✝

Take pains with these things; be absorbed in them,
so that your progress will be evident to all.

1 Timothy 4:15

Your brain is a remarkable machine, one that is constantly updating itself. Without any conscious effort, new neural pathways are constantly being formed. We create new thought patterns by repetition, meaning we can intentionally form new habits. A study from Dartmouth College revealed that a portion of the brain, the dorsolateral striatum, is stimulated when a new habit is formed.[10] The more you do this, the more the activity in this area increases, making behaviors more automatic. When the dorsolateral striatum is activated, it is difficult to be distracted from your current task because your brain has become accustomed to it.

When Paul wrote the words in 1 Timothy 4:15, he was referring to the things that, through discipline, would make Timothy a godly leader. Likely, Paul was referring to things like reading Scripture, teaching it to others, and using his spiritual gifts. He knew that the more intentionally Timothy worked on those important disciplines, the more they would become ingrained in him until becoming involuntary practices in his life.

If you want to live a mission-possible life, it's important to actively practice what God has instructed you to do. Sometimes He calls us to carry out actions that feel unnatural. Things like loving others when you would rather hate and being brave in the face of fear take conscious effort. Still, if you work on them enough, they will eventually become reflex.

What habits do you need to actively practice today?

Keystone Habits

✛

Only one thing is necessary; for Mary has chosen the good part,
which shall not be taken away from her.

Luke 10:42

When Paul O'Neill took his place as the new CEO of the Aluminum Company of America (Alcoa), an organization that had been around for almost a century, people had faith that he could get the job done. But when he shared his plans, stating that his top priority was the safety of Alcoa's workers, those who listened thought he was crazy. They were convinced he would run Alcoa into the ground.

But a year later, profits soared. When O'Neill retired in 2000, Alcoa's annual net income was *five times* greater than before he arrived. It's quite a success story, founded on what author Charles Duhigg called a keystone habit—changing one pattern that affects different aspects of patterns. In this case, the pattern was safety precautions.[11]

We must all develop good habits. If we're honest, there's a plethora of habits we need to change. For this reason, focusing on a habit that influences others is crucial. For example, working out is a big one. Many people naturally veer onto healthier paths when they begin to exercise (for example, eating cleaner, stopping smoking).

Jesus set in place keystone habits while He was on earth—things like committing to prayer and loving and serving others. Ultimately, He was always about His Father's business and did everything with it in mind.

What keystone habit can you think of implementing
that will help you move closer to living
a mission-possible life?

Get in Your Discomfort Zone

✛

If you know these things,
you are blessed if you do them.
John 13:17

For parts of my life, one of the things I was most willing to sacrifice for was sports. I didn't mind purposely making myself uncomfortable if it meant I would gain greater physical ability or the respect of my teammates.

During one of the first few weeks of my freshman year at the University of Florida, our coaches made us take ice baths for seven minutes. Ice baths are a killer method for athletic recovery. They're also *completely* not fun. Nobody wanted to get in. My teammates and I stared in fear at the freezing water. We all resisted what we were going to have to do eventually. I quietly stepped aside from the crowd and crept into the tub. My toes immediately contracted. Sinking deeper, my body instinctively recoiled over and over from the freezing temperature. No lie—it sucked, but it did make getting in the second time much easier. And the time after that.

There are better habits to start than taking regular ice baths. However, the point is, get uncomfortable. Regularly. Do it with purpose. Discomfort in the short term may produce more comfort in the long run. Instead of cozying up to your comfort zone, discover and hang out in your discomfort zone, whether that's going for a run, getting up earlier to spend more time with God, or socking away the money you were going to spend on another pair of black boots. Get uncomfortable doing things that will transform you into the man or woman you are called to be.

**Name three benefits that may come from making
a habit of being uncomfortable.**

Do It Again ... and Again ... and Again

✛

We have put our hope in the living God, who is the Savior
of everyone, but especially of those who have faith.
This is why we work and struggle so hard.

1 Timothy 4:10, CEV

I'm sure you may have heard at some point that it takes twenty-one days to form a habit. Well, that's not an entirely true statement.

Dr. Maxwell Maltz wrote a book called *Psycho-Cybernetics,* in which he introduced his discovery that patients take about twenty-one days to get used to seeing their new face after a plastic surgery. It is the same with patients who have lost a limb. It takes them about the same amount of time to begin to adapt to having no limb. Over the years, that statement got twisted. Popular authors and motivational speakers dropped the *about* and started announcing what many today believe is the truth: that it takes twenty-one days to form a new habit.[12]

Although that may be true for some of us, according to a study published in the *European Journal of Social Psychology,* "it can take anywhere from 18 to 254 days for a person to form a new habit and an average of 66 days for a new behavior to become automatic."[13]

Good habits are worth the work. Whether we're focused on tweaking our spiritual, emotional, or physical parts, we ought to do the most with what we're given. As Paul says, "This is why we work and struggle."

Instead of focusing on the end goal, divide the habit-making process into smaller parts and reward yourself after meeting your smaller goals.

No Is Not Always a Bad Word

✛

A prudent person foresees danger and takes precautions.
The simpleton goes blindly on and suffers the consequences.

Proverbs 27:12, NLT

As a self-diagnosed people pleaser, I'm not the poster child for saying no. If there's something I can do for someone, I'm happy to pitch in. I've realized, however, through some hard lessons, that I'm limited.

In the movie *Yes Man*, Jim Carrey plays Carl Allen, a man caught in a negative funk. While attending a self-help seminar, he learns that the secret to an amazing life is to say yes to everything. At first, the theory works and his depressing life takes an upward swing. Ultimately, however, Carl learns that saying yes all the time isn't the elixir for happiness as he had believed.

Jesus didn't say yes to everything. Here are some instances when He said no:

- Martha asked Him to tell Mary to help her
  (see Luke 10:40–42).
- The crowd asked Him to stay longer (see 4:42–44).
- The scribes and Pharisees asked Him for a sign
  (see Matthew 12:38–39).
- The demon-possessed man He healed asked to accompany
  Jesus on His journey (see Mark 5:18–19).

Not everything we say no to is necessarily wrong, bad, or sinful; it just might not be the best choice to make. If we find ourselves saying yes to every fun activity, every volunteer event, and every personal favor, we'll cause a head-on collision with a packed calendar, resulting in stress, frustration, and burnout. Decide your nos so you can choose your best yeses.

***Evaluate your process of discerning
when to say yes or no.***

Restrain the Rage

✝

Like a city that is broken into and without walls
So is a person who has no self-control over his spirit.

Proverbs 25:28

When's the last time you got cut off on the highway? Did someone make a turn in front of you without turning their signal on or stubbornly stay in their lane (the "fast" one) while barely going the speed limit? How did you respond? Maybe a loud groan morphed into colorful words, or maybe your hands gripped the steering wheel so tightly that your veins flared.

Rage, whether on the road or online, is common. Our culture seems addicted to it:

- A Christian leader falls from grace? Hurl snarky bits about hypocrisy in the comments section.
- Someone you know is taking a risk and trying something new? Be discouraging with one simple eye-roll emoji (not at them, of course), and then forward it to a third party, who'll share the laugh.

The options are endless. Sitting behind a windshield or a screen and engaging with others requires restraint, intentionality, and self-control. Without those attributes, you'll be left unguarded, defenseless, and vulnerable in your spirit.

In a world in which we are often encouraged to "Just be yourself!" and "Just do you!" or "Do what you want to do!" we would do well to consider whether these statements give us permission to let go of self-control and what we lose if we decide to give in to rage.

What areas of your life need more self-control?
Consider offering them to God.

A Prayer for Focus

✛

Thank You, Father, for loving me so much that You want me to live a life of significance. Please remind me each day to first seek Your kingdom, believing that You'll take care of the rest. As I wake each day, may my thoughts be aligned with what You say. You are the Lord of my life, heart, soul, and mind. Forgive me when my mind has been preoccupied with worry, questions, distractions, or lies from the Enemy. Thank You that Your will is for my thinking to be transformed day after day into Your likeness. I know transformation happens when I shift my focus from the things of this world to Your truth.

Show me the areas of weakness I need to change. Reveal to me the lies from the Enemy I have been believing that keep me stuck and distracted. Empower me to be self-disciplined and a master of my body and mind and remain centered on You. Remind me of my job to take my thoughts captive, and give me the strength to fix my attention on what is right, noble, and true. Thank You for actively working in my life. I trust that Your purposes for me will prevail.

In Jesus's name I pray. Amen.

Based on: Matthew 6:33; Ephesians 4:23–24; Romans 12:2; 1 Corinthians 9:27; 2 Corinthians 10:5; Proverbs 19:21

Created for Relationship

+

If one can overpower him who is alone, two can resist him.

A cord of three strands is not quickly torn apart.

Ecclesiastes 4:12

One of the loneliest periods of my life was when I was traded from the Denver Broncos to the New York Jets and moved to the northeast United States. Because coaches were concerned that my arrival would spark a media circus, I was strongly advised to stay away from public attention. I tried to do this, though I couldn't keep TMZ reporters from popping up on my lawn at random hours. It was hard. In maintaining low visibility, I often inadvertently started isolating myself from others. I wasn't involved in a church community. I didn't reach out much to those who were close to me. I'll admit, it was a dark time.

Here's what I learned during that lonely season: We need one another. God is a relational God. He made us to be in community. He made us to live in relationship with Him, first and foremost, and then also with others. While our society seems to emphasize the power of the individual, a stronger collective power erupts when we build and nurture a tight community. As you grow in your relationship with God, find others to experience this spiritual journey with you. Find people who will cheer you on, say the hard things you need to hear, pray for you when you're on the verge of quitting, and lend support when life throws inevitable curveballs. We are not meant to do life alone; we are meant to develop as individuals and emulate Jesus in the context of the people around us.

How have solid friendships
opened a path for your growth?

Courageous Conversations

✝

Speaking the truth in love, we are to grow up in all aspects
into Him who is the head, that is, Christ.

Ephesians 4:15

E vidence of a genuine relationship is when we know we can say
what the other person needs to hear—and vice versa. God calls
us to share truth and grace with people. There have been so many
times in my life when role models, family members, and friends
have had courageous conversations with me. From a perspective of
love, they've poured truth into me, telling me things I didn't like but
needed to hear. I can't say listening to their words was easy or that I
always received them well, but I've been influenced by these talks
because I know they're coming from love.

As believers, we ought to strive toward maturity. Sometimes it
takes being on the receiving end of courageous conversations, and
sometimes it means prayerfully taking a step to help keep our
brother or sister from making a huge mistake or entering an unhealthy path. Courageous conversations are a form of investment. I
know they can be uncomfortable and awkward, and they should
always be approached and received with prayer. Another piece of
advice: Don't initiate a courageous conversation because you may
be right about something; do it because it helps the other person.

Don't avoid courageous conversations. Instead, ask God to help
you identify the greatness and potential in others, call it out of them,
and put the right people in your path to do the same.

*Why do you think it's harmful to not speak truth
to those you love and not have it spoken over you?
Try to remember your answer the next time
you have a courageous conversation.*

Shut It Down

✝

Let no unwholesome word come out of your mouth, but if there is any good word for edification according to the need of the moment, say that, so that it will give grace to those who hear.

Ephesians 4:29

I f you don't have anything nice to say, don't say anything at all. The same adage applies behind screens. Technological advances have revolutionized communication as well as opened a new door for us to say nasty things seemingly in front of people but realistically while hiding behind screens.

I didn't frequent the internet when I was a kid, but I recall a few instances of my blowing up at someone in the not-nicest of ways. One such time was on a church bus. Somehow I found myself in a heated debate with a youth-group counselor who had a knack for talking down to kids. While I continue to stand behind my defense of Michael Jordan, our conversation did get ugly. I put the guy I didn't think treated us kids well on blast. I got loud—*really* loud. So loud, in fact, that all the other talking on that bus just stopped. All eyes were focused on me. I took my stance too far, and by the time we drove into the church parking lot, I was ashamed. I should not have been so disrespectful. I felt I had let God down.

Tearing someone down is never a win. As Christians, we need to be sure that our words, and the attitudes behind those words, are filled with grace, kindness, and respect. Saying nothing just might be the best defense sometimes.

Have you ever said something you later regretted?
What did you learn from that experience?

Tame Your Tongue

✛

The tongue is a small part of the body,
and yet it boasts of great things.
See how great a forest is set aflame by such a small fire!

James 3:5

Living on a farm while growing up kept things interesting. I'll never forget the time the weeds had grown like crazy in the pasture and Dad decided to start a controlled burn to get rid of them. Apparently, "controlled" is in the eye of the fire starter, especially when one forgets to place a forewarning phone call to the forestry department. We knew something went wrong when Dad rushed into the house, frantic. "Help! I need everyone's help!" he yelled in a panic. Turns out, our pasture was on fire! In fact, the fire was moving fast toward the woods. Staring at orange and red flames licking up toward the sky, we bolted into action, beating the edges of the fire with shovels while Dad tried to douse it with a gushing garden hose.

Through the grace of God and our efforts, the fire eventually died down. Though it had burned through the weeds in our neighbor's fields, our house was untouched by the flames. Afterward, Dad, in his inimitable way, used the opportunity for a teachable moment. He led us in a brief Bible study on James 3, in which we learned that just as a small spark can cause a huge fire, an uncontrolled tongue can breed great damage. Gossip. Passive-aggressive comments. Jabs excused under the guise of sarcasm. Words bear much power. Be intentional in how you use them (see also verse 6).

***Have you been gossiped about? How does this
motivate you not to do the same to someone else?***

Heart Wide Open

✝

Our mouth has spoken freely to you . . . our heart is
opened wide. . . . Now in the same way in exchange—I am
speaking as to children—open wide your hearts to us, you as well.

2 Corinthians 6:11, 13

A wide-open heart, what Paul wrote about in the above Scripture passage, is evidence of *vulnerability*. That's a scary word for some of us.

Many times, we avoid creating meaningful relationships because we don't want anyone getting too close, just in case they reject us or are put off by something in us they don't like. While I don't recommend becoming besties or sharing your deepest and darkest secrets with everyone you meet, consider the depth with which you approach relationships. Do you share your true self so people can recognize that you are more than the filtered highlights you post on social media?

When Jesus was in the garden praying before His journey to the cross, He poured out His heart to two of His disciples: James and John. The Bible tells us He was anguished and distressed. Jesus told them, "My soul is crushed with grief to the point of death. Stay here and keep watch with me" (Matthew 26:38, NLT). Those are gut-wrenching and vulnerable words coming from the Son of God. There are times we, too, will need to display our vulnerability. Don't be embarrassed when that happens. Invite others, those you respect and trust, into your pain. It might be the avenue to finding the strength you need.

**What is something you have avoided sharing
that you know must be said? Who can you tell
that will lend support in this?**

Get Sharp

✛

As iron sharpens iron,
So one person sharpens another.
Proverbs 27:17

I'm sure you're familiar with the phrase "Strike while the iron is hot." This ties in to the meaning of the ancient proverb written above. To be sharpened, iron requires intense heat and pressure. Once the metal is cool, you can't use a hammer or any other object to change its shape. The iron must be reheated and struck while it's hot.

Solomon, the author of Proverbs 27, focused much of his attention on relationships. He posited the value of an open rebuke from a trusted friend and compared a bickering spouse to a leaky roof. As the church—a body of believers, not a structure with four walls and a ceiling—we are called to inspire each other to dig deeper into our faith and grow in maturity. We don't build a community for entertainment purposes only, nor to create a cheerleading squad that agrees with everything we say. Furthermore, a blade will never be as sharp as possible on its own. We sharpen each other in the highs and lows of life. Sometimes we need a friend to encourage us when we're down. And sometimes we need to be that friend.

Navigating through friend and family struggles is an excellent recipe for learning how to be more like Jesus. Think of the relationships you depend on. Think of them as instruments to help you become sharper in your faith, and likewise do the same for others.

**Name three friends and write down
how each inspires your personal growth.**

Get It Together

+

How good and pleasant it is
when God's people live together in unity!

Psalm 133:1, NIV

O ne of the most memorable Tebow vacations was when we siblings, our parents, and some friends participated in a beach Olympics event. Whether we were playing *Minesweeper* or tug-of-war, paddleboard racing, or wrangling a snake—yup, you read that right—I made sure we started our morning with an adrenaline-rushing, heart-racing experience. But our competitive natures got the best of each of us quick, and not in a good way. Quarrels broke out. There were some name calling and accusations of cheating. What was intended to be a fun time morphed into a tense experience.

At one point, another family, flush with collegiate athletes, asked to compete against us. Music to the Tebow ear! When the news spread within our crew, we rallied together like a reckoning force. Whatever beef we Tebows had with each other was instantaneously quashed. We were ready to crush our challengers. We locked in and rallied strong. The first game lasted four minutes, and we won. We won the next one too. And the one after that.

How did that happen? How did we shift our family atmosphere from competitive fury to rallying and cheering each other on? We finally got on the same page. We had a common purpose to believe in and fight for. I know that at times believers seem more divided than united. Remind yourself that we are not fighting each other. We are uniting to love and serve God and others and make His glory known.

**Think back to a time when you worked together
with another believer or a group despite differences
in opinions. What was the outcome?**

Lead to Serve

+

Whoever wants to become prominent among you
shall be your servant.

Matthew 20:26

According to Matthew 20, as Jesus got closer to His date of death, He reminded His disciples of what would happen. He talked about being handed over to the religious leaders, condemned to death, beaten and crucified, and finally resurrected. At some point after this graphic mention, the mother of James and John rushed to Jesus with both sons in tow. Her question of choice was interesting:

"Um, so can my boys, like, sit right beside you, uh, in heaven?" (see verse 21).

I love how Jesus responded: "You do not know what you are asking" (verse 22).

I bet Jesus would say the same about those of us in positions of leadership who desire to be the star in every show or prefer the limelight of leading to the minutiae of service. Yet the latter is what Jesus calls us to. He came to earth to give us life as a ransom for our sins. That is service at its greatest. And He expects the same from us.

Whether you lead a family, a team, a small group, or a Fortune 50 company, those you lead aren't there to make your life easier. All real leaders must embrace the grind and the disappointments. We have not only a seat at the table but also a spot in the trenches to serve others. Encourage those you lead by letting them know that you're going to fight for them and with them. And do what you do for their good and for the glory of God.

***What can you do today for the good of those
you are serving, regardless of whether they or others
will ever find out?***

Preparation for the Purpose

✝

Say, therefore, to . . . Israel, "I am the LORD, and I will bring
you out from under the labors of the Egyptians, and I will rescue
you from their bondage. I will also redeem you with an
outstretched arm, and with great judgments."

Exodus 6:6

Born into slavery and slowed by a speech impediment, Moses
seemed an unlikely candidate to lead his nation to freedom.
Imagine the hesitation he must have felt when the Lord commanded
him to speak up against the most powerful ruler in the land. For
more than four hundred years, pharaohs of Egypt utilized every
resource available to them to maintain control over the nation of
Israel. Who was Moses—a fugitive outcast, an old shepherd—to approach Pharaoh, let alone make any demands?

However, in the eyes of the Lord, Moses was anything but common. Even though he didn't know it at the time, his entire life up to
that point had been for the purpose of becoming equipped. While
Moses was spending the past forty years of his life in obscurity in
the wilderness, God was preparing him to shepherd Israel out of
bondage and into the Promised Land. Before we can embrace bigger
responsibilities, we need to be able to handle and manage whatever
God puts in front of us, even though it may seem menial or boring.

Be all in with whatever you are doing. You have no idea how God
is going to use your experience as preparation for a greater purpose.

*You know that situation in your life right now
that makes you feel small and insignificant?
Choose an all-in attitude about it and persevere.*

No Small Role

✝

The one who is faithful in a very little thing
is also faithful in much; and the one who is unrighteous
in a very little thing is also unrighteous in much.

Luke 16:10

God tasked Moses with leading the nation of Israel out of Egyptian slavery, but God didn't leave him to do it alone. His own brother was called by God to stand by his side to speak for him on multiple occasions, including once to literally hold up Moses's arm when he was too tired to do so alone.

The Old Testament records a story about a battle between the Amalekites and the Israelites. As the battle raged, Israel prevailed as long as Moses held his hands up. But when his hands came down, the Amalekites prevailed. The Bible doesn't tell us how long the battle was waged, but at some point Moses's hands grew heavy. They started shaking like maracas, fatigued, and began to go numb. Aaron, his older brother, and an elder named Hur stood on each side of Moses and helped prop up his arms so Israel could claim her victory. With their help, Moses's arms remained steady for the rest of the battle, until the sun set.

God may call you to a mission in which you'll have to fight, strategize, pray, or hold up those who are carrying a heavy weight. Those jobs are all equally important. In fact, it isn't the job that matters; it's who has given the orders and the act of obedience of the receiver that makes the difference and results in a mission accomplished.

**Pray for God to open your eyes to
whatever He has called you to, great or small.**

The Art of Staying Grounded

✝

The LORD gave and the LORD has taken away.
Blessed be the name of the LORD.

Job 1:21

For most of us, our sense of security has been shaken over the last few years. Tragic headlines and constant fear-charged news feeds have triggered unprecedented anxiety in many of us. How can we feel settled when our world is rocked with tragedy and chaos?

One way to stay grounded is to live with open hearts, knowing that whatever we have and whatever we are given are not ours but instead belong to God. Our relationships, our possessions, our money, our jobs, our skills, our bodies—He gave these to us and He can take them back. He can give us fixed or recycled old things. He can give us new things. But they're His to give and His to take.

Some of us live like we have control over our lives, our communities, and the world. With closed fists, we grip tight our resources, our time, our talents, our skills, and our money. Yet all we can do is focus on today. Right now. This moment.

When we live this way, our grip loosens. Our fingers uncurl. Our hearts begin to open. We begin to live with open minds and open spirits. And when we do, we become willing to step out in faith in order to allow God to take us where He wants us to go and do the things He wants us to do.

Do you live as though what you have belongs to you or to God? What needs to change?

Do What's Necessary

✝

When you eat the fruit of the labor of your hands,
You will be happy and it will go well for you.

Psalm 128:2

There is nothing neutral about living a mission-possible life. Doing so is evident in more than the big moments when the things you have been praying for come to fruition or the dream for which you worked so hard comes to pass. A mission-possible life is lived each day at both practice and the championship game, in the rehearsal and during the performance, throughout the notes and in the first draft of the first edition of your book. What's just as important as game day is the cumulative value of the practices and training put in on Tuesday, Wednesday, *and* Thursday. In fact, the tip-off matters more when each day of the week you attacked your drills for hours, even when no one was watching.

Living a mission-possible life is about loving and serving God and others. It's not about accomplishing mission after mission of Tom Cruise–like stunts that defy gravity and impress the masses; it's doing what's necessary to move the mission forward. This looks different in different seasons. It can mean a consistent regime of praying, reading the Bible, and fasting (which, by the way, should be part of everyone's mission-possible diet). It could mean studying more than playing, focusing on planning, strengthening a certain habit, caring for a neglected part of your life, or tending to administrative-related responsibilities. The grind may not be exciting at times, but there is power in the details.

How can you change your mindset from being overwhelmed by a big goal to focusing on it one step at a time?

Grace Within the Grind

+

By grace you have been saved through faith;
and this is not of yourselves, it is the gift of God;
not a result of works, so that no one may boast.

Ephesians 2:8–9

D*o whatever it takes.* That statement is a philosophy of hustling hard that you may have heard used in business to get things done. If you know anything about me, I'm all about working hard for a purpose. We can't shy away from responsibility or the necessity of getting up earlier, staying up later, or sacrificing the things we want now for what we need later. That said, we can never worship the mastery of the grind to where we expect our efforts to always pay off exactly in the way we want. We can't do it all in our own power. This is also true of our salvation as well as living a mission-possible life.

Work hard? Absolutely! In fact, work as if the miracle depends on you. But know, and have faith, that the miracle will happen because of God.

When the stress piles up and you're tossing and turning in bed more than snoozing or if you find yourself constantly comparing your efforts to someone else's, take a breath. Remember, you're not in this alone. Turn your attention to the epicenter of it all: Jesus Christ. With Him, you have everything, including the grace you need to do what today is asking of you.

Make a list for the day or week ahead. Take that written list, cover it with your hand, and pray over it. Ask God for the strength you will need to get done what He wants you to do.

Break It Up

✝

Behold, I am going to do something new.

Isaiah 43:19

Sometimes the things we need to do daily become routine and, well, boring. They may matter. They may be important. We know we ought to do them. Yet the habit of doing the same thing day after day leads to predictability, which can lead to a mechanical way of being. This can be true of repeating the same pattern of emails and phone calls for work or running the same drills each day for practice, and it can even carry over into our spiritual disciplines. Sometimes we lose our zeal—not because we stop praying or reading the Bible but because we approach those practices with a kind of drudgery that results in a habit over a want or even a need.

Have you ever found yourself so inundated with the daily grind and an overcommitted calendar that your spiritual life begins to get stifled by the routine? This usually happens little by little, over time. However it happens, the results need rapid intervention. My advice? Interrupt yourself.

There's no need to do anything crazy or overcomplicate things. When you read a verse, really focus on how you can apply the principle to your personal life. How can you live it out? Or if you don't normally listen to worship music, try it. Or pray while taking a walk through nature. Routines are important, but sometimes they need to be interrupted on purpose.

How can you mix up your time with God today?

True Joy Comes from God

+

The joy of the LORD is your strength.

Nehemiah 8:10, NIV

Guest devo by Jennifer Dobson
Relationship to TTF: adoption-grant recipient

Joy is not always easy to find, but I've learned it's always there. My daughters have every worldly reason to be angry. We have turned their lives upside down with the choices we have made—choices to follow Jesus into a future unknown to them both. Our older daughter carried the weight of a seven-year journey to bring her adopted sister home. Our youngest has learned to come to terms with the future she has been given: leaving her birth country behind and learning to trust, let go, live in a biracial family, and believe that unconditional love does not quit. On top of all that, she is also in a wheelchair.

To watch our youngest struggle to put socks on her feet, feet that fail her, breaks my heart. But it doesn't break hers. She has an infectious personality that Jesus deposited deep into her soul that no messy journey could overtake. Her joy explodes despite all the obstacles she has faced. She has a joy that is supernatural, from a supernatural God. She has a joy that changes people—a joy that makes others take note that something is different. She is strong. And her strength comes from the joy that God has placed deep in her heart. Most days, instead of being angry and frustrated with her socks, she breaks out in song, "Mom, will you help me put on my socks?"

And the very thing that proves so difficult will inevitably end in a smile, a laugh, a joke, or a twinkle in the eye—a reminder that with God's power come strength and joy.

Where can you find joy today?

A Prayer for Community

✝

Dear Lord, thank You for creating me to be in relationship with You and others. Help me to be the friend I want to have. Forgive me for falling short in my relationships, where I have failed to forgive, show mercy, and be just and fair. Clothe me in compassion, kindness, humility, gentleness, and patience. Help me to freely forgive others as You forgive me. Teach me how to love others the way You love them and the way You love me when I am unlovable. You know the struggles I have in my relationships. Give me a soft heart and a wise mind to navigate those challenges.

As I approach each day side by side with other people, help me tackle each assignment, responsibility, routine, and task with excellence and intention. Help me be faithful in the little things. I thank You for gifting me with the ability to do the tasks put before me. Remind me there is purpose in all things. I commit today, and each day, to You. Thank You for ordering my steps.

In Jesus's name I pray. Amen.

Based on: Colossians 3:12–13; Ephesians 4:32; 1 John 4:20–21; Luke 16:10; Psalm 119:133

Created to Feel

✝

A time to weep and a time to laugh;
A time to mourn and a time to dance.

Ecclesiastes 3:4

Have you ever been caught off guard by a wave of emotion that came out of nowhere? Maybe you found yourself turning green when you heard the news about your friend's successful business venture or you received another wedding invitation in the mail and have yet another reason to long for your own. Someone else's good news can sometimes throw you for a loop and bring out a side of you that you usually try to hide.

To feel is to be human, and it's natural for emotions to come over us. Although there is danger in letting feelings like bitterness and envy take root in our lives, we don't have to be afraid of them. We don't have to suppress our sadness or anger and pretend they don't exist. We can sit with them and work through them instead.

God created us with feelings. They are gifts and something from which we can learn. That feeling of awe while looking out from a mountaintop at the incredible view. The feeling of joy while cradling a newborn baby or seeing a loved one after months apart. The feeling of unease that might keep you safe, of ache to alert your mind that something is wrong, and even anger at injustice, which can move you to action. We don't have to negate our feelings or pretend they don't exist. Our emotions are valid. They are gifts from God, and there is a time to feel each one of them, whatever it may be in the moment.

What do you feel today?
Take a moment to reflect on this.

Jesus Felt Things Too

+

We do not have a high priest who cannot
sympathize with our weaknesses.

Hebrews 4:15

God can handle our emotions so well because He is no stranger to them. The writer of Hebrews reminds us that we have the High Priest—Jesus—who can sympathize with us. This means He knows what we feel.

In Matthew 21, when the religious leaders allowed the temple of God to be used as a marketplace instead of a house of prayer, Jesus flipped tables to show His righteous anger.

The Bible tells us that though Jesus taught and healed crowds of people, He would get weary and need to slip away by Himself to pray. Jesus was also acquainted with deep sadness and grief. Although all powerful and fully aware of how the story would end, He wept with the others at the tomb of Lazarus. And when He prayed in the Garden of Gethsemane before His crucifixion, His soul was grieved to the point of death. (See Luke 5:16; John 11:35; and Matthew 26:36–44 respectively for those accounts.)

Jesus understands our feelings because He felt them too. We do not serve a God who is unfamiliar with our struggles; we serve one who knows them well. This is twofold: If Jesus was not immune to emotion, neither are we, but also we can really trust Him with our hearts. He doesn't look down on us or condemn us but comes beside us and works with us, because He knows exactly what we are going through.

*How does knowing that Jesus experienced emotion
affect your relationship with Him today?*

The Strength of Convictions

✝

Jesus Christ is the same
yesterday and today, and forever.
Hebrews 13:8

According to David Jeremiah, *conviction* is "a fixed belief, a deeply held set of certainties that lodges in the center of your mind and heart."[14] Convictions are not merely opinions you form in the face of debate, nor do they vacillate with your mood or depend on your outlook on a particular day. You do not arrive at your convictions without taking time to reflect and consider them. They go deeper and do not easily waver.

We have the ability to intentionally choose many of our convictions over time, and by them we can shape our perspective. They are stronger than our emotions, which change with our circumstances, and they remain consistent. Our convictions ground us and keep us focused on our aims even when we don't feel like working for them.

When your convictions are rooted in whose you are and living a mission-possible life, they will drive you toward your calling. As believers, our convictions must rest in our identity in God and who He is. We can trust, based on this verse in Hebrews, that Jesus is the same yesterday, today, and forever. This can be our unchanging, steady conviction. Anything else we set our foundation on will inevitably fail. Everything in this world will change. Personal truth and experience cannot keep us anchored. But when we live based on the Word of God, Jesus, we can remain steady, even when circumstances try to shake us or our feelings change.

What are your convictions?
How can they be your foundation for
what you need to do today?

You Have a Choice

✝

When [Jesus] came ashore, He saw a large crowd,
and felt compassion for them and healed their sick.

Matthew 14:14

When Jesus received the devastating news that His cousin John the Baptist had been killed, He wanted to retreat to the mountain. He was in deep grief. If people knew what He was going through, no one would have batted an eye if He decided to take a break.

But while He was going to the mountain, a crowd followed Him. They were getting to know Jesus and they wanted more of Him. Jesus knew why He was sent to the world, so having compassion on them, Jesus put His much-needed time of solace aside and fulfilled their needs.

There were thousands of people in the crowd. As He was teaching and healing them, it started getting late and the people grew hungry. Instead of sending them away, He took five loaves of bread and two fish and fed all of them—and had leftovers! Despite the hardship He was going through, Jesus performed a grand miracle and fed thousands.

Sometimes you may be justified in what you feel and it may be tempting to retreat. But Jesus's life is always our example. Like Him, you have a choice: hide away or keep going on your mission. When you know your assignment and put the purpose of God over your own emotions, willingly following where He leads, you allow Him to work through your obedience. You may be surprised how God uses you in those moments.

How can you lay aside what you feel today
and pursue your God-given mission?

Your Emotions Can Be a Weapon Against You

+

Be of sober spirit, be on the alert. Your adversary, the devil,
prowls around like a roaring lion, seeking someone to devour.

1 Peter 5:8

When a lioness hunts her prey, she lurks hidden in the background, quietly observing and assessing the weakness of her target as she slowly glides to it. Then, at an opportune moment, she makes her move and attacks the unsuspecting creature.

We have an adversary who prowls like a lioness planning her attack. Satan's aim is to get us off track of living mission-possible lives. He will use anything that God has given us for good, including our emotions, and distort it for his own purposes to use against us.

When your heart hurts, it's easy to seek vengeance or vindication. Anger easily lends itself to bitterness if it is not kept in check. The Enemy can use heartbreak as an excuse for us to seek temporary pleasures that the Bible warns against.

But at the root of it, when we are solely focused on our emotions instead of living the lives we are called to live in balance and health, we are ultimately focused on ourselves instead of on Christ. If the Enemy can get us distracted from our purpose and, moreover, our God, he can weaken and attack us. He can keep us from our mission-possible lives.

Be aware of the schemes of the Enemy, and don't allow him a foothold in your life. Turn your eyes from yourself and onto Jesus, even in those moments when your emotions incline you to feel otherwise.

How have your emotions been used against you?

When You Don't Feel Like It

✝

The heart is more deceitful than all else
And is desperately sick;
Who can understand it?

Jeremiah 17:9

Some days, you wake up ready to conquer the world. Living a mission-possible life is easy when you feel like that. Other days, though, you don't feel that way. Based on your emotions alone, it will feel impossible to live a mission-possible life. Exhaustion takes over. Selfishness rises to the surface. Worry tangles up inside your mind. Or it just feels as if the weight of the world rests on your shoulders.

The Bible tells us in the book of Jeremiah that the human heart is the most deceitful thing. For most Westerners, this concept is probably foreign. But what we think of as heart isn't what ancient Jews understood it to be. One study Bible notes, "The Hebrew term for the heart [here] metaphorically refers to a person's inner life—the will, thoughts, motivations, and emotions."[15] In this sense, the heart is where we feel feelings, think thoughts, make choices, use reason, and take action. It's similar to how we think of the brain today. Unfortunately, the bad news is that our "heart" is fundamentally broken. It's "desperately sick" because of our sin nature.

However, the good news is that God is the One who changes hearts (see Ezekiel 36:26). Our corrupt nature no longer rules over us. Negative thoughts, feelings, and emotions will come and go and change with the weather. Thankfully, we have a Savior who does understand our new heart, even with all our tainted motivations.

*Might your feelings be getting in the way
of living out your mission? How can you trust God
with those feelings?*

Bring Your Worst

+

Come to Me, all who are weary and burdened,
and I will give you rest.
Matthew 11:28

When emotions are overwhelming and you're not sure how to press on based on conviction, go back to the Source. We can bring everything to Jesus, including what we might feel is our worst. He can handle our childish tantrums, our hate-filled anger, and our crushing envy.

Sometimes the heavy burdens that weigh down your heart make it feel impossible to live from a place of conviction. The emotions you carry can be exhausting and eat you up until it feels as though you have the energy and strength to muster up only a half-hearted prayer. Whatever you have, it's enough for Jesus.

Our emotions are sometimes too big to deal with on our own, and in those moments, we don't have to pretend to be strong. Jesus promises to give us rest in exchange for our brokenness and burdensome loads. Instead of unending sadness, He will give us joy. Instead of pointless despair, He will give us hope. Instead of unguided anger, He will give us soft hearts. Jesus will always take the burdens that weigh us down and give us the rest we need because He loves us that much.

Running your race is so much easier without a heavy load on your back. If you feel too weak today to work through what you feel, lay it all before Jesus. He will show you His grace, reminding you of the reason He called you to pursue a mission-possible life.

Are you overwhelmed by your emotions?
How can you lay down your burdens today?

An Audience of One

✝

Whatever you do, do your work heartily,
as for the Lord and not for people.

Colossians 3:23

During college and early in my professional career, sometimes I felt crushing pressure to perform at my best. But I've gained a new perspective and come to realize that winning the trophy is not what matters most.

More than achieving success in this world, I want to be a believer—first and foremost, a believer in God. I also want to be a believer in the people around me and a believer in why we're all here. A believer who, more than anything else, is working for the Lord and serving His purposes.

Remember that whatever you do, your main audience is God, not others. That's why, in Colossians, the apostle Paul reminds us to live life *for* the Lord, with God's purposes in mind. As humans, we tend to want to parade our efforts and highlight our philanthropy. But it's not the likes of our family, friends, co-workers, community, or whoever we befriend on social media that deserve our energy. It is the love of our Father in heaven that we need. Live each day performing in front of an audience of one: God. It's His attention and approval that matter most.

What would your life be like if you lived for an audience
of God alone, not an audience of other people?

Be You

✝

I will give thanks to You, because I am
awesomely and wonderfully made;
Wonderful are Your works,
And my soul knows it very well.

Psalm 139:14

When I talk about how special each one of us is, I'm not talking about the way society sees us. We are not special because we graduated from Ivy League schools, own successful businesses, run marathons, or excel at whatever we put our minds to.

I'm talking about the uniqueness with which we were created—the innate gifts, talents, and abilities that make up who we are. Think about what you love to do. Think about what you're good at, the unique traits that are hardwired in you. Maybe you are a talented musician or athlete. You may have a unique way of teaching others or great communication skills. You may be compassionate, charismatic, or an amazing host. You might be a strategic thinker, skilled at building things, or creative.

We all have trouble accepting parts of ourselves that we don't like: perhaps our natural hair color, the shape and size of our bodies, or our physical limitations. Many of us get stuck in life because we compare ourselves to others and feel less than. Instead of worrying about not being as smart, compassionate, or creative as someone else, we must accept and maximize what we have to offer.

Instead of wanting to be like someone else, make the most of your own talents. Use whatever God has given you.

List three things about you that are unique.

Whose You Are

✟

I have set the LORD continually before me;
Because He is at my right hand, I will not be shaken.

Psalm 16:8

I know what it feels like to be adored, praised, and respected. I also know what it feels like to be criticized, made fun of, and fired. One of the greatest things I've learned is that neither the highs nor the lows in life define who I am. The same is true for you. Our lives are going to be filled with successes and failures, wins and losses, and although our feelings may fluctuate, one thing must remain steady: our identities. Our identities are shaped by our experiences, our backgrounds, culture, media, and our communities. We define ourselves by past events we can't change and in comparison to superficial variables, which are always changing.

Who we are is more important than what we do or even what happens to us. Our identities are tied to whose we are. I am a child of God. My identity is grounded in my faith in a God who loves me, who gives me purpose, who sees the big picture, and who always has a greater plan.

When you have an identity that's bigger than what you do or have, even when that fails or someone says you're not good enough or that you can't or you won't or you shouldn't, you can still prevail. Knowing *whose* you are sets the groundwork for *who* you are.

Write down a high and a low you've experienced.
Then try to imagine how an identity in whose you are
would shape your responses to both.

The Object of God's Love

✛

In this is love, not that we loved God, but that He loved us
and sent His Son to be the propitiation for our sins.

1 John 4:10

Feeling loved is a cozy emotion bundled in warmth and comfort. It's also an emotion that typically comes because of something we have done or said or what we offer to another person. We can know we are special when we see the difference between God's love and human love. Coaches might love us because we score touchdowns. Your girlfriend might love you because you're the quarterback of the football team. Your friend might love you because you're funny and always there for him.

But would they die for you? Would they give up their lives so that you could live? That's what Jesus did. That's some powerful stuff!

God doesn't love you because you are a Christian or go to a certain church; He loves you as an individual, just because He does. You are wanted. You are adopted into His family. You belong. A sense of belonging is a basic human need, just like food and water. But who you are is not based on what others say or think about you, on fitting in, on belonging to a certain crowd, or on what you do for a living. Your identity is based on belonging to God. And no one can take this foundation away from you.

***Think of a time when you hungered for belonging.
Jot down how it feels to know that you already belong
in the family of God.***

A Match Made in Heaven

✛

To Him who is able to do far more abundantly beyond all that
we ask or think, according to the power that works within us.

Ephesians 3:20

We get to live mission possible not because of how great we are or what we have to offer but because of who makes the mission possible.

You are not a mistake. You were created and put on this earth for a reason. The God of this universe says He has good works for you to accomplish (see Ephesians 2:10). You might feel that you don't have that much to offer. Yes, you do. You might not realize it, but you plus Jesus equals miracles.

Remember how Jesus once fed a crowd of more than five thousand people five fish and two loaves of bread (see Matthew 14:13–21)? The simple lunch was provided for Him by a little boy who was willing to give even though he knew the generous act would leave him hungry. This kid trusted Jesus with all he had. Even though he didn't have much, he ignored the rumbling in his own belly to see what Jesus would do with such meager provision. If you don't know the story, Jesus performed a miracle and fed every person in attendance that day—and there were leftovers!

A mission-possible life doesn't depend on you. The miracle of living that way depends on God. Trust Him enough and give Him all you have, and see what He can do with it!

***What's the most humanly impossible thing
you will ask God to do today?***

You Are God's Child

✝

You are all sons and daughters of God
through faith in Christ Jesus.

Galatians 3:26

A few years ago, I wrote a book called *Shaken: Discovering Your True Identity in the Midst of Life's Storms*. I got some questions about the title. The publisher, wanting something positive, suggested *Unshaken*. I get where they were coming from. They wanted a title that illustrated the strength and steadfastness of faith, a picture of someone who refused to admit disappointment or didn't need to ask God questions about why such and such did or did not happen. But at that particular time in my life, everything around me felt, well, *shaken*. I held on to a dream I believed was from God, yet I experienced one closed door after another. The space between the highs and the lows was extreme. I felt confused, not sure what to do. And for me, the title perfectly reflected the state of my emotions and circumstances.

That time in my life also forced me to recognize my identity in Christ and to remember that no matter what my emotions are saying or what is happening around me, who I am and whose I am is always secure. That part of me is anchored in the God who created me. Because you're a believer, nothing will change your status as an adopted child into the family of your Father in heaven. You are His son or daughter.

When you feel shaken in your faith,
what is one truth you can hold on to?

The Object of Our Faith

✝

We have peace with God through our Lord Jesus Christ,
through whom we also have obtained our introduction by faith
into this grace in which we stand.

Romans 5:1–2

"Faith over fear" is a slogan you see everywhere, from T-shirts to face masks to hashtags. That's an important, biblical truth. But there's a greater truth to that catchy statement. It's not so much that faith itself overcomes; it's the *object* of our faith that overcomes, and that's Jesus. I can have faith—faith in formulas, faith in other people, faith in a robust economy—but all those things fall short of the unchanging omnipotence of Jesus.

It is He who helps us overcome not only fear but our insecurity, confusion, doubt, pain, and dysfunction. As believers, we are connected to not only the Source of life but also Life itself. We are connected to our Savior by reading His Word, by praying, and by connecting with other believers. Anytime you get away from Jesus, you're getting away from what matters. You're getting away from the Person who went on the rescue mission to save your life.

The only way to strengthen your identity in whose you are is to deepen your relationship with Him. Don't just read books about the Bible; *read the Bible*. Don't just listen to podcasts about prayer; *pray*. Don't just immerse yourself in surfacy interactions; *surround yourself* with people who encourage and tell you the truth, even when you don't want to hear it. Finally, don't just fill your mind with positive affirmations; *fix your eyes* on the One who gave His life for you, trampled death, and is coming back one day.

**What is one of your first memories
of being drawn to Jesus?**

A Prayer for Grounding

+

Lord, forgive me when I have put my faith and trust in earthly things or my own achievements or skills. I commit to nurturing a heart, mind, and soul that delight and honor in Your ways. Thank You for being the anchor in my life that keeps me strong and steady. I know with You by my side, I will not be shaken. I may feel abandoned or betrayed by people or events that happen to me, yet I'm so grateful that it does not change who I am in You. As a believer in Jesus Christ, I am a child of God, connected to the very life of Your Son, who sustains my life. I am so sorry when I take for granted who You have created me to be. When I complain about what I have or what I don't have, remind me that I am fearfully and wonderfully made, and settle Your truths into my heart so my soul knows it well.

When my emotions overwhelm me, may Your convictions lead me. I pray the peace of Jesus Christ rules in my heart and leads me with wisdom to make the right decisions. Thank You that no matter the chaos that surrounds me, You will help me be steadfast, immovable, and continually striving to do Your work.

In Jesus's name I pray. Amen.

Based on: Proverbs 23:26; Psalm 16:8; John 1:12; 15:5; Psalm 139:14; Colossians 3:15; 1 Corinthians 15:58

Give It Up to Be Free

✝

It was for freedom that Christ set us free.

Galatians 5:1

reedom. It's a buzzword in society today—a word that ignites both strong feelings and strong conversations. Ask any two individuals in America their personal definitions of freedom, and you will most likely hear two different interpretations. It is a concept that is universal yet still deeply personal.

For the follower of Christ, however, true freedom is something different altogether. It's paradoxical in nature. It's a gift that is gained only in surrender, in submission, and in laying down your life and picking up your cross to follow the One who surrendered His own life first. It's a radical trust, one not built upon the lesser things that this world offers but instead rooted in the only One who truly satisfies.

The definition of *surrender* can be interpreted as having a negative connotation. At face value, the word conjures up negative images of waving a white flag, giving up, failing to overcome challenges, or being defeated. Surrender seems like an act of submission that we should avoid at all costs.

In its spiritual context, however, we must embrace surrender. In addition, to live mission-possible lives, our priorities must be in order. The first step is surrendering our wants and preferences, and even our steps, to God. Now when arriving at the critical juncture of acceptance and surrender, you will be able to wholeheartedly ask God to use you for His purpose regardless of your strengths and weaknesses.

How does the truth that surrender yields freedom enable you to live a mission-possible life?

Free to Hope

✝

May the God of hope fill you with all joy and peace in believing,
so that you will abound in hope by the power of the Holy Spirit.

Romans 15:13

For many individuals around the world, 2020 and 2021 were years in which hope was hard to find. Uncertainty, confusion, anxiety, depression, and fear took root in ways unseen in recent history and often eliminated any glimmer of hope. Yet if Christ has set us free, hope is already ours for both the giving and the receiving.

When we truly grasp that every moment of our lives is under the loving, watchful eyes of the Father—the Sovereign One for whom nothing is a surprise—how can we not have hope? Every one of us will walk through trials that might look like seasons of pain, loss, or grief. However, hope that is born out of the freedom Christ offers is never lost. He who promised is faithful.

When we surrender to His perfect plan and trust in Him completely, we find a freedom that empowers us to hope. What happens when we are filled with hope? God becomes more visible in our lives because we become more dependent on Him. We begin to experience His love so deeply and so personally that we become free to love others without limits and conditions. If you think about it, surrendering to God is empowering! In a world where uncertainty seems to prevail, that is something we ought to strive for.

Do you know someone who is caught in a
seemingly hopeless situation? Find a way to share hope
with that person today.

Jesus, the Master of Surrender

✛

Being found in appearance as a man, He humbled Himself
by becoming obedient to the point of death: death on a cross.

Philippians 2:8

From the classroom to the boardroom, from the big screens to our phone screens, we live in a society that tells us to look out for number one. It's about *us*. If we won't take care of ourselves first, who will? To the nonbeliever, a life surrendered to God and others makes little sense. Today's culture is certainly proof of that. But the life and death of Jesus Christ modeled for us a different way of thinking.

If anyone had both reason and ability to promote himself above all others, it was Jesus. He was the Son of God, after all, empowered to heal, save, deliver, and perform miracles that defied the laws of nature and physics. His very name made demons tremble. Instead, He did the very opposite of promoting Himself. He lived a life of sacrifice on behalf of others. And in what would become the single greatest act of service the world would ever know, He humbled Himself by becoming obedient to death—a gruesome, humiliating, and excruciatingly painful death that should have been ours to experience.

We will probably never be tasked with dying in another's place. However, those who know Him will be called countless times a day to think of others with humility, to surrender our own desires, to elevate the wants and needs of others above our own, and to submit to an authority who is above all others. In doing so, we will find that there is freedom in putting others first.

***Think of someone you can serve today,
even if it will cost you something, and do it.***

Purpose over Preference

+

Give me your heart . . .
And let your eyes delight in my ways.
Proverbs 23:26

When I was a teenager, summers offered me a couple of options. One of them was extra athletic training. Another opportunity, scheduled at the same time, was spending a few weeks on a mission trip in the Philippines serving those less fortune and sharing the good news. In the spirit of transparency, I must admit that my initial preference was to train. If I had a chance to become a better player, I was all in. At the same time, I knew there was a greater purpose at play. While summer training would elevate my muscle strength, my stamina, and my endurance to a greater degree, serving others for Jesus would leave a lasting impact not only on my life but on the lives of others, and for a lot longer than any training session in a gym would do.

A mission-possible life has less to do with us and more to do with others. Mission living means being motivated by something other than yourself. It requires submitting your preferences to God. Sometimes that doesn't feel very good or doesn't make you look as favorable as you'd like.

I don't know how to explain this, but every time I chose a mission trip over extra athletic training, I never returned to the States at a physical disadvantage. I still trained while overseas, even with limited resources. I did push-ups and squats as often as possible, carrying friends from youth group on my back. And each time, I'd return home stronger. Surrendering what we prefer may not come easy, but it'll always be worth it.

**How can you better surrender your priorities,
needs, and wants to God's purposes?**

Say Yes

+

Your kingdom come.
Your will be done.

Matthew 6:10

I'll never forget the day my dad called me from overseas and told me that he had just purchased the freedom of four young girls who were about to get sold into human trafficking. I was in my midtwenties at the time and was completely unaware that such a transaction was even possible. Yet I knew I had heard him correctly. My dad, in a situation hard for most of us to understand, had opened his wallet and bought as many girls as he could with the cash he had on hand—girls who would otherwise be sold in a human-trafficking transaction and forced to do unspeakable things. At that point in time, there was no safe house to take the girls to, so we built one.

There's a saying that evil triumphs when good men do nothing. My dad was not going to be the man who did nothing. Had he stood silently, who knows where the girls would have been taken to and what would have been done to them?

Honestly, we at the foundation weren't prepared. But through the years, that single moment in time—a moment in which my dad took a stand for what was right—was the beginning of a ripple effect still in motion today.

We must step into the darkness to be part of the solution that only God can make possible. We might not know the how or the why involved in the process, but what's most important in the moment is taking the first step: saying yes.

Do you recognize the still, small whisper in your heart? If so, what is God asking you to do?

Yes = Impact

✛

Our life for yours if you do not tell this business of ours;
and it shall come about when the LORD gives us the land
that we will deal kindly and faithfully with you.

Joshua 2:14

Hated because of her ethnicity and scorned because of her work as a prostitute, Rahab was a woman in the Bible who hid two Israelite spies in her home (see Joshua 2). She could have been killed for doing so, but she trusted that God had a purpose behind this mission. And in the process, she saved the spies as well as her entire family.

We know nothing about Rahab's life prior to this time. What we can safely assume, however, is that she was looked down upon, ignored, and certainly abused—a woman living on the very bottom rung of society's ladder. Yet God did not see her that way. He saw a woman to whom He had given both wisdom and courage.

At some point or another, you may have felt like Rahab. Less than. Unseen. Unwanted. Maybe abused in some way by others, perhaps even those closest to you. Rahab's story shows that God can, and will, use anyone to accomplish His will and play a significant role in His mission.

There's a reason why Rahab is listed in Hebrews 11 (commonly known as the "Hall of Faith") and why she is part of the genealogy of Christ. Her obedience—her yes—was used by God to bring about His purposes.

True, our yes to God may come with a cost,
but the impact is always worth the cost. Think back to
a previous yes—what happened in your or
someone else's life as a result?

Give God Your Pain

✝

God causes all things to work together for good to those who
love God, to those who are called according to His purpose.

Romans 8:28

Not every prayer is answered in the way that we want. Sometimes things happen for reasons we can't explain, that don't make sense, or that seem unfair. One of my favorite quotes is from my big sister Christy. Amid her health struggles together with the challenges of being a missionary overseas, she became convinced that "God will never waste pain that's offered to Him." I love that. God will never waste your pain. He will never waste your heartache. He will never waste your loss.

If you've lost something precious to you—a dream, a marriage, a child—I can't tell you exactly the purpose or plan or what the future holds. But I will say that God is loving, He is sovereign, and even though your heart may be broken in a million pieces, He will never leave nor forsake you. He can, and will, use even the bad in order to orchestrate good.

I know it's easier to hold on to the bad stuff, to control it to some extent, and to keep God out of the picture, but when we do, we're the ones who suffer. Trust God. Trust His heart. Trust that He loves you. Trust that He has a plan.

What hurt are you struggling with right now that you need to surrender to God? Make the decision to do it today.

God's Hands and Feet

✝

As God's chosen people, holy and dearly loved, clothe yourselves with compassion, kindness, humility, gentleness and patience.

Colossians 3:12, NIV

Guest devo by Kelli Smith
Relationship to TTF: mother of W15H recipient

We often hear that we should be the hands and feet of Christ, but what does that look like? As a mama who just ended a seven-year battle of trying to physically save my son from cancer, it looks much different than I used to envision.

As a believer, I thought that it meant that I would use my feet to walk and travel anywhere God called to reach His people. I also envisioned using my hands for manual labor to help God's people in need. I saw myself being on the giving side, physically sacrificing to fulfill God's beauty and love by serving His children. My life was pretty chill, and I felt I could serve indefinitely without ever needing to be on the receiving end. I was wrong!

During our seven-year battle followed by starting a new life without my sweet son, Chase, I have relied heavily on my Father's "earthly" hands and feet. So many people in our tiny school, small town, large state, and social media presence have extended their hands and feet to show us compassion and God's love. God continually sent an earthly physical dose of His grace and reassurance. He would send someone clothed in kindness and humility who had a gentle, empathetic ear to listen to our heartbreak and wipe away our tears. The compassion that Christ pours out through our family, friends, and strangers is such a gift! I am so thankful for others who are willing to be God's hands and feet.

How can you make a difference as the
"earthly" hands and feet for Christ?

Keep Taking the Loop

✝

Be strong and do not lose courage,
for there is a reward for your work.

2 Chronicles 15:7

Do you ever feel God nudging your heart to do something—talk to someone, send an old friend a message, take a different turn instead of the one leading home? I'll never forget being in downtown Austin one evening with some friends. On our way home after dinner, stopped at a traffic light, I saw a homeless man on the sidewalk. I felt an internal tug to pull over and go talk to him. I wrestled internally with that calling but made the decision to go to my friend's house. However, God's nudging was too powerful and I returned to downtown not long after.

I drove around downtown, taking the same loop around the city streets multiple times in my effort to find the guy. About the fourth time I looped around, still unable to find him, I happened upon a random side street that looked like a homeless community around an abandoned warehouse. It was an incredible opportunity to pass out bottles of water and encourage some people.

I believe God speaks to us in our hearts more than we realize. I feel His prompting often, but I don't always follow it. Don't be discouraged when you feel you've missed an opportunity God has presented. Here's what's important: Keep taking the loop. Keep getting back in the car. Keep trusting. Keep listening. Keep saying yes. It's never too late.

When was the last time you felt God speaking to your heart? What did you do about it?

Do It Anyway

✛

Be strong and courageous, do not be afraid or in dread of them,
for the LORD your God is the One who is going with you.
He will not desert you or abandon you.

Deuteronomy 31:6

E very now and then, I still get nervous about speaking in public, even though I've done it for years. It's because I care about the outcome. I want to do my best for God and for everyone who is listening. When we do something that stretches who we are, that demands courage, that pulls us into unfamiliar territory, that is uncommon and can make a difference, it's going to be worth it. Still, that first step is always the hardest.

When was the last time you did something beyond your comfort zone? Something that wasn't familiar but could do a world of good in the life of another? When you remain in your comfort zone, you don't grow. You're not challenged. You stay the same.

It's okay to feel afraid while taking the first step. Doing something against the flow of culture, society, or the crowd might tempt you to run and hide.

I think about the men Jesus took under His wing—the unorthodox group of fishermen, tax collectors, and revolutionaries. I wonder if they hesitated when Jesus asked if they would follow Him. Maybe Peter thought, for a moment, that he might be better off continuing his fishing business than following someone who was making some pretty controversial and crazy-sounding statements. He decided to follow anyway.

Don't fight against what's right or what's possible because the unknown territory freaks you out. Do it anyway.

**Write down a prayer for courage, as well as what it can
look like this week to be courageous.**

Do What You Love and Has Meaning

✝

I have seen that nothing is better than when a person is happy
in his activities, for that is his lot.

Ecclesiastes 3:22

I don't do things I don't care about. I don't endorse brands I don't care for. I want to do and support things that I love. Our time is so limited on earth, so for the time that I do have here, I want to do things that I'm passionate about. I want to do things that *matter*. I want to do things that have significance. For example, I love playing sports, writing, and motivating others, but I'm *most* passionate about bringing faith, hope, and love to those needing a brighter day during their darkest hour through the work we do at my foundation. So I base my priorities on what's in my heart based on my convictions, and I do my best to live out that passion through my conscious decisions. Choosing to do the things that are significant is what drives me most of all. Happiness can come in many ways, but fulfillment is always attached to a deeper purpose beyond self. Fulfillment and significance will come only when we do what makes us happy *together with* a greater purpose intertwined in those things.

My advice to you is to do what you love and what needs to be done. Seek out a mission and believe in it. You must find motivation in your mission, and you must be willing to sacrifice for it. When you believe in the mission, you will gladly embrace the grind that comes with it.

What is one thing that you enjoy doing that is also
something through which you can serve and love others?

No Bossing Around

✛

We are taking every thought captive to
the obedience of Christ.

2 Corinthians 10:5

I t's not easy to hear others say bad things about, make fun of, or belittle you. And thanks to social media, we have millions of talking heads that often have something bad to say about anyone at any time. However, sometimes the harshest words we hear come from our own minds.

What have you thought about yourself over the past week, or even in the last twenty-four hours, that may have been negative?

- *I won't get the promotion.*
- *We'll never afford that kind of vacation.*
- *I could never go to that school.*

Our forward movement is often stopped because we hold ourselves back, paralyzed. We compare our journeys, our marriages, our jobs, and our hopes and dreams with everyone else's. And in our minds, in some way, what's ours never matches up. We think we fall short: *I'm doing something wrong. I'm not enough. That person has it easier.* The trail that stems from these negative thoughts usually leads down a rabbit hole.

I love the intentionality with which Paul wrote "taking every thought captive." It's almost aggressive in nature. In other words, "I'm not going to let these thoughts boss me around."

Think about a time when you allowed negative thoughts to take you prisoner. I'm sure the outcome wasn't a good one. When toxicity seeps into your mind and determines to settle in that space, buck up. Remember the One who is really in charge. If the winds and waves obey Him (see Matthew 8:27), your thoughts can too.

What is at the center of your thought life?

Represent

✛

We are ambassadors for Christ, as though God were
making an appeal through us; we beg you on behalf
of Christ, be reconciled to God.

2 Corinthians 5:20

If you're creating awareness for a hair company, shaving your head probably isn't the first task you ought to assign yourself two weeks after signing the contract. That would be sketchy ambassador behavior. What you should do is post about how your morning shampoo smelled incredible and made your hair super shiny, not to mention that the gel you whisked into your mane locks your style in place without feeling like a helmet. Go ahead! Look into the camera and toss those silky strands into the breeze like a salad. This is what's required of brand ambassadors.

The dictionary defines the word *ambassador* as "an authorized messenger or representative."[16] I represent a few different companies these days, and part of the requirement of those relationships is to fulfill certain contractual obligations. A contract says, "If . . . then." In other words, "*If* I do a, b, and c, *then* you will do x, y, and z." I'm grateful I'm not in a contractual relationship with God. As believers, we are in *covenant*—a promise—with God, who says, "I will," regardless of our actions. He promises to love us even if we fail Him. It's the precise opposite of a conditional relationship. It's unconditional love.

It's an honor to be called an ambassador for Christ. It might be the greatest thing we do to show off Jesus. May we live in such a way that others want in on this kind of life.

What is your goal in being an ambassador for Jesus?

Fear Not

+

Fear not, for I am with you;
Be not dismayed, for I am your God.
I will strengthen you,
Yes, I will help you,
I will uphold you with My righteous right hand.

Isaiah 41:10, NKJV

Guest devo by Elise Lato
Relationship to TTF: mother of W15H recipient
who passed away from neurofibromatosis

I have always struggled with fear. When I was little, I was afraid of the dark. When I got a little older, my fear of the dark morphed into fears of conflict, decisions, my future—*Am I doing the right thing? Am I even a good person?*—and fear of becoming a mother. Or not being a *good* mother. In many ways, fear has been imbedded into many aspects of my life. There are times that fear has been healthy, and times where it held me back.

During our hardest time, our eldest daughter, Alexis, chose Isaiah 41:10 to be her inspiration to guide and comfort her through her journey. When we had been told Alexis was terminally ill, my other fears seemed so little compared to this new one of losing my child.

Now I look back and see that fear wasn't always a bad thing. It has challenged me, sometimes making me stop everything to think about and face it. And my fear did something more: It pushed me to really depend on God for answers, for strength, and sometimes even for comfort. More and more, I find that my conversation with God includes questioning my fears, asking for guidance, and laying those fears down before Him.

Make a list of the fears you are currently battling with,
and then talk to Jesus about each one specifically.

A Prayer to Strive Well

✛

Lord, there are times I haven't represented You well. I put my desires, my preferences, and my need to look good and be right over Your truth and what You value. Forgive me and help me to reflect You better as Your ambassador. May my life exemplify what it means to be reconciled to You through Jesus Christ. The mission to make my life count isn't always easy, so I thank You for Your promise to strengthen me, help me, and uphold me with Your right hand. As Your Spirit lives in me, embolden me to walk each day by Your Spirit. Remind me that trusting You is always best, even when I don't see it or understand. Thank You for being a God of hope who fills me with joy and peace so that I, too, may abound in hope. Place people in my path for divine connection, that through me, Your hope and faithfulness can be seen and sown. Thank You for being so faithful and teaching me the importance of being steadfast and courageous. Help me stay encouraged, knowing that living for You is always worth it.

In Jesus's name I pray. Amen.

Based on: 2 Corinthians 5:20; Isaiah 41:10; Galatians 5:25; Romans 15:13; 2 Chronicles 15:7

The Present Rescue Mission

✝

Vindicate the weak and fatherless;
Do justice to the afflicted and destitute.
Rescue the weak and needy;
Save them from the hand of the wicked.

Psalm 82:3–4

From beginning to end, the message of the Bible is one of rescue. Because of our inability to rescue ourselves from separation from God, the Father sent His only Son to pay the price for our sin, securing eternal life with Him for everyone who believes. But the stories of rescue began long before Jesus ever walked the earth. From the very moment Adam and Eve chose to go their own way instead of obeying the Lord, the ultimate rescue plan was set in motion.

In its most basic definition, *rescue* means "to free or deliver from confinement, danger, or difficulty."[17] However, in tracing the word back to its Semitic origins, the translation goes a step further, adding "to fortify, to arm someone for war."[18] It's an extension of the definition that is crucial to fully understanding not only our own salvation but also our calling to rescue others in Jesus's name.

The calling is not optional, and the opportunity will not last forever. One day the clock will run out, Jesus will come back, and God will make all things new. Until then and only in His power, we are called to defend the weak and the powerless. Now is the time to act.

With so many social issues in focus in our society today, is there one that has caught your attention?

Choose Now

✝

This is the day which the LORD has made.

Psalm 118:24

H ow many times have you heard, or even said, the phrase "Good things come to those who wait"? While there is certainly some truth in those words, the saying is more apt for a toddler looking to gobble an ice cream sundae before dinner than it is for a grown-up committed to living a mission-possible life.

We are not promised tomorrow. We are not guaranteed next week. We do, however, have *this* moment—the time we are given when we wake up each day. God gives us today as a gift. He wants us to pursue today, using the time we are gifted to grow, to love others well, to help someone, and to pursue a dream He's put on our hearts. Today is our day to live without fear of the unknown, to live without being chained by failures or what-ifs. No matter what today holds, we can choose to say yes to the opportunities of this moment.

The Latin aphorism meaning "Seize the day" comes from a longer sentence in the Roman poet Horace's work *Odes*: "Carpe diem quam minimum credula postero." It is translated as, "Pluck the day, trusting as little as possible in the next one."[19]

Good advice! Make the most of your life by choosing now to make the most of your day.

What would you do today if you knew you didn't have tomorrow? Make a list of how your priorities, conversations, and activities could change if you chose to seize this day for the Lord.

This Is a Race. Run.

✦

Let's run with endurance the race that is set before us.

Hebrews 12:1

Usain Bolt is arguably the fastest person in the world. He won his first-ever Olympic gold medal at the 2008 Beijing Games when he clocked a world record time of 9.69 seconds during the 100-meter race. The following year at the world championships in Germany, Bolt ran the 100-meter without slowing down. He broke his own world record, clocking in at 9.58 seconds. Amazing!

Most of us are not competing in track-and-field world championships. We all *are*, however, participating in the race of life. The author of Hebrews encouraged us to run that race with endurance. Not to jog. Not to take a thousand breaks. Not even to do the bare minimum to just get by. Endurance means a steady fight, a commitment to carry on even when you don't feel like it.

God has called you to live with purpose. You are not just wandering around in this life; you are on the track, making your way toward the triumph of a finish line. The race of faith is forged with intentionality. It's your chance to take the platform (big or small) that you've been given and make it count.

What obstacles have slowed you down on your faith journey? How can you avoid being sidetracked by them in the future and instead run with endurance?

Nonstop Urgency

✛

You are also to be like people who are waiting for their master
when he returns from the wedding feast, so that they may
immediately open the door for him when he comes and knocks.

Luke 12:36

Does your faith kindle urgency in your life? I'll never forget watching the Broadway show *Hamilton*, Lin-Manuel Miranda's unique retelling of the story of Alexander Hamilton. I enjoyed the show so much that I returned to see it on two more occasions. The third time I watched it, I was struck by the tune "Non-Stop." The song captures Hamilton's stubbornness and persistence. When the actor playing Hamilton sang the line "Like you're running out of time," I was transfixed by the urgency with which this pivotal political character had lived his life.

I want my journey of faith to be characterized by that nonstop urgency too. I want my life to magnify Christ's work as much as it possibly can. And I want Christ's message to be amplified by my mission-driven life for years to come. I'm not there yet, but this is an ongoing goal.

As believers, we know that one day Jesus is coming back. Until that time, we have a mission on this earth: to share His love. The world is filled with hurting people who need to hear the good news. We must live our lives with a sense of urgency in how we love, give to, and serve others. One day Jesus will return and time will run out. Does your life demonstrate this sense of urgency?

***What is one thing you can do, starting now,
to be prepared for when your Master returns?***

For Such a Time

✦

If you keep silent at this time, liberation and rescue will arise
for the Jews from another place, and you and your father's house
will perish. And who knows whether you have not attained
royalty for such a time as this?

Esther 4:14

S cholars believe Esther was a teenager when she caught the eye of the most powerful man in Persia, King Ahasuerus, and eventually became his queen. Unbeknownst to the king, though, she was Jewish. As history unfolded, there came a time when her ethnicity could no longer be hidden. Esther's husband's right-hand man had issued a decree declaring the mass murder of all Jewish people. This nightmare became an opportunity for one woman, Esther, to single-handedly save her people from genocide. She had to make a choice—and she had to act fast.

Forced to reveal her background, Esther asked the king to spare the lives of the Jewish people. Revealing the truth could have cost Esther her very own life, but the moment, the mission, to which she knew she had been tasked was greater. Esther bravely and humbly asked for the king to spare the lives of her people. God honored Esther's commitment to His call and saved the Jewish nation from annihilation.

There are times when we will have the luxury of time to make certain decisions. At other times, however, we must decide immediately and choose to do the right thing. Always remember that God has prepared you for such a time as this.

The unchangeables of your life—your race or ethnicity,
for instance—are God-given pieces of who you are,
purposefully. What are some ways that your unchangeables
could be (or have been) God's tools in your family,
social circles, or community?

Get Sent

✝

The harvest is plentiful,
but the laborers are few.
Luke 10:2

After a long day of interaction with staff and inmates on death row at a men's prison in Florida, my two friends and I were about to leave when one of them noticed a hallway we had not gone down. My friend asked the warden what it was. The hallway led to a part of the prison called "suicide watch." Despite our exhaustion, we felt led to encourage the prisoners in that corridor.

I'll never forget my interaction with the man in the third cell. The prisoner had been found guilty of murder. He had also killed a fellow inmate a few days prior. The warden mentioned that the prisoner was willing to try anything to kill himself.

The minute I peered through the small plexiglass window on the padded cell door, the man's eyes met mine and he burst into tears, crumpling to the floor like a rag doll. Once he composed himself, we talked for a few minutes. He told me that five minutes earlier, he had prayed to God for the first time in his life. He prayed, "I have no hope. If You're real, show me something! If not, I'm going to do anything I can to kill myself!" Five minutes later, there we were. I led the man to the Lord that day. I couldn't help but cry. God had a special plan for this young man. He had an appointment to meet with Jesus.

Lives are at stake. People need Jesus. Ask God to use you to help others move out of the darkness and into the light.

Who do you know that needs the light of Jesus?
Tell them about Him today!

Time to Work

✝

We must carry out the works of Him who sent Me as long
as it is day; night is coming, when no one can work.

John 9:4

In John 9, Jesus and His disciples were walking when they passed a man who had been blind since birth. Curious about the origins of his condition, the disciples asked Jesus why the man was blind. Had he or his parents done something wrong to deserve his condition? "None of the above," Jesus replied. It was so the work of God could be displayed in him (see verse 3), and He shared with them what is written in today's scripture. Jesus then healed the man by applying a peculiar (and rather gross) muddy concoction of His own spit and dirt from the ground.

Can you feel the sense of urgency in Jesus's words? It would be six months later that He would die a painful death on a cross. He knew His time on earth was limited. As such, Jesus's mantra was "Let's get to work!" He left us an example to follow in every area of life. He taught us how to love, serve, give, and pray. In fact, in this verse, Jesus tells us to work now for the kingdom.

It's not always about our timelines and which pleasures or plans we can squeeze in; it's about what we can do for the kingdom of God with the time we are given.

Is there something you feel led to do for the kingdom of God? Find someone with whom to talk to about it and ask if they can help you figure out how to get it done.

Do the Hard Thing

✝

Daniel made up his mind that he would not defile himself
with the king's choice food . . . ; so he sought permission . . .
that he might not defile himself.

Daniel 1:8

Daniel and his friends were taken captive to serve in Babylon under King Nebuchadnezzar. They were forced to take on new names and indoctrinated in the new land. Fearing God, however, they chose to remain close to their convictions.

As a slave, Daniel was allotted food that God had called unclean. Unable to go against what he believed, he made a request that could have cost him his life: to eat a modified meal. Where it would have been easy to just keep his head down and go with the flow, he chose to take a stand, not knowing where it would lead him.

As a result of Daniel's bold choice and desire to follow the Lord's commands, God gifted Daniel with wisdom and skill like no one else had and, because of his boldness, he was held in high esteem by the king, who put him in a position where he was easily able to show the glory of God through his life.

The hard choice may cost you, but God is gracious to those who honor Him. Like Daniel, do the hard thing, even if it's unpopular. Dare yourself to make the difficult decision, the one that will cost you the most. Walking the easy path only leads to mediocrity and monotony, and the plans of God do not settle for those.

***Are you willing to do the hard thing? How can you ask
God for help in making difficult choices?***

Know the Cost

✝

Which one of you, when he wants to build a tower,
does not first sit down and calculate the cost,
to see if he has enough to complete it?

Luke 14:28

Peter loved Jesus. That's why, when Jesus told His disciples of His impending death at the Last Supper, Peter made a passionate claim: "Lord, I am ready to go with You both to prison and to death!" (Luke 22:33). His bold claim came in an emotional moment, but when he was put to the test shortly after, he denied Christ three times for fear of what would happen to him.

It's easy to make extreme statements like Peter did when you are sitting close to Jesus. "I'll go anywhere You lead" and "You can have it all" seem like the right things to say in times of worship or at a church service. They sound really nice, and our hearts may even be sincere when we say them. But rhetoric gets us only so far.

Are we making passionate claims without considering what living them out would take? We mistake passion for exuberance when it means suffering. Many of us as Christians would be quick to say we are willing to lay down our lives and follow Jesus, but like Peter on the night before the Crucifixion, do we chicken out when trials come?

If we desire to follow Christ and live out the purposes He has for us, the cost will be our comfort. Are you willing to pay it?

In what way might God be asking you to get
out of your comfort zone today?

Boldness and the Holy Spirit

✛

When they had prayed, the place where they had gathered together was shaken, and they were all filled with the Holy Spirit
and began to speak the word of God with boldness.

Acts 4:31

The point of our mission-possible lives is spelled out in the Great
Commission at the end of Matthew 28. It is to spread the gospel
to the ends of the earth and make disciples. But this statement on its
own can seem daunting. The ends of the earth might seem foreign
to you. The idea of making disciples may be confusing. And who
knows what other people will say about us when we spread the message of Jesus?

In Acts 2, Peter delivered a sermon and after listening to his message, three thousand people got baptized (see verse 41). This was the
same guy who, only weeks before, denied Jesus three times after declaring his passion for Him. The difference between these two instances was that Peter was now filled with the Holy Spirit. The same
Peter who was always putting his foot in his mouth was now preaching to a multitude of thousands.

Choosing to get uncomfortable is hard on our own. The thought
of having to declare what we believe can make us weak in the knees.
However, one of the things the Holy Spirit does is give us the boldness to share what we need to share. Apart from Him, we may be
intimidated. But with the Spirit dwelling inside us, we can do far
more than we ever imagined we could.

***What can you do today to cultivate boldness
in your willingness to follow Jesus?***

Complacency

✛

Demonstrate the same diligence ... so that you will not
be sluggish, but imitators of those who through faith
and endurance inherit the promises.

Hebrews 6:11–12

Ever notice that just when you think the worst is over and you can breathe, crisis hits as you are suddenly unprepared? When you think you've reached the summit, there's still more to climb. When you thought you paid all your bills, one more comes from out of nowhere. You do the work you're supposed to do, and when you believe you are finished and start to relax, something else surprises you.

We sometimes feel like this in our walks with Christ too. For a while, we spend consistent time in prayer and reading the Bible. Then we feel like we've reached a healthy point and slack off. We skip our devotionals a few mornings and neglect to pray as much. We become comfortable with life as it is and feel no need to depend on God as we once did. We grow complacent, settling into a feeling of quiet security, believing that we are safe from any impending harm. We begin to let our spiritual guard down.

Don't give in to comfort, even when life is going easy. Continue to grow closer to God in the good times so that you can endure and inherit the promises.

Have you let your guard down spiritually? How can you remain close to God when life is comfortable?

The Safe Option

+

There is a way which seems right to a person,
But its end is the way of death.

Proverbs 16:25

When Abram originally received the call from God to go, his nephew Lot was with him. Both had been abundantly blessed by God, but the land they shared suddenly felt a little too small for the two of them. Abram suggested that instead of fighting they separate for the good of their relationship. Looking out at the land before them, he told Lot to choose (see Genesis 12–13).

Lot chose the way that seemed right to him. By looking out at the fertile land, he made the safest, best choice for him and his family, near Sodom and Gomorrah. But in the end, his choice led to destruction, not to flourishing, as he imagined it would.

Choosing to play it safe instead of following God can lead to danger, as it did for Lot. When we fail to seek God and choose based on our wisdom what we think is best, we often fail. Deciding to go down the path of least resistance seems comfortable for a moment, but we cannot grow while we are on it, and there is no prize waiting for us at the end.

Abram saw the land too. He could have gone with the safest option, but he had already made the decision to go where God would lead him. Because he trusted God, Abram eventually saw His promises fulfilled. When you make the decision to trust God in the unknown, you can also witness His will coming to fruition.

*Are you making decisions based on what you can see,
or are you relying on God to lead you?*

Train for the Prize

✝

Do you not know that those who run in a race all run, but only
one receives the prize? Run in such a way that you may win.

1 Corinthians 9:24

For a season in my life, the thing I was most passionate about was
sports. I would sometimes wake up in the middle of the night to
train just because I knew no one else was doing it. I knew I was
working toward something bigger, so I wasn't afraid to get uncomfortable. I made it my mission to train for the prize because it was
important to me.

What's important to you? Remember, as Christians, we have the
greatest prize waiting for us at the end of our race: eternal life with
Jesus. We receive the gift of salvation through faith, but faith is not a
onetime event. We need to practice our faith continually. This
means trusting God even when it makes no sense to us and going
where He leads even if we're not exactly sure where we're going.
This could mean striking up a conversation with your barista even if
you're an introvert, or tithing instead of holding on to every penny.

Like I trained for sports all the time, we must also practice our
faith constantly. This means trusting God and getting uncomfortable in small moments, not just in the big ones. Don't settle for ordinary. Go all the way, in every aspect of your life.

***In what small matters can you practice
your faith in God in big ways?***

Risk Looking Like a Fool

✝

*By faith Noah, being warned by God about things not yet seen, in
reverence prepared an ark for the salvation of his household.*

Hebrews 11:7

God had a strange command for Noah. In a world filled with
people so corrupt that God regretted ever creating them (see
Genesis 6:6), Noah stood out for his righteousness and faithfulness.
So when God told him to make a giant ark in the middle of nowhere,
possibly miles away from water, with enough room for his family
and two of every animal, because of an impending flood, Noah did it.

The project was a long-term project and, to be honest, it made no
sense at the time. Noah's neighbors likely looked at him like he was
crazy. To their natural eyes, there would have been no reason for
this man to build such an enormous boat so far from water and
minus the threat of a storm. He was possibly mocked by others who
did not revere God as he did and did not believe in a coming dooms-
day. But Noah's faith in God's word kept him doing something that
made no sense, even if there were days he felt like a fool doing it.

Do you feel as though God is instructing you to do something
that makes no sense to you? Are you afraid that if you start doing it,
people will judge and criticize you? God moves when we take risks
and trust Him, even if it makes us look foolish.

*Are you concerned about what others may think of you
if you step out in faith? Why or why not?*

Greater Than the Giants

✛

The land through which we have gone to spy out is a land that devours its inhabitants; and all the people whom we saw in it are people of great stature.... We were like grasshoppers.

Numbers 13:32–33

Guest devo by Dr. Rick Gardner
Relationship to TTF: physician at Tebow CURE Hospital
in Bulawayo, Zimbabwe

The Israelites were seeking to enter the Promised Land after forty years in the wilderness. They sent some spies ahead who returned with disturbing news: The land was occupied by giants, a seemingly insurmountable problem. The spies had a natural fear of the unknown and felt they had to tackle the challenges ahead in their own strength. Joshua, their leader, gave this response: "Do not be afraid . . . because we will devour them" (Numbers 14:9, NIV). Joshua knew that God was with them. He remembered the abundant miracles that led them away from Egypt and sustained them in the wilderness. He had a truly God-sized vision and knew they would be stronger for having defeated the Amalekites and that God would be glorified.

We see these giants in our own lives: situations that seem impossible to overcome. We also forget the way God has blessed us in the past. He does not promise us easy lives. He does not keep us from trials and conflicts. They shape us, our faith is strengthened by them, and we get to understand that dependence on God is where our focus we should be. We must look at the challenges we face not through our own frailties but in the secure knowledge that we have an amazing and faithful God who is with us every step of the way.

Seek out a prayer warrior who is willing to do
spiritual battle with you and, through the power of God,
help you overcome your giants!

Simple Love

✝

The one who does not love does not know
God, because God is love.

1 John 4:8

Guest devo by Maureen
Relationship to TTF: Night to Shine volunteer and
mom of special-needs daughter

One of the many blessings of having a special-needs daughter was her gift of unconditional love. Our sweet Brittaney did not recognize anyone's differences; she loved *everyone*. At the doctor's office one day, a precious girl sat in the waiting room with us. She had been born with severe facial abnormalities and was very shy. Her mom told us later that she was uncomfortable talking to people. Brittaney just started showing this little girl the teddy bear she always carried. Before long, this girl was smiling and laughing with her. Encounters like that happened often.

When God gives us children with special needs, He equips them with more gifts than we know. They could easily ask God, "Why me?" yet these precious children almost never do. They love in unique, special ways.

Brittaney showed us that it does not take a lot of material things to love people. Things like spending quality time with someone, listening, and holding a hand were natural ways for Brittaney to show compassion.

In 1 John 4:8, John wrote that if we are children of the One whose nature is love, then we will be like Him. But love like that is not automatic or effortless. There is always room for growth. Practice *simple* love. Learn to love in a way that when your presence is not there, the joy and love you experience in God remains with others.

How do you experience simple love with people
by showing compassion?

God Is for You

+

What then shall we say to these things?
If God is for us, who is against us?

Romans 8:31

R ead that incredible verse again. The same is true for you. Despite whatever is happening right now, God is by your side working. Whether you see it or not, He has amazing plans for you. What is happening in your life may be hard, heartbreaking, and painful, but it doesn't change your worth. It doesn't change the truth about how He feels about you. Isn't that encouraging? When life feels bleak, God is still there, rooting for His children.

Don't let mistakes, failure, or dysfunction keep you from experiencing His presence. God is so much more than we could ever imagine. He has no limits. He offers us more love, kindness, grace, and forgiveness than we could conceive of on our own. When you feel abandoned by those closest to you, trapped by a reality you can't comprehend, or suffocated by shame, there's Someone who has promised to never leave nor forsake you.

God isn't impressed with our spotless history or flawless performance. He doesn't wait to love us until we've gotten every area of our lives under submission. He just wants you. He wants your heart. It doesn't matter if you don't think you are good enough.

I get so excited even thinking about that. Probably because I need the encouragement!

When you experience failure, how can you remember
to run toward God instead of bolting
in the opposite direction?

A Prayer for Awareness

✝

Lord, there are seasons when I live as if I have all the time in the world—days I fill with mindless activities, days I simply occupy space without realizing the urgency to share hope with others or shine light in darkness. It's easy to get preoccupied with making my life as comfortable as possible. Forgive me when I have missed the mark and allowed my selfishness to take precedence over Your good news. Create in me an awareness of how much the world needs You. Open my eyes, my heart, and my hands to opportunities to reach others for You. The days go by so quickly, Lord. Help me see each one as a gift that You have created and filled with opportunity, with hope, with purpose—even the days that are hard and uncomfortable. Remind me that there is purpose to this life and that You have called me to run, not jog, stroll, or pause every few hundred feet and grab a snack. You have created me with intention and the capability to do the things that You have called me to do. I can know what they are and accomplish them, and even more, because of You.

In Jesus's name I pray. Amen.

Based on: Luke 10:2; John 9:4; Psalm 118:24; 1 Corinthians 9:24; Ephesians 3:20

It's Not a Popularity Contest

✝

*We have this treasure in earthen containers, so that
the extraordinary greatness of the power will be of God
and not from ourselves.*

2 Corinthians 4:7

We live in a high-pressure society where reputation is often determined by follows and likes and retweets. Many of us rely on the perception people have of us to determine our worth. We study algorithms to reach people, believing that if others could just see us, they would approve of us. But here's a hard piece of truth: You don't need everyone to like you. You don't need to fight for anyone's attention or people-please your way to a higher status. Your mission-possible life is about more than how others view you.

Desiring to be liked demands eyes set on us, but that's not our mission. We are called to be kingdom-minded people, shifting the attention away from ourselves and toward the King.

A mission-possible life is one that is continually focused on Jesus. We are earthen containers, potted clay formed by design. A flowerpot is not admired for its own beauty but created for a unique purpose: to hold a beautiful array of flowers. Like that flowerpot, we are simply jars designed to hold a precious treasure. The ultimate glory belongs to God, not us.

Don't fight for the spotlight. Life is not a popularity contest. Remember the humble strength of the clay pot, who holds a beauty that is not its own. Exalt God's beauty, then, not to get likes or approval for your own. All glory goes back to Him.

***Do you do what you do because you desire approval
from people or from God?***

Brace Yourself

✝

Be on the alert, stand firm in the faith,
act like men, be strong.
1 Corinthians 16:13

I t is your posture, not your strength, that enables you to withstand attack. It doesn't matter how much muscle you have built. If you are off balance or standing on one foot, anyone can run and knock you over. But if you are braced, feet right, shoulder down for leverage, even if you don't have the most muscle mass, it is harder for an enemy to topple you.

To be braced means that you are prepared for whatever comes your way. You are always ready and on high alert, knowing that as you live out a mission-possible life, you will face attacks. Even as you live God's purposes, you will not be immune to criticism and harsh words from the world and sometimes even from the people you love. You cannot predict or control the opposition you will face, but you can anchor yourself to receive it gracefully. You can get into the right posture to steady yourself in the midst of the struggle.

How do you find the right posture from which you can face the attacks of this life? When you meditate on God's Word consistently and pray without ceasing, you will stand tall in God's strength. From that stance of quiet trust, you will withstand the offenses that come your way.

Don't rely on your own strength. Brace yourself in God and remain steadfast in the unshakable foundation of His truth.

What opposition have you met in your mission-possible life? How can you prepare your heart to remain steadfast in the face of it?

You Won't Always Be Liked
(and That's Okay)

✝

If the world hates you, you know that
it has hated Me before it hated you.

John 15:18

Since I'm a people pleaser, I've aimed to get likes. It's human nature to seek validation and acceptance because we crave that sense of belonging. But at what cost? Many of my likes came after big wins or inspirational talks, but I quickly learned that likes were fleeting.

There is more to a mission-possible life than being liked. If our goal is to please everyone, we will end up swaying with the crowd on every issue instead of defending what we believe in. As Winston Churchill said, "You have enemies? Good. That means you've stood up for something, sometime in your life." When your conviction is stronger than your desire to be liked, it may provoke others.

God is going to call you to do some unpopular things, and you won't be liked by everyone. Jesus wasn't liked by everyone, and neither were His disciples. Many were persecuted and killed for proclaiming the gospel, but they knew that their mission was worth the risk.

There's a cost to following the call of Jesus, and sometimes the cost is our popularity. If Jesus was hated, as He says in the book of John, we will be hated too. Will we, like the first followers of Jesus, decide that our mission is worth that cost?

Would you rather be liked or actually do something
that makes your life count? Why?

Set Your Mind

✛

*Set your minds on the things that are above,
not on the things that are on earth.*

Colossians 3:2

When you feel the sting of criticism, it's natural to want to dwell on it. I struggle with this. I hear one negative comment and it's easy to let it change my entire mood, which can affect my day and even my relationships with loved ones. But I know one thing: I have a choice. So do you.

You don't have to let your mind be consumed with the negativity you hear. You don't have to play repeatedly in your mind that one remark someone made about your work or your ability or your personality. You can set your mind on something else, something that reminds you that you are more than someone's opinion of you.

Science supports this choice to reset your mind. Your brain is not rigid but is constantly changing based on your experiences. By consistently setting your mind one way, such as focusing on the goodness of God instead of the negativity in the world, you can literally transform your brain. So be intentional with what you allow in your mind. Whether it's listening to a podcast, a sermon, or worship music or reading Scripture, set your mind on the things of God. Keep your focus on Him and repeat truth to yourself until it silences the noise coming at you from other directions.

What you think about matters. Focus on the things above you and the truths that will last forever.

*How will you prioritize focusing on what's eternal
over what's temporal?*

Respect over Likes

✝

Only conduct yourselves in a manner worthy
of the gospel of Christ.

Philippians 1:27

Instead of looking to others for validation and acceptance, what if we aimed to earn their respect?

To earn a like or heart, all you need to do is give people something they can identify with—something that will spark a memory, cause a laugh, or tug at a heartstring. Earning respect is much harder. You need to work for it. You need to portray integrity, hustle, grind, tenacity, and grit and make the right choices. Not needing the approval of others is the mark of confidence, and it is evident to those around you. It's easy to gain someone's like—just post a cute dog picture or funny video on social media and you'll get a ton of likes!—but that doesn't mean you've earned their respect. People have earned my respect by making the right choices time after time.

Respect is so much deeper than a like, than just saying what people want to hear. What matters is your willingness to keep showing up and doing the right thing, regardless of what others are saying. This is what people will notice when they look at you.

You earn respect not by blending in but by standing out. Stand up for what you believe in, even when it's unpopular. Keep going in faith, even if there's no one with you. Make your mission to please God, not man.

How can you display integrity today that might earn someone's respect tomorrow?

Overcoming Opposition

+

The thief comes only to steal and kill and destroy;
I came so that they would have life, and have it abundantly.

John 10:10

W hen you start living on purpose, with purpose, you will find that opposition comes your way. You have an enemy. He doesn't want you living a mission-possible life, doing what Christ has called you to do. He wants you weighed down with negative thoughts and fears. He wants to get into your mind and wreak havoc there—to steal your joy, kill your faith, and destroy your spirit.

When you are fired up and ready to live the life that God is calling you to live, the devil wants to get you down. Although it is nice to believe that if you are following the path God has put before you, you will never encounter opposition, that's not what the Bible teaches. You *will* face resistance. You *will* deal with criticism. You *will* endure trials. There is no escaping it. But here's great news: You can overcome them.

You don't have to give in to the negativity that bombards you. Remember that Jesus, the Good Shepherd, who guides you with wisdom and gentleness, wants to give you an abundant life. He is bigger than what you face, and He offers freedom and life. They're yours for the taking. If you feel overwhelmed with negativity in your life, go to Jesus and receive the life He has to offer.

***When you are barraged with criticism,
how can you overcome it?***

He Cares

✛

Cast all your anxiety on Him,
because He cares about you.
1 Peter 5:7

People are people. This world isn't perfect, and you will feel the pain of rejection and the weight of relational hurt in your life. That may come from people who don't know you, or even the ones who love you and have good intentions. Humans will let you down at some point. So what do you do when you are insulted and offended?

As for all areas of life, we need to take it to Jesus. First Peter 5:7 tells us that God *cares* for us. Even when life hurts and we want to dwell on others' negative thoughts of us, He cares about us and wants us to tell Him what we feel.

When fishermen cast their nets into the water, they don't casually slip their nets in or drop them without thought. They chuck their nets into the sea with intention and aim, throwing them in for an actual purpose. So, when we cast our cares on the Lord, we don't simply tell Him in passing all that bothers us. We don't treat our cares lightly, because He does not treat them lightly. We thrust our anxiety deliberately into His arms, trusting that He will work with whatever we give Him and will care for us in the process. Make Jesus your first option, not your last resort, when you face hurt or ridicule.

Do you believe that Jesus cares for you? If so,
would you cast your cares to Him today?
Write down your prayer to Him.

One Step at a Time

+

The steps of a man are established by the LORD.

Psalm 37:23

The average person takes about 7,500 steps a day. If you consider the average life span to be eighty years old, once a baby learns to walk, that person will walk about a distance of 216,262,500 steps, or 110,000 miles.[20] We're talking as much as almost five times around the earth!

Walking around the planet a handful of times in one lifetime seems like a gargantuan task. It's much easier to process when you break it up, one step at a time. Yet, when we're in the thick of life, taking one step at a time doesn't seem like enough. We want to know the entire picture. What does God have planned for us next year? What are we supposed to be doing next month? How long will it take before our business becomes successful? It feels much safer to have a poster-board-sized master plan of our future, but the Bible is clear: God orders our steps.

One of the best ways to find the correct next step is through obedience to what God has put right in front of you. Here are a few questions I often ask myself when I need clarity on where to step out in faith:

- *How is God calling me to step out today?*
- *Who has He placed in my path to love right now?*
- *Where has He asked me to make a difference in this moment?*

Instead of worrying about your future, just say yes to putting one foot in front of the other.

What is something you feel in your spirit that God is nudging you to do right this moment?

Let God Be God

✝

Commit your works to the Lord,
And your plans will be established.

Proverbs 16:3

Human beings are created in the image of God, but one thing is certain: We are not God. We may hold on to certain dreams of how God should use us, but ultimately we are not in charge of that grand design.

There's nothing wrong with dreaming big. I do it all the time! But how God orchestrates the plan of your life is up to Him. Work on your gifts and talents in a way that challenges you. Don't compare your skill level to anyone else's. When we compare, sometimes it makes us want to give up. I hear this all the time: "If I can't be the best at something, why bother?" "Why bother practicing the piano if I'm never going to make it into Julliard?" "Why bother writing if my book will never hit the New York Times Best Sellers list?"

It's okay to want to be the best, but it's more important to want to be *your* best. I promise you this: God will use your gifts and abilities in His way and for His plan. Rather than trying to figure out or influence how He will make it happen, focus on *Him*.

Name and surrender the one dream, goal, or plan that you have not given over to God.

You Win!

+

In all these things we overwhelmingly conquer
through Him who loved us.

Romans 8:37

The *fog of war* is a military term coined back in 1896 by Colonel Lonsdale Hale. He described it as "the state of ignorance in which commanders frequently find themselves as regards the real strength and position, not only of their foes, but also of their friends."[21] It's a legit issue.

The chaos in battle can cause relevant and strategic information to become confusing. This fog distorts one's perception of what is happening. You basically can't see or hear or think straight. This limits your ability to do what you must do. You do the best you can to estimate the power of your troops and the enemy's, yet uncertainty often prevails.

This might strike a chord as you live trying to navigate through the fog of life.

Here's encouraging news: Even amid not knowing, feeling stuck, or nursing gaping wounds, the troubles of life don't end with tragedy. Life ends with triumph. When we know Jesus, we are more than conquerors. At some point, we come back. At some point, Jesus, the greatest general, steps in and fights for us.

It doesn't mean that walking through our trials is easy. But it means we can look past the fog with hope that can come only through Jesus.

Jot down some thoughts on how it feels to know that you are a conqueror in Christ. How might this help you get through the "fog" of your week, month, or year?

When You're Stuck, Serve

✝

Do not neglect doing good and sharing,
for with such sacrifices God is pleased.

Hebrews 13:16

Outside of God giving us crystal-clear, step-by-step instructions or guidance (which is not the usual experience of life), it can be tempting to get stuck. We don't know which direction to travel in. When do we stay put? When do we move on? What job offer do we take? Whom do we marry? Where do we go to school? Should we start this business? And sometimes in the absence of hearing specific answers from God, we do nothing. Certainly, there is a time to wait on Him, but rarely is there a time to do nothing.

You know what happens when we do nothing? *Nothing!*

Making your life count requires action. When you're at a crossroads, instead of being paralyzed by indecision, serve! Love. Give. In practical terms, position yourself to be a light where there is darkness. Take the time to listen to someone. Go out of your way to encourage a friend—or a stranger! Invite a neighbor who is struggling over for dinner. This is God's will, after all.

The little things we do each day add up to something greater and leave a legacy. Now, that's much better than doing nothing! Don't let uncertainty get in the way of choosing to influence others. There is always something to do.

**Name one thing you can do today to serve
someone else—and do it!**

Seek to Know God, Not the Details

✛

Oh, the depth of the riches, both of the wisdom and
knowledge of God! How unsearchable are His judgments
and unfathomable His ways!

Romans 11:33

Not knowing is uncomfortable. Among many other things, the pandemic of 2020 (and beyond!) taught us that. We found our-selves asking things like, *How many variants are there? How does it affect the body long term? When will the social fabric of society return to normal?* Most of us struggled with many unanswered questions as Covid-19 transformed the world as we knew it.

Ambiguity is a fact of life. The Bible offers great wisdom in its admonishment to "walk by faith, not by sight" (2 Corinthians 5:7). In fact, the Bible reminds us that God's judgments and ways are essen-tially unknowable to us—which is okay! God is great and unfath-omable; we can't comprehend Him. I'm grateful I can't comprehend all He is. If I could figure Him out, it wouldn't be much of a mystery or that big of a deal. But God *is* a big deal!

Although we can't know everything there is to know about God with our finite human minds, we can still know Him on a personal, relational level. This should be the goal of every believer. We should be encouraged by the fact that there will always be something more to learn about Him.

God has all the details figured out. Rest in this. Even though worry is natural, try to release it. Find peace that His knowledge is greater than ours.

What is one thing you can do today to increase
your knowledge of who God is?

The Bible, Our Guiding Light

✛

Your word is a lamp to my feet
And a light to my path.
Psalm 119:105

Each fall, Monarch butterflies gather at the top of the same mountain and migrate together from the United States and Canada to central Mexico. It's a phenomenon that happens year after year without the aid of GPS devices or maps. How do they do it? Coupling their internal circadian clocks and antenna-based compasses, they track their route using the sun. It takes that magical collaboration to get these black and orange beauties down to the south. One thing is certain: They wouldn't be able to do it without the light of the sun.

The Bible compares the Word of God to a lamp and a light. The same way we need light to guide our path into a room of darkness, we need God's truth to lead us, especially during times of uncertainty. It's easy to allow fear to keep us stuck, but this is the day to live without fear. It starts by diving into the Bible. Again, don't just read books about it; read *the* Book! As you allow God's truth to activate in your life, you will begin to be led not by fear but by what God says.

***How can you make meditation on Scripture
part of your daily habit?***

God's Already Written Your Story

✝

He guides me in the paths of righteousness
For the sake of His name.

Psalm 23:3

When I was playing baseball for the Columbia Fireflies, a reporter asked me something like this: "Has there been any moment where you said, 'Man, I should have stuck with baseball when I was young'?" This question about a possible regret got me fired up. I told him, "I think in life there are times when negativity and doubt and fear creep in. We have a choice in those moments. What are we going to do with those thoughts? How are we going to handle them? And what's the next step?"

Having regret or doubt isn't necessarily bad; it's what you do with those feelings that matters. To move past that negativity, I first remind myself of the truth that God works all things for His good (see Romans 8:28). Second, I choose to believe in the goodness of His plan. I took this crazy route filled with highs and lows for a reason. God wrote my story, and He is always working behind the scenes.

When we remember this truth, it can help us stay grounded no matter what we're going through or what we fear. God didn't make mistakes when I was going through the highs or the lows. He wrote my story before I was even born. With this in mind, I don't have to look back with regret. My job is to stay in the moment and do the best I can at whatever is before me. Likely, that's your job too.

How can you fully engage in whatever is before you knowing God's already got it figured out?

A Prayer for Trust

✝

There have been many times when I've looked outside of You to find direction, provision, comfort, rest, love, care, and hope. And each of those times, even if I felt a temporary relief, left me empty and longing for more. Your Word tells me that I am a conqueror through You, not through those other things. Forgive me for searching in all the wrong places for what I need and can be found only in You. When I am afraid of what will or will not happen, strengthen my trust in You. I pray that when I don't know what tomorrow brings that I begin to see it as an opportunity to trust in and lean on You. Thank You that whatever comes, You have promised to always be there and that You will not forsake those who seek You. Remind me that You are working all things for good in my life, even the ones that hurt and break my heart, and that You will somehow bring good from them. I thank You, God, that what You say in Your Word about me is greater than what people think of me. I commit to You what my hands find to do. Establish them according to Your will.

In Jesus's name. Amen.

Based on: Romans 8:37; Psalm 9:10; 56:3; Romans 8:28; Proverbs 16:3

Don't Stop Learning

✝

A wise person will hear and increase in learning,
And a person of understanding will acquire wise counsel.

Proverbs 1:5

Continuous education is essential in any industry to maximize one's experience and skills and adapt to change, which seems to be a constant thing. But you don't have to be a doctor, engineer, or CPA to glean the benefits of lifelong learning. You don't have to stop learning new things once you get that job or complete that degree. And as new creations in Christ, we are united to the Source of all growth, so we can always continue to improve and develop.

As Albert Einstein is reported to have said, "Once you stop learning, you start dying." Lifelong learning—whether fostered in a traditional environment like a college or trade school or organically by being curious, asking questions, and doing self-guided research to improve your knowledge about whatever is relevant to you—provides countless benefits:

- increases your self-confidence
- offsets age-related cognitive decline
- helps you live longer
- improves your mental health

And those are just a few.

Commit to staying in a constant space of learning. Read a book. Listen to a podcast. Attend a seminar. Take a course. Attend a workshop. Find and meet with a mentor.

You're never too young or old to learn more.

***Think of one thing this month that will teach you
something new. Make a plan to do it and to have fun!***

Get It Done!

✝

The desire of the lazy one puts him to death,
For his hands refuse to work.

Proverbs 21:25

When I was fifteen years old and on a mission trip in the Philippines, I met a boy named Sherwin and his two friends. Sherwin had a physical disability. His feet were backward and he couldn't walk. The people in his village looked at him as cursed, worth less than others, and insignificant. Sherwin moved my heart on the mission field. However, it would have been easy to return to the States and bury my good intentions underneath a pile of excuses. *I'm just a kid. How do I even start?* But God was pushing me forward. Sherwin inspired the creation of the Tim Tebow Foundation, an organization that, through specialized programs and ministries, fights for children and adults who cannot fight for themselves.

I've often heard people say things like "Oh, so-and-so has a lot of heart" as a way of apologizing or making an excuse for someone who wanted to do good but for whatever reason didn't. Having an open and tender heart is important. So is cultivating the intention to do the right thing. And what ties the two together is execution. Jesus didn't just *intend* to die for our sins; He actually *did*!

Don't settle for good intentions. Go after what you desire to start and get it done.

What is one positive thing you have wanted to do but have avoided or put on hold? Do it!

Finish Strong

✝

[Look] only at Jesus, the originator and perfecter of the faith.

Hebrews 12:2

I n the National Championship Game of the 2009 Bowl Championship Series (BCS), the Florida Gators (the team I was playing on) faced the Oklahoma Sooners. Three minutes into the fourth quarter, we drew even at 14–14 but took the lead ninety seconds later, 17–14. With just over three minutes to go in the game, I threw to David Nelson for a four-yard touchdown. We won 24–14, our second championship title in three years.

Near the end of the game, the coach came up to me and said, "I love you. I'm proud of you. You finished strong." His words were heartfelt and struck a chord in that moment. Someone I respected had asked me to do something for him, for the team, and I had come through. The coach acknowledged my efforts. I realized something deeper in that moment. When I get to the end of my life, I want to be greeted by my Father in heaven with a big hug and a genuine "Attaboy, Timmy—you finished strong."

Often, it seems easier to start something than to finish it. As time passes, distractions set in. Life happens. We get impatient. Progress seems slower than expected. Focus on the goal. Set your eyes on the prize. When your momentum starts to fade, focus not on your own strength but on the Author and Finisher of your faith.

What would it look like for you to finish strong in whatever season of life you are in right now?

The Power of Together

+

I urge you, brothers and sisters, by the name of
our Lord Jesus Christ, that you all agree and that there be
no divisions among you, but that you be made complete
in the same mind and in the same judgment.

1 Corinthians 1:10

Relationships are messy. They require work, conflict resolution, hard conversations, and navigating through discomfort. They are also one of the most rewarding parts of being human beings. We were wired to connect—to share, give, serve, love, encourage, and learn from others. God created us to be in relationship.

Jesus didn't need His disciples to fulfill His mission on earth, which was to save humankind, yet He let them be an integral part of spreading the gospel. They helped push His mission forward.

It's one thing to be a nice person. It's another thing to be intentional about rallying people to be united—to believe in a mission or be builders of bridges instead of blowing them up when we are quickly offended or refusing to engage with others because our hands might get dirty. An old saying goes, "A rising tide lifts all boats." When we stand together in unity, fighting for instead of against one another, we make our lives and the lives of those around us count.

Are you facing a relational challenge today?
Invite God into your situation and pray for peace,
guidance, and a tender heart.

Maximize Your Talents

+

Well done, good and faithful servant.
You have been faithful over a little; I will set you over much.

Matthew 25:21, ESV

In Matthew 25, Jesus tells a parable about a businessman. Before leaving on a trip, he gave three of his employees an assignment. To one he gave five talents, two to another, and one to another, according to each one's ability. The man expected his employees, in his absence, to do something wise with the money they were given—to make a prudent investment. When the businessman returned, he was thrilled to see the employee who was given five talents had earned five more and the one who received two talents had earned two more. But the employee who was given one talent buried the money out of fear and returned to his boss the one talent he was given. The first two employees were praised for their efforts, and the third was admonished.

We are responsible to do the most with whatever God has given us, a little or a lot. When we don't use the gifts, the time, or the resources He has blessed us with, it's equivalent to telling Him, "Thanks, but no thanks."

What has God put *you* in charge of? Whether much or little, are you being a faithful steward and earning a return on the investment you're making? Are you honing your gifts, sharpening your skills, leading by example, and using the money you make in a way that is productive and not frivolous? Don't hide what God has given you—multiply it!

***When you have done something useful for God
or others, how does it feel?***

Make Yourself Available

✝

I heard the voice of the Lord, saying, "Whom shall I send,
and who will go for Us?" Then I said, "Here am I. Send me!"

Isaiah 6:8

When we think of abilities, most of us think of things that steal the limelight: a musician performing onstage, an orator who can engage a crowd without much effort, or a preacher traveling the globe and sharing the good news. But there are many abilities that don't require showcasing or a degree from an Ivy League university. One of the greatest abilities we have is our availability.

When we live in a space of availability, we are attuned to God's prompting. We meet a need that is brought before us. We listen. We encourage. We say yes.

Isaiah was a prophet when the nation of Israel was in a state of turmoil. At the time the northern kingdom was taken captive, the Assyrians were attacking the southern kingdom. Isaiah prophesied the fall of Israel as well as the restoration of God's people in the future. When Isaiah received this vision, he responded, "Here am I. Send me!" He made himself available even though the future was bleak. The outlook didn't matter as much to the prophet as who was in control.

Be open to changes in your schedule, plans, and preferences. And pray for the courage and the strength to be aware of opportunities to serve and love God and others, and take those opportunities!

How do you exhibit availability in your day?

Never Forget

+

Samuel took a stone and placed it between Mizpah and Shen,
and named it Ebenezer, saying, "So far the LORD has helped us."
1 Samuel 7:12

Nischal Narayanam, a child prodigy from India now in his mid-twenties, is the youngest double Guinness World Record holder for memory. When he was twelve, he won his first world record for memorizing 225 random objects within 12.07 minutes. At thirteen, he clinched his second Guinness title for the longest sequence of numbers memorized in one minute.[22] While your memory may not be as sharp as this mathematical genius, it's an essential part of your mission.

The ancient Israelites remembered the miracles God had performed by laying stones as a memorial to Him. In the scripture above, right before the prophet Samuel placed a stone between the cities of Mizpah and Shen, what was possibly a settlement, something incredible had happened. In a dramatic fashion, God had defeated the Philistines, who had attacked the Israelites. He had confused the enemy to the point they were unable to battle. To commemorate the victory and God's faithfulness, Samuel laid down a stone as a memorial.

Don't forget the moment God changed your life. Don't forget the moment He challenged you to join the fight. Don't forget that you have a specific role to play in bringing faith, hope, and love to a world in need. May you always remember that God loved us first and called us to love others.

What are some practical ways you can remember
what God has done for you to position you in a
continual state of gratitude?

The Honor of Humility

✝

He gives a greater grace. Therefore it says,
"God is opposed to the proud, but gives grace to the humble."

James 4:6

There are moments in life that seem unfair. We believe that we are doing everything right but feel as if the world is working against us. In those times, we may plead with God to come to our aid and prove that we are not at fault.

However, although God is for you, He does not take sides. Instead, we need to get on *His* side. We do that by remembering that the world does not revolve around us. We take the focus off ourselves and set Jesus as the focal point of our lives.

The verse above is one of the first my parents made me memorize. They taught me the importance of humility. Humility usually isn't a laudable characteristic. It means admitting our weaknesses and our defeat. There is no glory in it for us. When we humble ourselves, we realize the limited power that we have. We surrender all to Jesus, waving our white flag, hoping for a truce.

When we do this, a miraculous thing happens. The moment we stop demanding that God be on our side and instead come alongside Him, He gives us grace—unmerited favor that we could never deserve. The only way we can learn to transcend the journey is to be covered in His grace, which we must do by humbling ourselves before Him. As much as we may fight it, being in this place of submission is how we can best experience the fullness of God and what He has for us.

**What areas of your life do you need
to humbly submit before God?**

Beyond Personal Gain

✚

No one is to seek his own advantage,
but rather that of his neighbor.
1 Corinthians 10:24

I f you've ever watched a horse race, you may have noticed small leather squares near the horses' eyes. These squares serve an important purpose in the event. With these blinders on, horses are unable to see anything around them or behind them, thus keeping their attention on what is directly in front of them.

Most days, we walk around with our blinders, keeping our focus on only the things that directly affect us. When our field of vision is so limited, it's easy to forget there is a world around us and people who are hurting. It may be time to take the blinders off. We are called to live for more than ourselves.

Although humbling ourselves before God is important, it's also necessary to practice humility with others. When we do that, we think of ourselves less and wonder more, *How can I serve others?*

The greatest form of love is choosing the best interests of other people and acting on their behalf, as Christ did for us when He laid His life down. Look for the people around you. When you see that they need help, go out of your way to love and care about them. Show others the love of Jesus by making your life less about you and more about your willingness to be His hands and feet.

How can you lay aside your personal interests today
in favor of someone else?

Rise Above

✝

Everyone who hears these words of Mine, and acts on them,
will be like a wise man who built his house on the rock.

Matthew 7:24

There were two men who both set out to build a house. The first one got everything he needed for the job and took care to lay a foundation before constructing his home. The second man also got everything he needed to build a new place, but he could not be bothered to lay a foundation. Eager to start, he began construction directly in the sand. When a storm eventually came, the first guy's house remained steady. The second guy's? Not so much. As you can imagine, it blew over with the squall, leaving the man homeless on his bed of sand (see Matthew 7:24–27).

Between the first and second man, there weren't too many differences. Their houses were the same age. They likely used the same building materials. And the storm that hit them was the same one. The only difference was the foundation.

When our lives are founded on Jesus and we build upon Him, we are like the man whose house was built on the rock. Storms may come, but they cannot shake us like they could if we were living apart from Him. When we dwell with Jesus, we don't have to give in to the circumstances around us. We can rise above them and transcend the journey. Don't let your situation define you. Be anchored in Christ in such a way that He defines you.

On what foundation are you building your life?

Attitude

✛

Each one must do just as he has decided in his heart, not
reluctantly or under compulsion, for God loves a cheerful giver.

2 Corinthians 9:7

Jesus spotted a poor widow placing two measly coins into the collection box at the temple (see Mark 12:42). Many people had already put their own offerings into the box before that, in amounts far larger than what this woman gave, yet Jesus looked at this woman and commended her. Although the amount was a pittance to most people, He remarked that she gave more than any of the others (see verse 43). Her offering, as little as it was, was all that she had. As Jesus does, He looked beyond the act itself into the heart behind the act. Attitude matters!

Why do you want to live a mission-possible life? Do you want to show others how good you can be? Does your interest lie in impressing anyone or fulfilling an obligation? Choose to do the right thing over what feels good or comfortable, whatever that might mean for you. It didn't matter how much the widow gave in terms of numbers; it mattered that she gave her all because of her devotion to and trust in God.

God loves a cheerful giver. He is pleased when we devote our lives to Him out of our love for Him. Worry less about how much you can do for God today and focus more on setting your heart on Him. Give of yourself—no matter what you lack—not out of compulsion but out of the desire to please the Lord.

In what ways is God leading you to give cheerfully today?

Your Public Self and Private Self

✝

As for you, when you pray, go into your inner room,
close your door, and pray to your Father who is in secret;
and your Father who sees what is done in secret will reward you.

Matthew 6:6

There's something inspiring about going to watch a show and have reality suspended. For a moment, all that is real is whatever is happening onstage. All the cast is in costume, portraying different characters with various personalities. For a while, you believe that the actors you see really are who they are pretending to be. It's part of what makes live shows so delightful.

The thing is, this often happens offstage too. We walk around putting on different airs, acting our way through life. Many times, we portray the kind of people we want others to see us as. We post our best moments on social media and take thirty-eight selfies before deciding on the most perfect one. We put on an act in the attempt to please others.

But having integrity is being the same person no matter where you are. Train yourself to hold fast to your convictions. Remain tenacious and faithful regardless of who is watching or what they see. You can fool others by putting on a front, but you will never be able to fool God. He sees what happens behind closed doors.

Living a mission-possible life is not about gaining favor from others; it's about living in obedience to God. Walk in His way and remain faithful to Him today.

Who are you behind closed doors?
Is it the person you want to be?

Give Life, Don't Just Take It

+

Those who refresh others will themselves be refreshed.

Proverbs 11:25, NLT

Have you ever been around someone who sucks the energy right out of the room? Maybe they can't stop talking about themselves or they're not shy about sharing their (usually negative) opinions with anyone who will listen. It's hard to hang with people like this because they seem to drain the oxygen out of the air. I call them life takers.

Then you have the other kind of people, the life givers. Their spirits and speech are full of optimism and hope. They genuinely care, and it shows. They make you want to be a better person. Truly, it is a joy to be around them.

Every opportunity we have with someone is an opportunity to influence that person for the good—to give life and not just take it—because whether we realize it or not, people are watching us. What we say and what we do matters. When we live with purpose, we can make a difference that will leave a lasting impact.

Jesus is the Author and Giver of life. Consider making a choice to follow His example and be a blessing to someone else. Breathe life into whatever space you set foot in.

***What can you do today to put a smile
on someone's face?***

Jesus Cares for the Broken

✝

The King will reply, "Truly I tell you, whatever you did for one of
the least of these brothers and sisters of mine, you did for me."
Matthew 25:40, NIV

Guest devo by Jason and Tracy Raitz
Relationship to TTF: adoption-aid recipients

We will never forget standing in Kai's orphanage in Nanjing, China, on his family day. We were there to thank his nannies for taking such wonderful care of him for his first three years of life. The experience of meeting him was overwhelming. For months, we had prayed over pictures of this little boy on the other side of the world, and now we were standing in the very room where those pictures were taken. Kai has phenylketonuria, and because of this, he was in a special-needs room.

We stood in the middle of this room with special-needs babies surrounding us all over the floor—babies with Down syndrome, cerebral palsy, and heart issues next to our son, who has a rare genetic disorder. Kai's nanny looked at us and saw the tears in our eyes. "Only Christians adopt these broken babies," she said gently.

In all our years of following Jesus and working in ministry, we have never felt the presence of God so powerfully than in that room with those "broken babies." But Jesus not only cares for the broken, the abused, the abandoned; He desperately loves them and brings hope into their lives. I hope today you will be encouraged to care for and love the broken people in your family, workplace, and neighborhood. When you do, you are representing Jesus and doing what "only Christians" do.

How can an act of obedience morph into something greater than the act itself?

A Prayer for Understanding

✝

Thank You, Lord, for being the creator and supplier of all wisdom and understanding. Forgive me when I rely on my own insight apart from Yours. Help me to continually hear and increase in learning so that I develop into the person You have created me to be. Remind me that Your ways and thoughts are higher than mine. That is why I can trust You instead of relying on what I think is or should be. I know and am grateful that the mission You have planned for me on this earth has a deeper purpose than what I may think it is. Fill me with the wisdom You have stored up for me and that is in abundant supply when I ask. Your Word tells me that lack of knowledge is a deadly threat. Help me to become more than just book smart or well versed in worldly knowledge. Give me a hunger and thirst to dive deeper into what it means to follow You, take charge of who I am on the inside, and gain valuable knowledge so I might be a light in darkness. Clothe me with a spirit of wisdom and revelation in the knowledge of who You are and what You have called me to do. I am so grateful.

In Jesus's name I pray. Amen.

Based on: Proverbs 1:5; 1 Corinthians 1:25; Proverbs 2:6; Isaiah 55:8–9; Hosea 4:6; Ephesians 1:17

A Love Like No Other

+

God so loved the world,
that He gave His only Son, so that everyone who believes
in Him will not perish, but have eternal life.

John 3:16

Right before the BCS National Championship Game between Florida and Oklahoma in 2009, I wrote out John 3:16 in eye black under my eyes. Ninety million people would Google the scripture that day. Exactly three years later, during my first NFL playoff game, which was with the Denver Broncos against the Pittsburgh Steelers in 2012, the strangest things happened, which I can only attribute to God:

- I threw for 316 yards.
- My yards per rush were 3.16.
- My yards per completion were 31.6.
- The ratings for the game were 31.6.
- The time of possession was 31:06.

That sure seems like more than a coincidence. But this verse means much more to me than a football statistic. Though I'd memorized it when I was a little boy, it was only a few years ago that something clicked. When Jesus was on the cross, dying for our sins, He cried out, "My God, My God, why have You forsaken Me?" (Matthew 27:46). God, His Father, had turned His back on Him. That's terrible! A good dad would never do that. But as Jesus was dying, the sins of the world were upon Jesus. And God knew that for that moment, He had to forsake His own Son so He would never have to forsake us. God's biggest love, the love He has for His Son, is the love He offers to us, the sinners of the world, forever. Now, that's a love like no other.

What does that kind of love make you want to do today?

The Nature of God

✝

God is love.

1 John 4:16

Have you ever wondered what God looks like? The ancient Greek philosopher Xenophanes once wrote,

Had the oxen or the lions hands,
Or could with hands depict a work like men,
Were beasts to draw the semblance of the gods,
The horses would them like to horses sketch,
To oxen, oxen, and their bodies make
Of such a shape as to themselves belongs.[23]

The point is that we usually think of God as being like us. It's all too easy to mold our vision of Him based on our own biases and identities. Maybe we picture God as an idealized version of ourselves. Maybe He has a Midwestern accent or cheeseburgers are His favorite food. Maybe He spends His days in a long flowy robe and sandals.

But the Bible does tell us what God looks like: love. God is love. The Bible doesn't just describe love as an attribute of God but uses love to define His very essence. Love is who God is. It is His nature. Love is what God is and how He shows up.

A mission-possible life is steeped in love, which means choosing the best interests of other people and acting on their behalf. God chose the best for us when He sacrificed His Son to save us from our sins. Each day that we choose the best for others, we see what God Himself looks like, because God is love.

How does God's love nature inform the choices
you make every day?

Our Picture of God on Earth

✛

[Jesus] is the radiance of His glory and
the exact representation of His nature, and upholds
all things by the word of His power.

Hebrews 1:3

While in the Upper Room during Jesus's final meal before His arrest and crucifixion, His friend Philip said, "Lord, show us the Father, and it is enough for us" (John 14:8). Jesus replied with these blunt words: "Have I been with you for so long a time, and yet you have not come to know Me, Philip? The one who has seen Me has seen the Father" (verse 9).

Philip wanted to know what God is like, and Jesus basically said, "He is like Me, and I am like Him." Philip didn't quite understand, but Jesus's response sheds light on His true nature. There is no divine difference between the Father and the Son. They are both God, equal in essence and power. Wow!

The author of Hebrews further illustrated this by saying that Jesus is the "exact representation" of God's being. The Greek word for "exact representation" is *charaktér*. A *charaktér* was originally an engraving tool used in ancient coin making. It later came to mean a stamp or impress used on a coin or seal.[24] Essentially, after a precious metal was melted, it would be poured into a mold, and once cooled, it would possess the exact image of the mold. So, just as a coin bears the image of the original mold, Jesus shows us exactly who and what God is like. Although no one has ever seen God, the reality of God's likeness is precisely represented in His Son.

In what ways can you follow Jesus's example
as seen throughout Scripture?

His Loyal Love

✝

Give thanks to the LORD, for He is good,
For His faithfulness is everlasting. . . .
Give thanks to the God of heaven,
For His faithfulness is everlasting.

Psalm 136:1, 26

A few months after Demi and I got married, we welcomed three adorable puppies into our home: Paris the dalmatian, Kobe the golden retriever, and Chunk the Bernese mountain dog. Each one is unique and special to us! Paris is Daddy's little princess. She loves to snuggle and is so sweet (*most* of the time). Kobe is the playful one. He's always jumping into the pool and looking for a nice head scratch. Chunk, well, he's a big ole teddy bear! (Don't tell the others, but I think he's Demi's favorite!)

What I love most about our dogs is how loyal they are. One of my favorite things when I return home from a long work trip is pulling up in the driveway, seeing my babies looking at me through the window, opening the door, and receiving countless slobbery kisses!

Their love is unconditional—and sometimes wet and hairy! No matter how I'm feeling, our dogs want to be around me. I imagine God's love is similar but to a much greater extent! In Psalm 136, *twenty-six times* the author states how God's "faithfulness is everlasting." Other Bible versions translate it, "His love endures forever" (NIV) or "His loyal love endures" (NET). Just like this line is repeated throughout the chapter, each and every day God's love is repeated for you and me. It's steadfast. Personal. Loving. Loyal.

How have you seen God's loyal love in your life?

He Is Trustworthy

✝

My blessing is on those people who trust in me,
who put their confidence in me.

Jeremiah 17:7, NET

As an unwanted Israelite priest, the prophet Jeremiah coura-
geously embraced God's call on his life when given the difficult
task of delivering unpopular news—warning the southern kingdom of the coming judgment. Because the Israelites had repeatedly
broken God's covenant, they would eventually be conquered and
dispersed.

But before that would happen, Jeremiah experienced the trust-
worthiness of God in a unique way. While in a courtyard prison
during a time of war, he was approached by his cousin and asked if
he wanted to buy his land. You might be thinking, *Surely, Jeremiah
would not want to buy property in a war zone . . . while he was in jail.* But
here's the kicker: Jeremiah had already been warned by God that the
cousin would show up to make such an offer. So, when it happened,
he wasn't surprised. Jeremiah got the money together and made the
transaction. See, as strange as the query sounded, God knew something: Even though the nation of Israel would be defeated, their land
would eventually become their own again. Years later, the dust
would settle, and the people of Israel would be free to return home,
just as God promised (see Jeremiah 32:42–44).

Jeremiah was literally making an investment in faith. He was
choosing to believe that God's promises would come to pass. And
they did! After seventy years of exile, the Israelites would eventually
be welcomed back to their land under Persian rule.

Nothing is too difficult for God. When God gives us His Word,
He keeps it. Even when what happens makes no sense, we can trust
Him, because often He knows something we don't.

How can you choose to trust God today?

A Good, Good Father

✝

The LORD is good,
A stronghold in the day of trouble,
And He knows those who take refuge in Him.

Nahum 1:7

I remember reading a story about a teenaged girl who was stopped for speeding, given a ticket, and told to appear before a judge in court.[25] On the girl's court date, the judge read her citation and asked, "Guilty or not guilty?"

The girl simply replied, "Guilty."

After hearing the girl's plea, the judge hit the gavel and fined her a hundred dollars.

Then the judge did something amazing. He stood up from his chair, took off his robe, stepped down from the bench, took out his wallet, and paid the young girl's fine. Strange, right?

Well, the judge was her father. He loved his daughter, but he also knew that she had broken the law and had to pay the consequences. He couldn't make an exception just because they were related. It was his job to keep and enforce the law. But this judge was also a good, good father! Stepping down from his seat of authority, he paid the fine so that his daughter would be free!

What a perfect picture of the gospel. God the Father stood up from His throne in heaven, looked down at His children, and saw that there was a penalty to be paid. And out of His love for us, He took the form of man and gave His life on the cross as a ransom to set us free from sin and death (see 1 Timothy 2:5–6). Now, that's a good, good Father.

How have you seen the goodness of God in your own life?

Unmatched Holiness

✛

There is no one holy like the LORD,
Indeed, there is no one besides You,
Nor is there any rock like our God.

1 Samuel 2:2

H*oly* is not a word we use every day, or if we do use it, we typically don't use it correctly. *Holy* can be defined as "sacred," "distinct," and "set apart." It implies difference, purity, and reverence.[26]

Throughout the Bible, God is often referred to as *holy*. Holiness is the very essence of His nature and character. He is sacred, sinless, distinct from all else, set apart, and profoundly different from any man or anything. His holiness is more than His perfection; it embodies His divine mystery and majesty. God's holiness is not something we can comprehend, but it should open our eyes to the reality of our human condition. In his book *The Journey: Living by Faith in an Uncertain World,* Billy Graham wrote, "Only when we understand the holiness of God will we understand the depth of our sin."[27]

I love that! The holiness of God demands our need for a Savior. There is nothing we can do to be good enough to make ourselves holy. Therefore, God "made Him who knew no sin to be sin in our behalf, so that we might become the righteousness of God" (2 Corinthians 5:21).

It's because of Jesus's death and sinless life
that righteousness is attributed to us through faith.
How would you describe God's holiness?

Rich in Mercy

✛

God, being rich in mercy, because of His great love with which He
loved us, even when we were dead in our wrongdoings, made us
alive together with Christ (by grace you have been saved).

Ephesians 2:4–5

I n one of my favorite passages in the Bible, Ephesians 2:1–10, God
is described as being "rich in mercy."

When we were dead in our trespasses and, by nature, children
deserving of God's wrath (see verse 3), God stepped in. He didn't
leave us the way we were. He intervened! Out of an overflowing
abundance of character and compassion, He had a desire to help. He
brought us from spiritual death to life—not by anything we have
done or will do but completely by His great work and goodwill toward the afflicted.

In *The Bible Knowledge Commentary* on Ephesians, Dr. Harold W.
Hoehner noted that the Greek word for mercy is *eleos* and means
"undeserved kindness."[28] As God has exhibited undeserved kindness to us, we are called to do the same for others. For Jesus said in
His fifth beatitude, "Blessed are the merciful, for they will receive
mercy" (Matthew 5:7). As God's children, we're supposed to reflect
His mercy because we have come to receive it from Him.

*Again, God's mercy is not earned by any merit or action.
It's been freely given through the finished work of
the Cross. How can you demonstrate
"undeserved kindness" today?*

Our Forerunner

✝

We have this as a sure and steadfast anchor of the soul, a hope
that enters into the inner place behind the curtain, where Jesus
has gone as a forerunner on our behalf, having become a
high priest forever after the order of Melchizedek.

Hebrews 6:19–20, ESV

In the book of Hebrews, the message is clear that Jesus is superior
to all things—to angels, to leaders, to the law, and to the Jewish
priesthood. As you may know, following Him isn't always easy. And
we shouldn't expect it to be. But we can endure, be patient, and persevere because Jesus did what we couldn't.

In the verse above, Jesus is described as a *forerunner.* The Greek
adjective translated here is *prodromos,* which depicts one who runs
ahead or goes before others to prepare a way.[29] In ancient Greek-
speaking cultures, *prodromos* was often used to describe a small boat
that was sent into a harbor to help larger ships get safely and securely into the port.

It seems as if the author of Hebrews was using the last usage to
paint a picture of what Jesus did for us regarding our salvation. Jesus,
being the runner boat (*prodromos*), was sent to earth, took our anchor of hope, and by His death and resurrection leads us safely and
securely into the harbor of heaven! He is the One who has shown us
the way. The One who goes before us. The One who pulls us in.
That's the character of our God.

*Our anchor is the hope we have in Jesus rooted in
God's promises. Trust that He's pulling you in the
right direction. How have you experienced
the Lord go before you?*

Trusting in the Waiting

✣

Wait for the LORD;
Be strong and let your heart take courage;
Yes, wait for the LORD.

Psalm 27:14

Where do you feel like you are waiting for God? Is it in a prayer that you've had for years that hasn't been answered yet? A longing or a desire that has yet to be fulfilled? Are you waiting for direction from God as you decide the next step to take?

When we talk about waiting for God, it's not that He isn't there already. He is always with us. We don't have to wait for His presence. We can trust that God is still with us even if He feels distant. We trust that He isn't finished with us. We trust that He is still working even if we don't see it. And as we trust Him, we are able to wait patiently for what He is going to do in our lives.

While waiting at a bus stop, we know the bus is coming and that it's abiding by its schedule, not our own. If we carry that same confidence to our relationship with God, if we trust that He is going to work in His timing and will reveal Himself in His way, we can wait for Him without getting weary. We can be strong while we wait, as we keep our trust in the Lord.

What is your biggest challenge when waiting?
How does knowing and experiencing God's character
strengthen your waiting period?

Today's Call

✝

Whatever you do in word or deed, do everything
in the name of the Lord Jesus, giving thanks
through Him to God the Father.

Colossians 3:17

When we first meet David in the Bible, he is just a shepherd boy, the youngest of eight brothers, and he suddenly has a rags-to-riches story and is anointed the next king of Israel in the middle of his shift, in front of his family.

But David doesn't go straight from tending sheep to sitting on a throne. There's a moment of celebration. And then David goes back to his current job. Although he was just declared the next king, he didn't see shepherding as a task that was beneath him.

What is God's big call on your life? Maybe you've already received it and you're waiting for the wheel to be set in motion. Maybe you feel like there is no major call God has for you. Either way, no matter what's in store for you, whatever is in front of you deserves your full attention.

If you're working part-time in retail, do it with a smile. If you're in school, study diligently. If you're in between jobs, make use of your time by serving others. Purpose is intertwined in where you are right now. Make an intentional decision to work heartily, as for the Lord, in whatever He has called you to do.

***Take a moment to reflect on what your call
may be today. Write it down.***

Behind the Scenes

✛

It is God who is at work in you,
both to desire and to work for His good pleasure.

Philippians 2:13

After David was anointed king and went back to the sheep, he went to help his older brothers. His brothers were supposed to be at war, but like the rest of the Israelite army, they were hiding in the barracks from a giant named Goliath. After David brought his brothers a home-cooked meal and asked them some questions, as little brothers do, he decided that enough was enough. An entire nation was terrified of the giant, but David accepted the challenge of fighting Goliath.

Despite pushback from others, David stood firm in his mission. He knew what he was up against. But he had been here before. In his work as a shepherd, he chased off lions and bears and killed them with his bare hands, so he was confident that God could help him defeat this giant. David's present-day job as a shepherd was much more than a menial job; it was the exact preparation he needed for a task he didn't know was coming.

Waiting is more than waiting; it's preparing. God is not a God of accidents. Even when you don't see it, you can trust that He is working behind the scenes in your life for His purposes.

***How has God worked behind the scenes
in your life in the past?***

A Bunch of Little Calls

✝

He said to them, "Go into all the world and preach
the gospel to all creation."
Mark 16:15

Maybe you feel like you don't have a big call like David did. Maybe you're not anointed to be a king like he was or called to preach in front of large crowds or lead a massive organization that works to end injustice. Maybe you feel that God is calling everyone else but misplaced your phone number and hasn't called you.

When it comes to calling, we as Christians all have the same mission: to spread the gospel to the ends of the earth and make the name of Jesus known. While you may not be called to all the ends of the earth, you are always called to your community, your neighbors, your family, your school—right where you are. Think about it: If God called everyone to the mission field in Africa, how would people in *your* neighborhood know of the good news of Christ? To God, there is no small call. Each one is of utmost importance in His eyes because each one revolves around people getting to know Him, and He desires that all come to Him.

You might not get this one big phone conversation with God, but maybe He is texting you a lot of little things. Think about what you believe He might be saying, and then respond to Him, even if it feels unimportant.

If you're in a waiting season, what can you do to shine
the light of Jesus and focus on the people around you?
What changes will you need to make to do this?

God Provides in the Waiting

✛

He rained down manna upon them to eat,
And gave them food from heaven.

Psalm 78:24

After miraculously leading His people out of slavery in Egypt and through the Red Sea, God brought them straight into a wilderness, where they would wander as nomads until they eventually came home to the Promised Land.

It was a long wait for them to get home to the place God had promised them and that they had dreamed of for so long. But it took more than an overnight trip to get there. More like 14,600 nights, or roughly *forty years,* even though the route there could have been completed in a matter of weeks. Their wandering sojourn to the Promised Land took a lot longer than it should have because of their disobedience and forgetfulness of God's faithfulness. But God didn't leave them. While they waited and wandered, He supplied. Where there was nothing for them to eat in the middle of nowhere (not even any delivery service to bring takeout from the next town over), God provided for them with food straight from heaven, exactly enough for each day.

If you feel like you're waiting on God to tell you when to take the next step, look around you today. How is He providing? What has He given you exactly enough for? He doesn't leave us in the wilderness and expect us to fend for ourselves. Like with the Israelites, He wants us to be fully reliant on Him. Even in the waiting, He is faithful and good.

Reflect on God's goodness, thanking Him
for all He's provided for you.

God Is Always Leading

✝

The LORD was going before them in a pillar of cloud by day
to lead them on the way, and in a pillar of fire by night to give
them light, so that they might travel by day and by night.

Exodus 13:21

Sometimes the hardest part about waiting is not really knowing what you're waiting for. In life, we have so many unknowns and, whether we expect them or not, we are bound to get a few wrenches thrown into our plans.

When we decide to live mission-possible lives and follow where God leads, He doesn't always tell us exactly where He is leading us or when we will get there. The Israelites knew that there was the Promised Land awaiting them, but they had no sense of direction as they wandered the wilderness. With no GPS to help them out, they had to rely on God's guidance.

Even when they weren't sure where they were going, the Israelites knew that God was with them. He was in the cloud at daytime and in the fire at night. If He stayed, they stayed. If He moved, they moved.

A life of faith does not require you to know where God is leading; it requires trusting *that* He is leading. You may not know exactly where you are going, but if you have decided to follow Jesus, you can trust that He is always with you. He will get you where He wants you to be. You simply have to go with Him.

**Examine your life today. Do you see evidence
of God's presence?**

The Ultimate Outcome

✛

*We ourselves groan within ourselves, waiting eagerly for our
adoption as sons and daughters, the redemption of our body.*

Romans 8:23

We get impatient in waiting because we want a specific outcome. Whether it's a relationship, a job, or just clarity for the next step in our lives, we have an aim and set our focus on it, holding our breath until we can finally attain it. We grow antsy, with no guarantee of the outcome and desperate hope that it's what we want. But what do our souls really wait for?

We aren't citizens of this world. Our time here will end. But if we believe in Jesus as Lord and Savior, we know the ultimate outcome: We get to be with Jesus in all His glory.

The apostle Paul goes on to say in Romans 8 that though we do not yet see what our hearts ultimately long for, we can wait with expectation and confidence for the day we will see Jesus. If nothing else is guaranteed in life, our salvation and eternity with Him are. With this perspective, whatever else we wait for pales in comparison.

***Think about what outcomes you tend to focus on.
What would it look like to focus on this
eternal outcome instead?***

A Prayer for Restraint

✝

Lord, Your Word tells us that You make everything beautiful in its time. While I recognize that truth, sometimes impatience gets the best of me. I get angry and frustrated. Instead of waiting on You, sometimes I intervene in my painful situations on my own, which doesn't result in Your best for my life. Forgive me, God, and help me not to stay in that space. Give me an eagerness in my spirit to be self-controlled and not foolishly wound up by my intolerance— that I would trust the waiting process instead of trying to control outcomes. Thank You for Your great mercy that is infinite and inexhaustible and for being my Father in heaven, who never changes. Even when I stumble, miss the mark, or rely on my own resources to forge ahead, You remain steady and faithful. Teach me to likewise remain steady in my journey with You on earth. When I am tempted to turn to idols like shopping, food, substances, and love in all the wrong places, remind me it is always, and has always been, You. Thank You for the open invitation to come to and remain in You, for You are forever good.

In Jesus's name I pray. Amen.

Based on: Ecclesiastes 3:11; Psalm 27:14; Ecclesiastes 7:9; Deuteronomy 4:31; Malachi 3:6; 2 Timothy 2:13; Psalm 34:8

Don't Let Your Age Stop You

✛

Let no one look down on your youthfulness,
but rather in speech, conduct, love, faith, and purity,
show yourself an example of those who believe.

1 Timothy 4:12

Guest devo by Victoria Franzen
Relationship to TTF: ministry partner, Impact Baby Rescue,
Johannesburg, South Africa

As a sixteen-year-old missionary born and raised in South Africa, I often felt intimidated trying to figure out my place in the world and how I could make a difference. In addition, having parents who had accomplished so much for the kingdom stirred up fear and insecurity that I wouldn't quite measure up.

I've come to realize I can't waste my time and days wishing to be older, smarter, or more talented before I can do something important. God can use me; He can use *you*! It isn't dependent on our age, experience, or geographical location. What matters is that we have an open heart to whatever God calls us to do and are willing to take a step no matter how big or small.

I've realized that God can use me in so many ways to bring Him glory. Things like loving on abandoned babies at our baby home, telling Bible stories to kids in the impoverished communities, praying for the sick, and showing kindness to my two-year-old foster sister are ways I live authentic love.

God has plans for us since the day we were born, plans we are intended to fulfill. Be open and faithful to His way as He sees the bigger picture and has a purpose for all of us no matter our age.

Have you been afraid to take a leap of faith
because you're intimidated?

He Was, Is, and Always Will Be

+

All things have been created through Him and for Him.
He is before all things, and in Him all things hold together.

Colossians 1:16–17

When life doesn't turn out exactly as we wanted or had planned even after praying and feeling pretty sure about God's directions, the questions come. A lot of them. And fast.

It's what happens when you finally get the job and then get let go three months later or your spouse of twenty years tells you she's leaving.

When life throws us curveballs, some devastating, it's easy to allow doubt to creep in, no matter how strong we think our faith is. We doubt ourselves, we doubt God's plan, and oftentimes we doubt God.

Hey, I've doubted. I've asked many a time, *God, where are You? I was depending on You. I thought You had this.* Sometimes I wanted something so bad that I took the reins to make it happen, only to fall flat on my face.

When we ask questions, when we doubt, when we wonder if God is going to pull through or why He didn't pull through or why our miracles are taking so long or why the miracles never came at all, remember that doubt is normal. God isn't scared of your questions. Bring them to Him. But don't let doing so stop you from fighting the good fight and keeping the faith. It may seem that life is a bundle of chaos and problems and questions, but God was, is, and always will be. He is the one you can count on.

What have you doubted God about?
How have you learned to trust Him in the meantime?

Only God

✝

Jesus said, "With people it is impossible, but not with God;
for all things are possible with God."

Mark 10:27

I n 1986, right before a certain missionary went onstage to preach before a crowd in a remote village on an island of the Philippines, he began to uncontrollably weep. He felt like God was putting it on his heart and in his head that babies all over the world were being aborted. And then God put it on his heart and in his head that he needed to have another baby. He already had four kids that were home on another island in another village with his wife, but he felt this need so strongly. He and his wife began to pray for the baby they hoped to have, and a while later, she became pregnant. They were so excited.

When they saw the doctor, however, their excitement deflated. The doctor believed the baby wasn't in fact a baby but a tumor. A bit later, more news: The tumor was, in fact, a baby, but the baby wasn't healthy, and should the mother continue with the pregnancy, it could cost her life. The mother chose to trust in God and keep the baby. Her entire pregnancy was rough, filled with one ailment after another. But miraculously and much to the doctor's amazement, the mother gave birth to a perfectly healthy boy. And she, too, survived.

That day, I got to meet my mom. That's right. That "tumor" was me.

God has the power to accomplish what we cannot. Choose to trust Him, even when where you're standing seems impossible.

What impossible prayers do you have
to choose to trust God for?

The God Who Opens Doors

✝

I have set before you an open door, and no one can shut it;
for you have a little strength, have kept My word,
and have not denied My name.

Revelation 3:8, NKJV

Guest devo by Ockert Potgieter
Relationship to TTF: Night to Shine host, Reni, Ukraine

I remember that evening so clearly. It was the night before my wife and I had to fly out to Ukraine to work on the mission field. We had been struggling for months to obtain visas. We ran out of time. Enemies in Ukraine had bribed the right people, and the official told us clearly when we called that afternoon, "You will never get this document!"

However, the Lord reminded us of His promise. When we left for Ukraine as an inexperienced young couple, He said that it was He who opened the door before us and no man would be able to close it. And even though it was well after closing hours, we called the consulate number. To our surprise, the consul picked up the phone, and to our even greater surprise, after we explained the dilemma, he calmly answered, "Bring your passports tomorrow morning and I will issue you visas within fifteen minutes." We were ready to fly. Once again, the Lord held the door open! Nobody and nothing was able to close the doors to Ukraine to us because the Lord put an open door before us.

There aren't guarantees about outcomes. But one of the assurances we have when we follow Jesus is that He will open doors before us that seem impossible to open. And when a door closes, we are at rest because we know *He* closed the door and we trust Him. Even when we have little strength, if we keep believing Him and His words, He will finish what He started.

What door has God closed that you are grateful for?

The Gift of Trust

✦

He who supplies seed to the sower and bread for food
will supply and multiply your seed for sowing and increase
the harvest of your righteousness.

2 Corinthians 9:10

"**P**lease get me a drink of water," he asked. "Oh, and some bread" (see 1 Kings 17:10–11). It was a simple request—at the worst possible time. During a famine, a widow was preparing the last meal she and her son would ever eat, when Elijah knocked on her door and said he was hungry. I mean, the mother and son were literally about to die. The widow's response was rather shocking. She didn't slam the door in his face. She very matter-of-factly, it seems, told the truth: "I've only got enough ingredients to make bread for my son and me, which we plan to eat, then die" (see verse 12).

Elijah told her it wasn't a problem and to go ahead and make the bread but give some to him first and then she and her son could have the rest. He said that if she did that, she'd never have to worry about running out of food, even in a famine, because God would always provide for her and her son. For some reason, she slipped out of her suffering to show this man, a stranger, compassion. Likely, she believed and trusted God. The Bible tells us that "she and . . . her household ate for many days" (verse 15). Sometimes God will ask us to do or say things that breach our abilities or defy common sense. But that's just Him asking us to trust that He'll make possible what we see is not.

What miracles can God do with your gift of obedience?

Death Is Never the End

✝

All creation is waiting eagerly for that future day when God will
reveal who his children really are. Against its will, all creation was
subjected to God's curse. But with eager hope, the creation looks
forward to the day when it will join God's children in
glorious freedom from death and decay.

Romans 8:19–21, NLT

The story of the widow who prepared what she believed to be her
last meal for her and her son didn't stop at the miraculous outcome. Sometime after the inexplicable provision that kept her and
her only child alive, tragedy struck. The boy got sick and died. Talk
about a sick joke! Why would God do that? She had just rounded the
corner of a dark time thanks to divine deliverance, so why the sudden sucker punch? How cruel!

But life's like that at times, isn't it? The minute we're exhaling
after a crisis, a new one erupts. While one day we will join all the
saints, past and present, in heaven, free of death and decay, tears and
pain, for now we remain on earth. And as we breathe through the
hard things, we are invited into opportunities to trust in Him. For
the widow, it was a bleak moment. For God, it was a chance to show
off.

Elijah threw himself over the dead boy and began to pray. As the
desperate and faith-charged words surged from the prophet's lips,
the boy's lungs started to rise and fall. And in that moment, death
did not have the final word.

For believers, death never does.

How does knowing that God has prepared for believers a
place for them in heaven encourage you
during tough times?

Your Power or God's?

✛

With people this is impossible,
but with God all things are possible.

Matthew 19:26

After crossing the Jordan River on dry ground and witnessing the walls of Jericho fall, Joshua knew that God was with the Israelites. When it came to the battle of Ai (see Joshua 7–8), though, Joshua took matters into his own hands. He sent out a couple of spies and relied on their advice for devising a battle plan, which ended in great loss. Suddenly the Israelites who had witnessed God's hand miraculously lead them were terrified. Joshua, in despair, turned to God. After repenting for the nation, he received a new battle plan from Him. When Joshua obeyed God's voice, his army was again led to victory.

Often, you may try to move forward in your own strength and realize that, in spite of how simple the situation seemed, you can't. Even if you have seen God move before in your life, it's important to remember that your ability to overcome did not come from you but from God alone. Like Joshua, we may be confident in God, but if we do not consult Him before making our next move, we will not be working in His strength.

Living a mission-possible life is not about the humanly possible but the God-possible. Walking in sync with God is more important than being able to conquer your battles on your own. Don't rely on your own power. Continually go to God and seek Him for direction in all things.

**Are you relying on your own power or God's power
for your next move?**

Eating Solids

✝

Solid food is for the mature, who because of practice have
their senses trained to distinguish between good and evil.

Hebrews 5:14

G rowth is a part of life. We're born as infants, helpless, unable to fend for ourselves. Eventually, we become toddlers learning to explore, then older children with questions, until we finally emerge into adulthood, when we are more self-sufficient than ever and able to pass down our knowledge to a younger generation. All living things have life cycles and growing processes.

But too many Christians are content to be stagnant in their faith. Although the best and biggest decision we can make in our lives is to say yes to Jesus, we can still grow from that place. We can do more than sip milk whenever we feel the urge. Our faith needs to grow.

The only way to grow is to nourish our souls. To do so, we need full meals to satisfy our longing for God. The occasional snack on a Sunday morning is not enough to strengthen us the way we need to be strengthened. To become mature Christians, we need to eat solid foods.

Don't just read the verse of the day; study the Bible with a group of friends. Don't just pray before dinner; carve out intentional time to communicate with God. Without these nourishing meals, we are bound to stop growing in faith and become stagnant in our walks with Christ. But we're created for more than lives of stagnancy. Hunger for more so you can grow in ways you never imagined possible.

**What can you eat today to ensure you are getting
the spiritual nourishment your soul needs?**

Bread of Life

✝

Jesus said to them, "I am the bread of life; the one who
comes to Me will not be hungry, and the one who believes
in Me will never be thirsty."

John 6:35

What do you want most in life? Where do you invest the majority of your time and energy and seek gratification? We all
crave something. It may be fame, fortune, love, or acceptance. Deep
down, we desire to be known, seen, and heard, and we make it our
aim to obtain the things we want, hoping they can fulfill us.

At the root of all we desire is the only One who could bring us
peace and rest. In fact, Jesus remarked multiple times that in Him we
would find peace. Fame and fortune are nothing apart from Jesus.
Status and acclaim are empty without Him. Accomplishments don't
satisfy, and compliments are hollow after a while.

Ultimately, our hearts aren't set on any of the things we chase but
rather on fulfillment. Jesus called Himself the Bread of Life. He
knows our hunger and tells us that He is what we long for. Jesus
is more than salvation for our souls. He's more than a teacher. He
is daily nourishment for us, the only One who could satisfy our
hunger.

The next time you are feeling unfilled in life, recognize your
soul's desire for Jesus and turn to Him. Spend time with Him and let
Him be the fuel that keeps you going.

**Is your soul malnourished? How can you make space
for the Bread of Life today?**

Blessed Hunger

+

Blessed are those who hunger and thirst for righteousness,
for they will be satisfied.

Matthew 5:6

If you know me, you know what a fan I am of living healthily. One practice I often put into play is intermittent fasting. A few times a week, I may fast for sixteen or more hours a day to give my body a boost. Research shows there are many benefits to this. It helps your body get rid of toxins and gives you mental clarity. Additionally, by practicing intermittent fasting, you begin to reduce your hunger, making you less prone to reach for a snack when your body doesn't really need it. By decreasing your appetite, you're less likely to over-eat.[30]

Spiritually speaking, though, it is dangerous to curb our appetites for the things of God. Just like with our natural bodies, the less we consume, the less we want to consume. In the same way, the less we fill ourselves with the things of God, the less hungry we will be for them. Jesus said that spiritual hunger is a good thing. He called those who hunger for God's righteousness blessed. The more we hunger for God, the more He will fill us.

Keep your spiritual hunger growing by continually keeping yourself in the Lord. Read your Bible daily. Make prayer a constant habit. Choose to worship even if you don't feel like it. Whatever you do, make it a point to consume more righteousness, ever increasing your appetite for it.

How can you increase your spiritual appetite today?

Wonder

✟

Your light must shine before people in such a way that they may
see your good works, and glorify your Father who is in heaven.

Matthew 5:16

Before the Israelites finally crossed the Jordan River to go into the
Promised Land, they were instructed to take twelve stones, one
for each tribe, and make a memorial with them. The stones were to
serve as a reminder to future generations of the miraculous power
of God. He led these people through the Jordan River on dry ground,
just as He had led the previous generation through the Red Sea in
their exodus from Egypt. God worked wonders, and the Israelites
were to keep their wonder alive. (See Joshua 3:1–17 and Exodus
13:18 to read those accounts.)

Think of what God has done for you. Have you set up a memorial
to remind you of His faithfulness? When people see your life, do
they see the emblem of God's goodness? Whether it's as simple as a
fresh start to a new day and the breath in your lungs or a true Red
Sea miracle He's performed in your life, reflect on God's goodness.

As your wonder grows, live the type of life with Jesus that will
cause others to be curious about the God who is at work in your life.
Shine the light of God by declaring the things that God has done for
you. Do this in such a way that your wonder is contagious.

***How can your life act as a reminder to others
of God's faithfulness?***

Wisdom

+

If any of you lacks wisdom, let him ask of God,
who gives to all generously and without reproach,
and it will be given to him.

James 1:5

God appeared to King Solomon in a dream. He offered him anything. Solomon asked for one thing: Knowing he had big shoes
to fill and grateful for the blessing of his role, he asked God to grant
him wisdom to be able to do his job well. Out of anything he could
have possibly had, an understanding heart was the most important
to him. Pleased with his request, God gave wisdom to Solomon.

Solomon's desire for wisdom was coupled with his desire to
carry out his role. He did not ask God to do his job for him; he asked
God to equip him with wisdom so he could do it well.

You have a responsibility to fulfill as a follower of Christ in your
mission-possible life. You may find that He leads you into places of
uncertainty that stall your momentum. You have two choices in
those moments: you can settle into the confusion, overwhelmed
with fear and apprehension, or you can seek wisdom.

The good news is that wisdom isn't difficult to seek. As Solomon
asked God for wisdom, we can do the same and expect God to grant
it to us. He will not do our job for us, but when we ask Him, He will
generously give us what is required for us to make the next choice.

**Where do you need God's wisdom in your
life today? Ask Him for it.**

Treasure Hunt

✝

The kingdom of heaven is like a treasure
hidden in the field.

Matthew 13:44

W hat would you do if someone handed you a treasure map, like the kind you see in old storybooks, with an X that marks the spot? Would you hold on to it for a little while, then toss it in the trash, brushing off the map as a hoax? Or would you drop everything to go search for the gold, dreaming of all that you would be able to do with the fortune when you find it? I'm sure most of us would go on the treasure hunt. We would be fools to know that something of that worth exists and not search for it.

There is something infinitely greater than a buried chest of gold. The kingdom of heaven itself is a treasure, and we have access to it, no treasure map required. Salvation and eternal life with Jesus are worth more than anything of value you could ever hope to find in this world.

As believers, we know the way to heaven. His name is Jesus. Do you recognize what a priceless prize a relationship with Him is? Would you lay down everything in your life to seek and obtain it? Often, the only risk involved is your time as you learn to devote yourself to following Him. And the reward is more than worth the risk.

Where is your treasure?
What do you seek most in this life?

A Prayer for Greater Faith

✛

Father, though I know You call me to live by faith and not by sight, I'll admit, it's hard! Circumstances and relationships cause me to waver in my belief. Forgive me when I fail to trust in You. I believe in You, in Your power, in Your love, in Your divinity and Your omnipotence. And in the moments when my faith slips, help me overcome that unbelief. Help me to remain anchored in You despite what I see or don't see. Arm me with a growing confidence that makes me believe I can do whatever is before me because You arm me with strength. Thank You for the power You infuse into my being. I know that it is greater than the wisdom of humans because it comes from the Holy Spirit. What greater way to grow my faith than to know You more! Create within me an insatiable hunger for Your Word because it's in Your truth that I will find my daily sustenance and always be satisfied.

In Jesus's name I pray. Amen.

Based on: 2 Corinthians 5:7; Luke 17:5; Mark 9:24; Philippians 4:13; 1 Corinthians 2:4–5; Deuteronomy 8:2–3; Matthew 5:6

Sacrifice Is Inevitable

✝

No servant can serve two masters; for either he will hate the one
and love the other, or he will be devoted to one and despise the
other. You cannot serve God and wealth.

Luke 16:13

Most people understand that if you want to achieve greatness,
you will have to give up other things in life, like laziness and
scrolling social media for hours. There's too much work to do to get
caught up in those kinds of things.

But there's another side to sacrifice. Because you can choose
what you want to do in life, you may decide that you want to spend
your days lying on the couch or catching up on online videos. When
you do that, you end up sacrificing the things you could be doing
instead. Staying out late partying means you sacrifice getting an
early start on your day. Choosing to play video games instead of
studying means you might sacrifice doing well on your exam. When
you choose mediocrity, you sacrifice greatness.

Sacrifice is inevitable. There is a cost to every choice you make. If
the point of following Jesus is to lose your life, you cannot follow
Him and keep your idea of a good life. If you keep your idea of a
good life, then you are not fully submitted to Christ. If you are submitted to Christ, you need to put aside other things.

You cannot serve two masters. Either way you choose to go, you
will be sacrificing something. Make sure that whatever you sacrifice,
it's worth the gain.

Think about how you spend your days.
Are you making choices to sacrifice greatness
for mediocrity? In what way?

Living Sacrifice

✛

I urge you, brothers and sisters, by the mercies of God,
to present your bodies as a living and holy sacrifice, acceptable
to God, which is your spiritual service of worship.

Romans 12:1

In the Old Testament, sacrifices served many purposes. There were some sacrifices for atonement, some for praise, some as fragrance, and some for thanks. In the Law, the Israelites were given drawn-out and very specific lists of sacrifices they could offer God depending on the occasion. There were instructions for how to slaughter the animal and how to present it to God. In each of these sacrifices, the blood from the animal would be strained out and offered to the Lord.

On the cross, Jesus became our atonement once and for all. His blood covered all our sins, making such other sacrifices obsolete. He was crucified and died a sinner's death but was raised again to life on the third day. Now, just as Jesus is alive, we are also to present ourselves as living sacrifices to God.

To be living sacrifices for God means to submit to His authority in our lives. We do this by choosing to follow Him even when it's hard—by putting our own desires second and trusting Him with the direction of our lives. Living mission possible means being consumed with Jesus to the point that there is no room for us. When we get to that place, we will see His glory on display in our lives.

What does it mean for you to be a living sacrifice today?

Count It All as Loss

✝

I count all things to be loss in view of the surpassing value
of knowing Christ Jesus my Lord, for whom I have suffered
the loss of all things, and count them mere rubbish,
so that I may gain Christ.

Philippians 3:8

I remember walking into the Dallas Cowboys complex one day when I was scheduled to speak at the Omni Hotel years ago. At first, I didn't realize that the hotel and the stadium were part of the same facility, but touring it all was fascinating. Walking around, though, I started to miss football. The more memories that I had, the more frustrated I got at God. I wished in the moment that He'd had different plans for my life, ones that had me get everything I wanted.

I'm sure you've felt the same in your life, wondering the purpose for everything that God has brought you through. When you try to live a mission-possible life, you live one marked out by God, following directly in His footsteps. It may mean that He sends you down roads that you would rather not walk down. It might mean letting go of certain activities, habits, or tendencies. It might mean that something you long for doesn't come to pass in the way you'd hoped. But loss in this context is not without value. It pales in comparison to what you gain: Jesus Christ.

Ultimately, when we desire to follow Jesus, we willingly give up our desires for the sake of following Him. We trust His leading, and we obey. And though losing something we wanted may sting for a while, our gain supersedes the pain.

What do you need to count as a loss today?

Delayed Gratification

✝

Esau . . . sold his own birthright for a single meal.

Hebrews 12:16

I n a well-known social experiment, kindergartners were each given a marshmallow. They were told that if they did not eat the marshmallow, they would be given an extra one. Then they were left alone for a few minutes. Some children squirmed and toyed with their snack, while some waited patiently. Others didn't miss a beat and ate the marshmallow as soon as the coast was clear. For the ones who waited, more was given. But the ones who could not wait to eat their treats were given no more.[31]

Choosing to live a faith-based life means being willing to give up something now for something better later. It takes more than just old-fashioned willpower and self-control to practice delayed gratification. It takes understanding the why behind your action and using that, and the power of the Holy Spirit, to say no now for a yes later.

In the Bible, a man named Esau traded his birthright for a cup of lentil stew. He was hangry and, in that moment, putting his lips around a spoonful of beans meant more to him than his position of leadership in the family. I doubt he thought the trade was worth it when he stared at the bottom of the empty bowl. God has so much more in store for you than you have for yourself. Through the blood of Christ, you were given new life—eternal life. Before you give in to your craving, consider the cost.

*What makes you willing to lay down your desires
for today and trust God to fulfill them tomorrow?*

Obedience Is Always Best

✝

Samuel said,
"Does the LORD have as much delight
in burnt offerings and sacrifices
As in obeying the voice of the LORD?
Behold, to obey is better than a sacrifice,
And to pay attention is better than the fat of rams."

1 Samuel 15:22

God was specific in His commands to Saul, Israel's first king. Through Samuel, God had instructed Saul to go into the city of Amalek and devote everything there to destruction. So, Saul went to Amalek and destroyed *nearly* everything. He kept the king alive as a prisoner and kept the best livestock from the enemy. There is no such thing as partial obedience. We either obey, or we do not. And in Saul's case, he did not. Saul did not follow through with God's command, and it cost him his kingship.

We don't know exactly what Saul was thinking when he put his own slant on what God told him. We do know Saul had the idea to sacrifice the animals as an offering. God, however, was totally disinterested in the spoils. He was more concerned with Saul's disobedience. And through the prophet Samuel, God made clear His disappointment with Saul's decision and declared His regret at making him king (see 1 Samuel 15:11). Ouch.

Be obedient in what God is asking of you. If you refuse, do things your way, and plan to make it up to God afterward in big way, you'll fail. Obedience is a form of sacrifice; in fact, it's even better than many of the things we think of as worship. If you know God is telling you to do something, do it all!

**What step of obedience do you need to take that
you may have been avoiding?**

Handing Over Authority

✝

Whoever wants to save his life will lose it;
but whoever loses his life for My sake will find it.

Matthew 16:25

Elijah was on the run from Jezebel and came to a town called
Zarephath. There was a famine in the land, so food was in short
supply. He was hungry, so he asked a widow for a little bread. Remember this faithful woman from an earlier devotion? Disheart-
ened by his request, she explained that she had enough flour and oil
for only one last meal for her and her son. However, she chose to
trust God and prepared it for the prophet anyway. Because of her
willingness and faith, God blessed her. Through a miracle, she never
ran out of oil or flour (see 1 Kings 17:8–16).

What do you have in your possession that God is asking you to
give up? If you look closely enough, you may find that, like the
widow, you have enough for only one more meal. As good as it may
be, it will not sustain you. It may be scary to let it go, but when we
make the decision to sacrifice the little bits we have, we find that
God supplies us with an overabundance of His grace.

When you sacrifice for the Lord, you get Him. With nothing in
the way, you get direct access to Him. You have the assurance that
He is in control. You have the peace that He is with you. You get
Jesus, which is infinitely more than you could have ever tried to earn
on your own.

What is God asking you to sacrifice?
Take a leap of faith, and trust Him and obey.

By Our Love

✝

By this all people will know that you are My disciples:
if you have love for one another.

John 13:35

They will know we are Christians by our *love*. Not by our hashtags. Not by our T-shirts. Not by the highlights in our Bibles or how many scriptures we post on social media. The one thing Jesus will use to let the world know that we follow Him is our love for others.

When Jesus spoke the above words from John 13, He was sitting with His disciples at their last Passover meal. He knew what the next few days would hold: His imminent crucifixion, the fear the disciples would walk through, and His impending resurrection and victory. This would be one final pep talk that He would give them before He accomplished what He came to this world to do. Before He left them, He gave them a new commandment: "Love one another; just as I have loved you" (verse 34).

That is how Jesus told us to love others: the same way He loves us.

How does Jesus love you? Has He given you mercy when you deserved punishment? Has He bestowed grace when you were least deserving of it? Has He forgiven you? Has He invited you to come as you are?

We are required to love others with that same kind of love. It is hard because it feels so unnatural to our flesh. Even when it is difficult, we get to go to Jesus and ask Him to fill us up with this kind of love. Ask Him today to help you love others as He loves them.

How can you practice the love of Jesus today?

Can't Pick and Choose

+

My brothers and sisters, do not hold your faith in our glorious
Lord Jesus Christ with an attitude of personal favoritism.

James 2:1

As humans, we tend to stick with the people who resemble us most. Look at who you follow on social media. Do they have the same values as you? Do you like their content because it aligns with your worldview? Now look at your phone contacts. Do those you talk to the most also share your ideologies?

We need those people in our lives to encourage us and hold us accountable, but we also need to branch out. The world is filled with many different people with many different backgrounds, views, and experiences—and they need Jesus too. We must be intentional about seeking relationship, regardless of our differences. We can play favorites with friends and decide who we do or don't want to vacation with, but we shouldn't play favorites with whom we are called to love.

Jesus modeled what it was like to love the ones who are not like us. While He walked this earth, He visited the home of tax collectors (see Matthew 9:10–13; Luke 19:1–10) who were seen as traitors and thieves. He started a conversation with a Samaritan woman (see John 4:1–42) despite centuries of civil unrest between their cultures. He even washed the feet of His own betrayer (see John 13:1–17).

We can't play favorites. Jesus commanded us to love others, with no loopholes that allow us to pick and choose whom. Trust that the people God has put in your life are there for a reason, and look continually to Him for grace to love them as He loves.

**How can you show love to a person
who offends you today?**

Don't Get Discouraged

✝

*Let's not become discouraged in doing good, for in due time
we will reap, if we do not become weary.*

Galatians 6:9

From the time it is planted, an acorn takes four to six weeks to germinate. During this time, the seed in the acorn begins to sprout. First, a root shoots downward, ensuring the future oak tree receives nutrients from the ground beneath it. While the roots continue to grow in the depths of the soil, hidden from the human eye, a sprout eventually emerges, making its way to the surface. Only at that point, more than a month after planting the original seed, is there something to show for all that happened.

Jesus talks about planting seeds, about people hearing the Word of God and the way it may take root in their lives. Sometimes the seeds land in fertile soil. Other times, they don't even have the chance to sprout. As you plant seeds and share the love of Jesus with others, sometimes you might see a heart change right away. At other times, you might not see any evidence that people are receptive to what you're saying. You might wonder what the point of planting seeds is. However, you wouldn't plant an acorn and expect an oak tree to immediately spring up.

You might not see the fruit of your mission right away. But in those moments, remember that a mission-possible life is, above all, about obedience to what God has called you to do. Focus on your mission and don't get carried away with its results. Those are best left in God's hands.

*Are you feeling discouraged? What would it look like
to overcome that and obey Jesus's call anyway?*

What's in a Name?

+

Jesus said to her, "Mary!" She turned and said to Him in Hebrew,
"Rabboni!" (which means, Teacher).

John 20:16

On the Sunday after Jesus's crucifixion, just before the sun peeked over the horizon, Mary went to the tomb where His body had been buried. It was customary to bring spices to the gravesite to anoint the deceased's body. But to Mary's dismay, as she drew closer to the tomb, she saw that the stone was rolled away. In a panic, she ran to get a closer look and saw that Jesus's body was gone and in its place was left a couple of folded garments. Her distress grew. She ran out to a gardener in the yard and begged him to tell her where the body of her precious Lord had been taken. Looking at her, the man said one word.

"Mary!"

Instantly, Mary came undone. This person knew her name. She knew who this person was. He was no gardener. He was Jesus.

Jesus could have said anything to Mary that morning to let her know who He was. He could have talked to her about the prophecies and asked her if she remembered them. Instead, He just spoke her name.

Never underestimate the power of such a simple act. Something as small as learning someone's name and repeating it back to them can remind them of their value in this world. Obviously, the way we say someone's name versus how Jesus does doesn't lend quite the same impact, but when we do it, it at least shows someone we care enough about them to know them by name.

**How can you give that same care and attention
to someone today?**

Be Intentional

+

Little children, let's not love with word or with tongue,
but in deed and truth.

1 John 3:18

When you are living a mission-possible life, are pumped up about the gospel, and want the world to know about the hope you have and can offer others, you may be surprised to find that those who need that hope aren't exactly lining up at your door to ask you about it.

There is no doubt that darkness exists in this world and that people feel hopeless, but when you are living in the dark, you have no idea that you are in darkness until you can see the light. People who wander through life in that bleak state often don't realize that they need a Savior or that there's another way to live. As Christians, our call is to spread the gospel. We can't sit back, twiddling our thumbs and whistling our favorite tunes, while we wait for people who need the gospel to come to us. We need to be intentional and seek out the lost.

This means acting as if every moment with a stranger is an opportunity from God to share the message of hope. Whether it's the man sitting next to you on the plane, the teenager taking your order at lunch, or the woman in the next cubicle, take ten minutes to invest in the people on your path. Ask questions. Get to know them. Don't be pushy; instead be intentional with your conversation. Offer a listening ear. You may be surprised by what God can do with your obedience and your willingness to get to know others.

**What does being intentional with others
look like in your life today?**

Share the Good News

✝

The Spirit of the Lord God is upon me,
Because the Lord anointed me
To bring good news to the humble;
He has sent me to bind up the brokenhearted,
To proclaim release to captives
And freedom to prisoners.

Isaiah 61:1

I f the heart of spreading the gospel is loving people, then sharing the gospel should be about sharing our hearts and not memorizing lines. That Isaiah verse gives us a good depiction of the strategic gospel and how to share it:

- "Bring good news to the humble." In this context, the Hebrew word for humble means poor and needy. The more you talk to people with intention, the easier it is to know when a person is in need. These are the people who need to hear the good news that you have experienced in your life. Share with them what you know.

- "Bind up the brokenhearted." If you see someone in pain and going through a hard season, sharing the gospel in that moment might look like holding their hand through it and sticking around when everyone else leaves.

- "Proclaim release to captives and freedom to prisoners." Where people are bound up, they need to know that freedom is an option. Be the person to remind them that they don't have to stay stuck. Tell others about Jesus and the freedom that is found in living with Him. Think about who Jesus is to you and share that with others who need to know those aspects too.

*How has the gospel transformed you,
and how can you share that with others?*

Let Your Life Be Your Message

✝

You are the light of the world.
A city set on a hill cannot be hidden.

Matthew 5:14

Sharing the gospel is not about saying the proper words or having the right conversation. It's not about developing gimmicks and tricks to get people to invite Jesus into their lives. When we talk of a strategic gospel, we do not mean there is a formula to follow but instead a principle. At the root of it, your life is the message. If you're only interested in gaining converts, your life will reflect your inauthenticity. People can sense fakeness from a mile away. If you really want people to come to the knowledge of the saving power and grace of Jesus Christ, your love needs to be genuine. In other words, it needs to come directly from Jesus. Be willing to stand up with courage and tell people the good news, but also live it.

Jesus said in Matthew 5:14 that we "are the light of the world." Simply by following Jesus, we become His ambassadors and shine His light through our lives. When we live from that truth, others will see that our actions and conversations aren't just ploys but that we hold something different. The glory of God will be evident through our actions alone, especially through the way we behave with others.

What do you want your life message to say?

A Prayer to Imitate Jesus

✝

Lord, what a great example You left for us when You walked this earth. You gave it all up to come down from heaven to love, teach, guide, serve, and ultimately give Your life for us in the greatest form of sacrifice in history. Like a sheep led to the slaughter, in humility and obedience, You came to die, and live again, so we can live with You in eternity. Help me see the sacrifice You made for humankind—not just sealed in Your death but also overcome through Your resurrection. When I get discouraged from doing what You have called me to do, fortify my spirit and remind me that the time to reap is coming. Remind me that You look for a spirit of obedience in our hearts, that You value our submission and surrender to You above making grand sacrifices that make us look good in public. Help me to think of others more than myself—not in a boastful way but because it is Your model of mission-possible living. Finally, when the pressure is on and the darkness around me builds and binds my mission, remind me that within me is the Light of the world. Strengthen my heart, mind, body, and spirit to overwhelm the darkness with light.

In Jesus's name I pray. Amen.

Based on: Philippians 2:5–8; Isaiah 53:7; Galatians 6:9; 1 Samuel 15:22; Romans 12:3; 21; John 8:12

Hold Fast

✢

Let's hold firmly to the confession of our hope without wavering,
for He who promised is faithful.
Hebrews 10:23

Guest devo by Rich and Michelle Franzen
Relationship to TTF: ministry partners, Impact Baby Rescue,
Johannesburg, South Africa

In the world we live today, the daily pain, suffering, and death we see around us seems to be increasing. Living nearly eighteen years in Africa, we have definitely seen our share of hardship. Poor education, abuse, and poverty denote the impoverished communities in which we work. Most often the victims of these atrocities are babies, children, women, and the marginalized.

There are days it is just too much. I'm sure you have felt the same way. Amid the maelstrom, we need something to grab hold of to keep us secure, focused, and operating in the Lord's strength.

The author of Hebrews was clear in saying, "Hold firmly to the confession of our hope without wavering" (10:23). A different Bible version says it this way: "Let us seize and hold tightly the confession of our hope without wavering, for He who promised is reliable and trustworthy and faithful to His word" (AMP).

As we grab hold of the truth of God's Word, it helps us steady our wobbly legs and stand on His promise to be reliable, trustworthy, and faithful. In turn, it helps us bring hope to the hopeless by giving them something to grab hold of as well: Jesus!

What are you grabbing hold of amid the storm?
How are you helping others grab hold of the truth?

Let God Use Your Pain

✝

Rejoice to the extent that you partake
of Christ's sufferings, that when His glory is revealed,
you may also be glad with exceeding joy.

1 Peter 4:13, NKJV

E than Hallmark was nine when he was diagnosed with stage IV
high-risk-of-relapse unfavorable-histology neuroblastoma. The
cancer was very lightly scattered in his marrow, and a softball-sized
tumor sat in his abdomen. At Ethan's age, the cancer was more difficult to treat than in an older kid or adult, and therefore the odds of
survival were significantly diminished. He would leave this earth and
enter the arms of Jesus only four years later.

Over a third of Ethan's life was spent in the trenches of cancer as
he faced endless rounds of high-dose chemo, stem-cell transplants,
multiple surgeries, more than one hundred days of radiation, and
travel for trial after trial. On the surface, his life was marked by suffering, but that was only part of the fight. Ethan wanted people to
know the truth that the glory to come, the glory found in the priceless gift of Jesus Christ, far surpassed any amount of suffering endured in this temporary world.

While Ethan waited to beat cancer, he used the darkness—what
the Enemy meant to destroy him—to bring others closer to the light
of Christ. Through his life and death, Ethan affected so many people, even bringing countless men and women, as well as boys and
girls, to make the decision to trust in or rededicate their lives to
Jesus.

Pain is painful. But God will use even the hardest and most deso-
late parts of our lives for a purpose far greater than we can imagine—
but *only* if we let Him.

What is the worst pain you've ever experienced?
What helped you endure that pain?

Stay in the Heat

✝

He knows the way I take;
When He has put me to the test, I will come out as gold.

Job 23:10

In Bible times, high-temperature flame was a process used to purify gold. Gold was first mined from the earth, cleaned of dirt and debris, then crushed to break down the particles. The next step was one of the most important and involved removing the dross, which was the gold's waste product and had no value. The clean gold was placed in a crucible over a hot fire or in a hot furnace. After a period of time, dross formed on the surface, and the refiner skimmed it off, leaving behind only pure gold. This process was repeated, as different impurities were released at different times and in different temperatures. I've read that some refiners considered their work finished when they could see a reflection of themselves in the crucible-cradled gold.

The Bible is replete with images containing "refining by fire" language. It's a process that obviously is uncomfortable and excruciating at times but requires a greater work than exacting searing pain. It bears a refined image of Jesus Christ in our lives.

Whatever struggle we endure, God will nudge certain weaknesses or unhealthy dependencies that need to be exposed to the surface. When it gets too "hot," our natural tendency is to run. But when we stay and trust the process, yes, even in the pain, we will become more and more like Jesus.

**What did you learn through
a "refining by fire" experience?**

On Whom Is Your Hope Set?

✝

We despaired even of life.... We would not trust in ourselves,
but in God who raises the dead, who rescued us from
so great a danger of death, and will rescue us,
He on whom we have set our hope.

2 Corinthians 1:8–10

In this message to the church at Corinth, Paul was candid about his troubles. He didn't shy away from the bad stuff. In fact, he wanted the people he served to know that he and the ones who served alongside him had been wrecked beyond their expectation. The Passion Translation puts the above scriptures like this: "All of the hardships we passed through crushed us.... It felt like we had a death sentence written upon our hearts."

This is intense! Scholars have different theories as to what was happening with Paul. Perhaps it was physical pain. Perhaps persecution. Whatever the reason for what felt like a death sentence to Paul, it was a rough time. Yet it was also an opportunity for him to set his hope on God. I can't tell you the purpose for your or a loved one's pain, but I can say that it reminds us to trust less in ourselves and more in the God on whom Scripture promises we can set our hope.

*Think about a present situation in your life, or that
of a loved one, that is causing pain. Then ask
the Lord to help you set your hope on Him.*

The Message in Your Story

✟

*Let's consider how to encourage one another
in love and good deeds.*
Hebrews 10:24

My dad is one of my greatest heroes. For my entire life, I've watched him choose the path that's worth it—the one that usually bears struggle, pain, and hardship. Over the years, Dad has told us a ton of stories from the mission field. One story that stuck with me was when right before he was due to preach, some armed men rushed him and said, "If you preach, we're gonna kill you." Dad's response was steeped in courage. He walked up to the podium and told those men and the others who came to listen to him how much God loved them.

There were times in that season when my parents had only cents in their bank account. Dad chose to give whatever we had away, believing that God would provide. When he got Parkinson's disease, his doctors told him to stop traveling and take it easy. He didn't. He told me he was going to keep sharing the gospel the same way he had done for the past several decades: flying overseas. I can't help but be encouraged by his story and want to follow in his footsteps—to believe in God's promises and share the hope of Christ no matter what.

The Bible is full of stories that can inspire, encourage, and challenge us. Don't view your struggles as one dimensional. Reframe them into vessels used by God to share hope with others.

**What do you hope people can gain when
they hear about your story?**

It Is Well

✦

Behold, I extend peace to her like a river.

Isaiah 66:12

We won't always know or even understand the purpose of our pain until we get to heaven, but God cares for us in the midst of heartbreak.

Horatio Spafford was a lawyer who lived in Chicago with his wife and five kids. In the early 1870s, his four-year-old son died of scarlet fever. Just a short while later, the Great Chicago Fire destroyed practically everything they owned. Horatio kept his faith and did the best he could to make the most of his life in light of those two terrible events. Two years later, the family took a trip to Europe. Horatio stayed behind and scheduled to meet up with them in a week or so. Soon he received a message from his wife. It read, "Saved alone." The ship that had carried his wife and four daughters had been struck by another vessel and, in only a few minutes, sank deep into the ocean. Two hundred twenty-six people lost their lives in that accident, including Horatio's young girls.

A few days later, Horatio left for England to meet his wife. When the captain of the ship showed him the place where the ship that had carried his family sank, the man burst into tears. He then penned the hymn we know today as "It Is Well with My Soul." As wrecked as he was from the pain of loss, Horatio was able to live in the strength of the only One who could make his soul well.

Create a list of the heartbreaks you've endured.
Next to each heartbreak, write down someone or
something that, at the time, brought you encouragement
or peace. Pray and thank God for His felt presence.

The Bigger Picture

✠

"I know the plans I have for you," declares the LORD,
"plans to prosper you and not to harm you,
plans to give you hope and a future."
Jeremiah 29:11, NIV

Guest devo by Ansley Jones
Relationship to TTF: W15H recipient

Two weeks after my fourteenth birthday, I was diagnosed with acute myeloid leukemia, a very aggressive blood cancer. Two months after my sixteenth birthday, I relapsed. Altogether, I have spent nearly a year of my life in a children's hospital, endured extensive amounts of chemotherapy, received a bone marrow transplant, and suffered from almost every possible side effect that could have resulted from my intensive treatment. Throughout my cancer journey, this verse solidified my faith in God and gave me comfort in knowing that He has good things planned for my future.

On February 15, 2021, I celebrated my fifth anniversary of being cancer-free. I'm not glad that I got cancer, but because I did and survived what felt like a never-ending uphill battle, I have grown more as a person, and for that I am thankful. God was there when I was at my lowest, and He gave me strength when I needed it most.

This verse reminds us that even when we are suffering or in pain, the Lord has plans to give us hope and a future. God has a purpose for our lives, even though we may not be able to see what it is in the moment.

How did God show you that He had designed a
different path during a time that did not go as planned?

The Gift

✝

"My grace is sufficient for you, for power is perfected in weakness."
Most gladly, therefore, I will rather boast about my weaknesses, so
that the power of Christ may dwell in me.

2 Corinthians 12:9

Guest devo by Rachel Hallmark
Relationship to TTF: mother of W15H recipient Ethan Hallmark

After four years of fighting cancer, my thirteen-year-old son, Ethan, had run out of options. During his palliative care, we took a trip to a Christian camp in Colorado. When the counselor asked each teen what their gift was, Ethan's reply left him speechless: "Cancer is my gift." How could a dying teenager view cancer as something to be used as a gift?

What if creating a life that counts involves unimaginable suffering?

Are you weak and weary today? Maybe you are dealing with financial devastation, deep grief, or your own cancer diagnosis. Sisters and brothers, your story has never been one of despair but rather one of hope. While your heart aches and tears fall, the very power of Christ rests upon you. In His sustaining grace, you can create a life that shows others there is so much more than this world. His power is evident when people see that nothing—not a terminal illness or any other trial you walk through—can take your eyes off the prize of Christ.

The gift for Ethan was never in his dreadful disease but in the hope of Christ that others saw in him despite his suffering. As those powerful words came out of his mouth, Ethan knew the gift was in using his cancer to glorify God as he pointed others to Christ.

No matter how big or small the trial before you,
how can you use it to glorify God and lead others to Him?

Give God Your Weakness

✛

My flesh and my heart may fail,
But God is the strength of my heart and my portion forever.
Psalm 73:26

A man I admire is the father of one of my best friends. His story is of trauma and great transformation. Throughout his childhood, this man had multiple stepfathers in and out of his life. All of them were violent. An average day for him included a beating. On a few occasions, he was hit so hard that he had to go to the emergency room. As he grew up, he began to train in martial arts. Fighting became an outlet for his anger. The discipline became more than a line of self-defense; it became a channel for retaliation and rage. Years later, he ran into one of the men who had beaten him up as a boy. My friend's father returned the favor that day and sent the older man to the hospital. But the satisfaction he expected from tasting revenge was short-lived. He remained angry and empty and bitter.

Finally, he met Jesus and began to develop a relationship with Him. Over time, this man learned to surrender his bitterness to God. He realized that committing to trust in Jesus wasn't a partial promise. He had to be all in. Everything had to change, even releasing what he was holding on to so tight. It took a lot of inner work, patience, and time to process the trauma. Watching this man love God and let go of his bitterness has had a profound effect on my life. The aftermath of painful experiences may seek to destroy our lives, but we can always depend on a God who will give us strength.

What bitterness is God inviting you to surrender today?

Great Is God's Faithfulness

✝

The Lord's acts of mercy indeed do not end,
For His compassions do not fail.
They are new every morning;
Great is Your faithfulness.

Lamentations 3:22–23

When Thomas Chisholm penned the lyrics to the classic hymn "Great Is Thy Faithfulness," he understood what it was like to suffer greatly on this earth even as he found God to be unswervingly faithful. With only a minimal education as a child, Chisholm lacked any foundation for worldly success. He served as a minister for a year. Then health problems, including the sudden and uncurable loss of his hearing, derailed his ministry. He moved from Kentucky to New Jersey, working odd jobs through the years just to make ends meet. Though no longer a minister, his devotion to God never waned even as his illnesses forced him to be bedridden at times. Through the ups and downs, Chisholm found solace in the Bible. The above passage in Lamentations had a special place in his heart. His song "Great Is Thy Faithfulness" remained relatively unknown until Billy Graham started using it in his revival crusades.

God's faithfulness was Chisholm's personal anthem throughout his life. And for more than a century since then, his song about God's faithfulness has given others a reason to hold on to hope.

We don't always discover the faithfulness of God when our prayers are answered exactly how we want them to be. Alternatively, when hope seems hidden and then God's presence becomes inexplicably apparent, we find hope after all. Life is hard, painful, and confusing, but God is good. He can be trusted, even when circumstances seem to say otherwise, and His faithfulness will never fail.

***Recall moments of God's faithfulness to you
even when you felt hopeless.***

The Place of Strength

✝

If I have to boast,
I will boast of what pertains to my weakness.
2 Corinthians 11:30

When we think of sharing our stories, most of us prattle on about the crowd-pleasing moments. The overcoming. The successes and triumphs. The photo of our date night. The snapshot of our toes in the sand and a clever hashtag. The moments that made us cringe—when we weren't great Christians, when we ignored the right thing to do—tend to stay in a dust-covered box in a locked closet.

But Paul didn't hide certain parts of himself. This was the guy who wrote in honest exasperation, "The good that I want, I do not do, but I practice the very evil that I do not want" (Romans 7:19). And that wasn't his pride talking. Paul wasn't the kind of guy to humblebrag about the depth of his suffering or the breadth of his imperfections to look good. The exposure of his weakness aimed the spotlight on God's strength.

It's hard to share where we fell short, how we cut corners, or that our best effort produced an inadequate result. When we do share those, it's not because God wants us to broadcast what losers we are. It's not about us. It's about showing how perfect the God is whom we serve, believe in, and trust in our weakness. Be bold. Don't cower from admitting a truth that could give hope to someone else. Weakness is not the end of the story. God shows up and in that exact place perfects His strength.

Practice telling yourself the stories of your own weaknesses.
For every story of weakness, tell a story of God's strength.

Greater Than Our Hearts

✝

LORD, You are our Father;
We are the clay, and You our potter,
And all of us are the work of Your hand.

Isaiah 64:8

God is always in the process of molding us. This process is not easy. Some might say that walking by faith is simple—or that it should be. But most things that are worth doing aren't simple. Sure, think how easy it was for me to get super pumped and put Bible verses on my face when I was winning championships and scoring touchdowns. It's easy to praise God when you're crushing life, when everyone loves you, when you're in perfect health, when money is in the bank, and when stress is absent. But when a giant stands in front of you, whether in the form of cancer or a career that's collapsing, what does your faith look like?

A friend of mine likes to say, "God is greater than your heart." We can quickly dwell on circumstances or our feelings when we're overwhelmed or drowning. If you lose your job, worry can consume you. When your child is born with a disability, it's easy to fear the future.

But God is greater than our hearts. Always.

When hardships show up—and they will—they can manifest in our responses, our reactions, our management of relationships, whether we allow our hearts to remain in a state of emergency or we choose to believe, minute by minute even, that God is greater than whatever is disrupting our stability.

We must choose faith—choose to believe in Him whether we feel like it or not.

How has God molded you through a difficult time?
Can you say you are better for the experience?

The Power of Weakness

✝

I delight in weaknesses, in insults, in distresses,
in persecutions, in difficulties, in behalf of Christ;
for when I am weak, then I am strong.

2 Corinthians 12:10

Guest devo by Robyn Clarke
Relationship to TTF: W15H recipient

I've lived with cerebral palsy for twenty-one years. As I've become an adult, I've wrestled with others' perceptions of me. Does needing help with physical tasks make me a burden? Do people talk to me out of pity, or are they looking to form a genuine connection?

Not long ago, a thought crossed my mind that flipped my internal narrative on its head. What if the purpose of my disability is to lead others to God? What if my physical weaknesses are intentional so that I can witness His power as He guides me through obstacle after obstacle?

God never makes mistakes. Everything about you—your hobbies, your passions, your dreams—are threads in a larger tapestry, one that He has woven to bring a greater plan to fruition. When you find yourself wondering if God is working through you, find peace in the knowledge that you are His. He has chosen you. He created you in your mother's womb for a reason that only He knows, and He has not left any detail untouched. Everything about you, even the qualities you define as weaknesses, are part of His higher purpose. One day you'll look back and realize that what you considered your biggest flaw may be your greatest asset.

*How have you seen God use your weaknesses
to make a difference in someone else's life?*

We Are Not Crushed

✝

We are pressed on every side by troubles, but we are not crushed.
We are perplexed, but not driven to despair.

2 Corinthians 4:8, NLT

Guest devo by Slone Kays
Relationship to TTF: W15H recipient

In my short twenty-five years of life, I have suffered and survived more than I could have ever imagined. At the age of fifteen, I had brain surgery, received a brain-and-spinal-cancer diagnosis, and started chemotherapy. As a child, I was resilient and knew I would beat this disease. However, with a relapse at age twenty-four, I found myself with a much different mindset. *I'm going to die. This cancer is going to kill me this time* were the words I told myself most days in the beginning. I felt like a pincushion and believed that suddenly everything was falling apart all around me.

Soon into my second time having chemotherapy, that "Why me?" mindset changed. I began to think, *Why not me? I can do this! I will persist. I have no choice but to persist!* I fought because I knew God had a plan for me. I knew there was a reason He kept me fighting. I wasn't, and still am not, going to give up this fight as long as I have God by my side. He has shown me that no matter the situation, I will not be crushed. I will persist.

Has God put you in a situation recently where you felt crushed? How can you call upon Him to help you persist through this season?

Joyful Suffering

✝

*None of these things move me; nor do I count my life dear
to myself, so that I may finish my race with joy, and the ministry
which I received from the Lord Jesus, to testify to the
gospel of the grace of God.*

Acts 20:24, NKJV

Guest devo by Hanna Liv Workman
Relationship to TTF: Joint Venture Ministry,
Tebow Okoa Philippi Campus, Masaka, Uganda

In our first six months of living in Uganda, we faced what felt like insurmountable challenges. People tried to throw acid on us, kidnap our daughter, poison our water supply, destroy our ministry and reputation, and put us into prison. So many days I wondered what was happening and why!

In the verse prior to this one, Paul said that the Holy Spirit had assured him that chains and tribulations awaited him on his way to Jerusalem. Yet he was going anyway. Why? Because he counted his life as no value to himself. In plenty and in suffering, preaching God's grace to people was the only thing that mattered, not his own needs, feelings, or well-being.

It's important to look at *how* Paul wanted to finish his race: with joy! A joy that cannot be explained in words and can come only from God.

When we live with an eternal perspective, we find peace in knowing that our lives are not about us. Keeping our eyes on heaven helps us remember that life here on earth is short compared to eternity. There is no greater joy or satisfaction than knowing that we are living, celebrating, and suffering with an eternal purpose.

When in your life have you experienced
unexplainable joy during hardship?

What Are You Talking About?

✝

We proclaim to you what we have seen and heard, so that you
also may have fellowship with us. And our fellowship is
with the Father and with his Son, Jesus Christ.

1 John 1:3, NIV

Guest devo by Mike and Missy Wilson
Relationship to TTF: ministry partners, myLIFEspeaks

When our family first moved to Haiti, we knew that the remainder of our lives would not be easy. But one thing we did (and still do) know: We would rather be where God has called us than anywhere else. The longer we have lived here in Haiti, the more we know that God's call is not to make Haiti more comfortable. Instead, our call is to tell everyone of the great things we have seen and heard God do in our lives and in Haiti.

We believe God is the only true hope for the world, and because we believe that to our core, we often talk about His goodness, the gospel, and the salvation that only He can bring. When you choose to make Jesus your Lord, Savior, and Everything, people often look at you like you're crazy. The world sees us that way, but God sees us as right where we need to be. It's not human nature to choose the things of God over the world, but God's call is more than any human could ever provide.

Your life speaks greatly to what your heart is truly about.

Today, choose to shout about the goodness of God with your entire life and not just your words.

Whose story are you telling, yours or God's?

A Prayer for Strength

✝

My God, do not be far from me today! Come close and come quickly, for I am tired and worn out. I've come to the end of all my trying and acknowledge I cannot do it all. I desperately need to be reminded that You, and You alone, are my ultimate source of strength. As my heart and mind grow weary, I find renewal in how You are an ever-present help in times of trouble.

Lead me to Your dwelling place, for in my weakness, Your power is perfected. Apart from You, I can do nothing. Your name is a strong tower, a shelter for when I am hurting. You hear my cries. You listen to my prayers. Fill me with courage and an awareness that You are with me wherever I go. May I run, as one pursuing righteousness, into the refuge of Your loving arms. It is there where I find comfort amid my pain. Your grace is sufficient, for when I am weak, then I am strong.

In Jesus's name. Amen.

Based on: Psalm 22:19; John 15:5; Psalm 46:1–3; 61:1–4; Proverbs 18:10; Joshua 1:9; 2 Corinthians 12:9–13

The Privilege of Prayer

✛

Let's approach the throne of grace with confidence, so that we
may receive mercy and find grace for help at the time of our need.

Hebrews 4:16

In the Old Testament book of Leviticus, we read about purification rituals for the Israelites as they learned to live under God's rule. Because God is a holy God, it was necessary for them to keep themselves and everything they associated with completely holy and physically clean. Although there were rules for rightful living to benefit themselves and others, there were also particular instructions for the Levitical priests regarding sacrifices and how to present themselves. The stringent rules were a tall order to follow, but it was the only way they would be guaranteed access to God without being consumed by His holiness.

When Jesus gave His life on a cross for our sin, He took the place of all those written laws. Sin had separated us from the Father, but Jesus's sacrifice restored our relationship with God. It was the only way to seal the debt, once and for all. When Jesus died, He made a way directly to the Father. Because of that, we now can enter freely into the presence of God, exactly as we are.

Prayer is not a religious ritual but a privilege. Through it, we can remain in direct communication with God. We can tell Him anything and everything and listen expectantly for His response. As you live a mission-possible life, it's important to remain in touch with God. Jesus has made that possible. Remain close to Him through prayer.

Do you view prayer as a privilege or a chore, and why?

Constant Access

✢

Pray without ceasing.

1 Thessalonians 5:17

How often do you talk to your best friend? Maybe you don't always call each other up and talk for hours, but if you were to scroll through your texts, you would probably find that you "talk" a lot. When you are in constant communication with someone, it's almost like you are in a conversation that has no end.

That's what our prayer life should be like. It should be a constant habit of yours, always keeping the line of communication open. We do this not for God's benefit but for our own. This doesn't mean that your prayer life is limited to on-the-go prayers when you're in the car between appointments or when you need an immediate favor from God. Just as you still schedule time to meet with your best friend, you should carve out time to meet with God intentionally. This means that wherever you are, you can always talk to Him. Think how awesome it is to be connected to the source of life itself! We get to talk to God in the middle of our crazy day, when we're struggling with temptation or trying to wrap our mind around unexpected and upending news.

If you have a worry, you can bring it to God then and there. If you want to thank Him, you don't have to wait until later that night. If He is constantly on your mind, you can constantly tell Him whatever you want to say. The more we take advantage of this access, the more prayer becomes a reflex instead of a ritual.

What prayer do you want to bring before God right now?

Hallowed Be Thy Name

✝

Pray, then, in this way:
"Our Father, who is in heaven,
Hallowed be Your name."

Matthew 6:9

Have you ever stood on the sandy shore of a beach at sunset and had your breath taken away by the colors of the sky or climbed to the peak of a mountain and looked out at the beautiful view in amazement? Do you ever look at the moon in wonder or notice how tall trees can grow? And do you think, *Who created all this?*

When Jesus died to restore relationship with God, He didn't simply restore access to our Father in heaven; He gave us the ability to get to know the Creator of the heavens and earth personally. Prayer is more than just a conversation with God; it is the recognition that He, holy and righteous and mighty, desires to have relationship with us. The same God who placed the moon in the sky and drew the boundary on the shore wants to converse with us. The same God who split the Red Sea, sent fire down from heaven, and raised an army of bones to life wants to form a connection with us.

Prayer is about setting our focus back on God. First and foremost, we need to acknowledge all that He is. To pray without ceasing does not mean that we pray flippantly or focus on only ourselves. While He loves to hear our hearts and desires relationship with us, He is still God. When we pray, we should have a sense of reverence. Out of that reverence, we learn to submit to God, and through our submission, we will see the transformative effects of prayer in our lives.

What can you worship God for today?

Bring It to Him

✢

My God, my God, why have You forsaken me?
Far from my help are the words of my groaning.
My God, I cry out by day, but You do not answer;
And by night, but I have no rest.
Yet You are holy,
You who are enthroned upon the praises of Israel.

Psalm 22:1–3

Have you ever been angry with God or felt hurt at something that happened or because of what someone said? How do you handle the emotions that can so easily overwhelm? Sometimes we attempt to pray those feelings away or hide them because we don't want to be angry at God. Other times we turn to others and complain about what we feel. But have you ever prayed those thoughts to God?

If you read through the book of Psalms, you'll find that David often cried out to God in his despair. His cries were filled with accusations of abandonment and grief. David did not hide what he felt from the Lord—he brought it *to* Him. In doing so, David always remained secure in the presence of God. Even in his distress, he declared God's holiness. David, a man after God's own heart, knew that the Father could handle his rich emotion.

Some seasons in life are tough and prayer may feel impossible. But in those seasons, God accepts our cries and laments. Go directly to Him with your weakness and frustration instead of trying to sort through it yourself. When we present everything to God in prayer, He gives us peace in return (see Philippians 4:6–7).

***When you are in distress, do you tend to run
toward God or away from Him? Why?***

Powerful and Effective

✜

Confess your sins to one another, and pray for one another so that
you may be healed. A prayer of a righteous person, when it is
brought about, can accomplish much.

James 5:16

When Elijah earnestly prayed for a drought on the land, rain
did not fall for three and a half years (see 1 Kings 17:1–7).
Then when he prayed that it would rain, it suddenly did (see 18:42–
45). James reminds us that Elijah was just as human as we are, but
his prayer had tremendous power. Just like Elijah, when we are made
righteous through the blood of Christ, we can pray bold prayers and
expect them to accomplish much.

Prayer is an extremely effective tool. To keep prayer as just a
means of communicating your desires and needs to God means that
you are missing out on the tremendous power that prayer can have.
The Bible teaches us to confess our sins to one another and pray for
one another. It says that when we, as people made right in God's
eyes through salvation in Christ, pray, our prayer can accomplish
much.

Think about the people you love. What do you want for them in
life? The same Jesus who died for you and saved your soul died for
them too. The same God who has given you a purpose to live out
has also given them purposes.

When we pray, whether for loved ones or ourselves, we can expect God to move because He cares. We can trust that, even when it
seems impossible, our prayers can accomplish much.

**Have you ever seen God move in great ways
through prayer? Reflect on this.**

For More Than Ourselves

✝

I urge that requests, prayers, intercession, and thanksgiving
be made in behalf of all people, for kings and all who are in
authority, so that we may lead a tranquil and quiet life
in all godliness and dignity.

1 Timothy 2:1–2

If you were to keep a journal of all your prayers over the past
month, who would you see that you prayed for the most: yourself
or others?

We are called to *intercede* for others, which, according to Merriam-
Webster, means "to intervene between parties with a view of recon-
ciling differences; mediate."[32] We are commanded to pray for others
on their behalf, to act as a go-between for God and that person.
Prayer involves more than just ourselves and God. Through it, we
can stand in the gap for another person.

When we intercede, we can pray for the ones we love and care for.
But we are also called to pray for people we may not know personally. The Bible instructs us to pray for our leaders and whoever is in
authority. Whether we voted for them or not, whether we like them
or not, whether we agree with them or not, we are to pray for them,
to act as mediators, asking God to give them wisdom and grace in
how to lead.

Prayer, in general, is humbling, as it reminds us that God is God
and we are not. It may feel strange at first to pray for others if you are
not in the habit of it, but ask God for wisdom and guidance for doing
so. Seek His heart and let Him reveal Himself to you.

Who might God be asking you to intercede for today?

Listen for the Answer

✝

I will stand at my guard post
And station myself on the watchtower;
And I will keep watch to see what He will say to me.

Habakkuk 2:1

I magine you're lost on a road you've never been on before. It's un-familiar and your phone has no service, so you can't look up di-rections. Eventually, you find someone who knows her way around the area and you, relieved to get some help, ask her for some direc-tions. After you ask her, would you leave before she had a chance to give you an answer? Chances are, no. You would wait for her re-sponse. Yet so many of us act that way with God. We pray to Him and ask Him for direction and then walk away and carry on with our lives, confused and upset by His silence.

Prayer is not just a one-way conversation with God. Like Habak-kuk, we can make our requests to God and ask Him questions, but we need to stand still and wait for His response. Too much of the time, we hope that He will chase us with His answer, but just as you wouldn't walk away from someone after asking a question, you don't want to walk away from God before He answers.

God always answers prayer. The answer may not be what we are hoping to hear, but we can be expectant for His voice. If it feels like He has been silent lately, go back to where you last spoke to Him. Remain there until you hear His response. Talk to God, but also give Him a chance to talk to you in your heart or through His Word.

**How can you focus on what God
is speaking to your heart?**

Even on Your Best Days

✛

Moved with compassion, Jesus touched their eyes; and
immediately they regained their sight and followed Him.

Matthew 20:34

In Matthew 20:29–34, Jesus and His disciples were leaving Jericho and heading toward Jerusalem for what would be Jesus's final Passover celebration. I imagine the atmosphere was electric! Large crowds followed, many of whom probably had seen His miracles, heard His convicting teachings, and experienced His deep love for people. By now, Jesus's reputation was greater and more widespread than ever.

But on this day, on this road—before Jesus trotted into Jerusalem on a donkey to be praised as a Savior—He was interrupted by a loud cry. "Lord, have mercy on us, Son of David!" According to Matthew, the scream came from two blind men—men who had probably been overlooked, deemed as cursed, and ostracized from society. Embarrassed by the men's efforts to get Jesus's attention, the crowds tried to hush them up. But they cried out all the more. This time Jesus heard them. He stopped, called to them, and asked, "What do you want Me to do for you?" In response, they simply said, "Lord, we want our eyes to be opened."

In that moment, being moved by their belief, Jesus showed *compassion*, touched their eyes, and immediately healed them. What I love about this is the fact that even on one of Jesus's best days—a day when He was probably being praised—He still chose to put the best interests of others ahead of His own. Instead of asking, "What can you do for Me?" Jesus asked, "What can I do for you?" Even on our best days, we don't stop living mission possible!

***When times are good and things are going your way,
will you still choose compassion?***

Are You *Moved* Enough to Act?

✝

When Jesus went ashore, He saw a large crowd, and He felt
compassion for them because they were like sheep without a
shepherd; and He began to teach them many things.

Mark 6:34

Have you ever seen something that touched your heart or made
you want to do something to help? I imagine you have! Well,
throughout the Gospels, there's this interesting word that may describe the way you feel at times. Bible geeks, you'll *love* this. It's a
word that commonly described the way Jesus felt. It's the Greek verb
splanchnizomai (splawnk-nitz-oh-my).

Splanchnizomai appears twelve times in the New Testament and is
traditionally rendered "moved with compassion" or "felt compassion." It's built on the root word for a person's internal organs (heart,
liver, lungs, and so on). Figuratively speaking, it means the center of
deep emotions and feelings.[33] So, when the word *compassion* appears
in our English translations, it means "to be moved from our inside
parts."

The word precedes accounts of Jesus's healing (see Matthew
14:14; 20:34; Mark 1:41), raising a widow's son (see Luke 7:13), feeding people (see Matthew 15:32; Mark 8:2), and teaching crowds (see
Matthew 9:36; Mark 6:34). It's also used to describe a person's attitude in three of Jesus's parables (see Matthew 18:27; Luke 10:33;
15:20).

But what I find most interesting is that in every occurrence of the
word, when someone is "moved with compassion," it is immediately followed by an action! This word reminds us that to truly have
compassion means that every fiber in your body is compelled to do
something! It's one thing to say you have compassion, but it's another to actually take action.

Can you think of a time when you were
moved enough to act?

To Suffer With

✝

Do not plead with me to leave you
or to turn back from following you; for where you go,
I will go, and where you sleep, I will sleep.

Ruth 1:16

W hen famine hit the land of Judah, Naomi, her husband, and their two sons left Bethlehem and settled in Moab. It was supposed to be a fresh start. However, shortly after they arrived, Naomi's husband died. Roughly ten years later, tragedy struck again. Naomi lost both her sons. The people she loved were gone, and she was then left to fend for herself.

Or so she thought.

Still in the picture were her two widowed daughters-in-law, Orpah and Ruth. Naomi insisted they leave her and be remarried, but Ruth wouldn't listen. Speaking to Naomi, she promised to stay with her, even to the end of Naomi's life (see verse 17).

Ruth, a Moabite woman, was serious about staying with Naomi no matter where her mother-in-law went! If you know the story, she was willing to sacrifice her own identity, dreams, and ambitions for the sake of Naomi's best interests. As I mentioned in a previous devo, our English word *passion* comes from a Latin word meaning "to suffer." Well, we get our English word *compassion* from *passion*. It means "co-suffering" or "to suffer *with*."[34] Ruth was willing to suffer *with* Naomi—in her grief and in her eventual new life back in Bethlehem.

Has there been a Ruth in your life?
Have you ever been a Ruth for someone else?

There Is No "Yet"

+

The LORD is near to all who call on Him,
To all who call on Him in truth.

Psalm 145:18

My friends Jeff and Becky Davidson got married in 1991. With corporate dreams and family aspirations, they planned out the rest of their lives. However, they quickly realized they had much less control than they thought.

Becky's first pregnancy ended in a miscarriage. Then when they finally had a son, Jon Alex, it was discovered he had cerebral palsy and autism and would be unable to walk, talk, or function independently.

Fast-forward to 2009, when Jeff got sick. What began as a chronic foot problem over the years required a leg amputation and turned into renal failure with chronic kidney disease. For years, Jeff was in and out of the hospital. From 2015 to 2017, Jeff was unable to care for himself, and Becky became his caregiver while also remaining Jon Alex's.

In one instance, a social worker from the hospital asked Becky, "Who will take care of Jeff when you return home?"

Becky answered, "I will. We've been married more than twenty-five years, and I'm not going anywhere."

The social worker responded, "Yet."

It was a sarcastic way of saying, "Sure, Becky—it's only a matter of time before you leave." But the social worker didn't know Becky, who very directly responded "There is no yet" and went on to explain how leaving her family was not an option.

Becky's story is a telling example of what it looks like to be all in—to suffer with and have real compassion for people. There was never a time when she was going to stop caring for those she loved.

There is no "yet." Who or what is God asking you to have compassion for?

The Prodigal's Father

✝

*He set out and came to his father. But when he was still a long
way off, his father saw him and felt compassion for him,
and ran and embraced him and kissed him.*

Luke 15:20

If you grew up in church, you've probably heard the story of the
prodigal son. As the parable goes, the son asked to receive his father's inheritance and then went off to a distant land, where he
wasted it all (see verse 13). When a famine hit, he went to work at a
nearby farm to feed pigs. While in the fields reflecting on life back
home, he realized that he'd made a big mistake. Dying of hunger
and filled with shame, he quit his job and trudged home to beg for
his dad's forgiveness.

Verse 20 tells us that while he was still a long way off, his father
saw him, felt compassion for him, and ran to him! For his father to
see him, his father had to be looking. And when the day came that
his son returned, he was moved so deeply that he couldn't help but
sprint toward his son.

What I find fascinating is that in the first century, a Middle East-
ern man never ran in daily life. If he were to run, he would have to
pull up his tunic so he would not trip. By doing this, he would ex-
pose his bare legs, which in that culture was shameful for a man to
do. The father took on indignity rather than shame his son.[35]

***How does this story shape your understanding
of God as a Father?***

Fall on Your Knees

✝

Moved with compassion, Jesus reached out with His hand
and touched him, and said to him, "I am willing; be cleansed."

Mark 1:41

In Mark 1:39–45, while Jesus was preaching in Galilee, a man with leprosy approached Him. For whoever was around Jesus at this moment, this would have been a shocking sight to see!

In the first century, leprosy was likely considered a curse of God, often associated with sin. It was a skin disease that lingered for years, causing nerve damage, skin bumps, loss of feeling, and body deformations. Given that leprosy was spread by repeated skin-to-skin contact or by coughing and sneezing, those who had it were ostracized from society.

So, I imagine that when this man fell to his knees, begging Jesus, "If You are willing, You can make me clean," everyone in attendance would have taken several steps back. Fearing that they, too, may contract the disease, some probably left the area completely. But not Jesus.

With compassion, He moved toward the man. Reaching out His hand, Jesus did what no one thought He would do: He *touched* him, making Himself "unclean," and said, "I am willing; be cleansed." And immediately the leprosy left the man!

See, Jesus is willing. He's willing to heal, love, forgive, and show compassion. He was even willing to become what we are (sin) so that we can become who He is (righteous) (see 2 Corinthians 5:21). But becoming righteous starts with a choice to move toward Him and ask God to do what we cannot.

**When's the last time you fell on your knees and
cried out before God? Perhaps today!**

The Science of Compassion

✦

Rejoice with those who rejoice,
and weep with those who weep.

Romans 12:15

According to a Harvard medical study, 56 percent of physicians said they lacked the time to be empathetic with patients.[36] Let that sit for a moment.

This study, among others, is noted in Dr. Stephen Trzeciak and Dr. Anthony Mazzarelli's book, called *Compassionomics*.[37] These two medical doctors have spent the past several years researching the effects that compassion has had on patient recovery and the overall health-care system. Specifically, they wondered how long it takes for a meaningful expression of compassion to happen.

They cited work from Johns Hopkins University, where researchers had physicians conduct randomized consultations with breast cancer patients. At the beginning and end of these interventions, the oncologist would read from a standardized script, using words of empathy and compassion to see if doing so would reduce patient anxiety.

In all, this "script" took roughly forty seconds to recite! That's it. Conclusion of the study: *Forty seconds* of genuine care and compassion from the oncologist saw a statistically relevant decrease in cancer patient anxiety![38]

See, showing compassion isn't just talk; it has meaningful impact. When you step into someone else's life—not only in the moments of rejoicing but also in the moments of weeping—your presence and support can be the reason people get through difficult times.

Take forty seconds today to be intentional with someone who is hurting or just needs some love.

A Prayer for Impact

✛

Lord, first and foremost, I am so grateful You have rescued me. I was once dead in my own sin but am now alive in Christ. With a big smile on my face, I humbly say, "Thank You!" I'm now part of Your rescue team, and You've given me a simple mission: to love You and to love people! By the power of Your Spirit, may I go into my home, school, workplace, community—everywhere—proclaiming Your good news, for it is in You that man finds complete joy, hope, and satisfaction.

As I go, strip me of all selfishness so that I may influence as many people as possible. Let this be not for my own glory but for Yours! I pray that as I enter the dark and hard places, Your Light shines bright for all to see. I want my life to truly matter. I do not want to chase after the temporary things anymore (like money, fame, and power). When my feet hit the floor in the morning, I want to make my life count. I want to pursue the things that last forever: You, Your Word, people, and eternal rewards. May my life be defined by these things.

In Jesus's name. Amen.

Based on: Ephesians 2:1–5; Mark 12:30–31; Matthew 28:19–20; Acts 1:8; Matthew 5:16; 1 Corinthians 9:25; 1 John 3:11, 16; 1 Corinthians 9:19, 23

A Lopsided Life

✝

Seek first His kingdom and His righteousness,
and all these things will be provided to you.
Matthew 6:33

Finding balance is less about having everything equally spread out on your plate and more about having everything in its proper place. Balance doesn't mean that everything in your life gets the same attention; it means that you have your priorities straight.

It's easy to get overwhelmed by life's demands. There is no doubt that food and shelter are necessities, but when we put all our focus on surviving, it can feel like we are drowning in our obligations instead of rising above and living mission-possible lives. Instead of focusing on our needs, we are called to look to the One who supplies all of our needs.

The secret to finding balance is to live a lopsided life, one centered on Jesus only. He takes care of what we need, physically and spiritually, because our bodies and souls need to have rhythm in a changing world to be used for God's glory.

God cares about the small things in our lives so much that He promised to provide us with all the essentials when we seek His kingdom before all else. This means you don't have to strive to attain perfection. You need only to trust Him with your life and allow Him to have control over every aspect of it.

What does it mean for you to live a lopsided life?

The Glorification of Busy

✝

The Lord answered and said to her, "Martha, Martha,
you are worried and distracted by many things;
but only one thing is necessary."

Luke 10:41–42

Martha was stuck with the cooking after her sister decided to sit with the guests. Between basting the roast and dressing the salad, she would sigh just loud enough so that Mary, in the next room with the guests, would get the message that she clearly needed help.

Finally, Martha had enough. "Jesus," she called to the guest of honor. "Please tell Mary to help me out." Jesus looked down at the sister who sat at His feet to learn from Him and back at Martha and smiled. He knew that she didn't understand that Mary was the one who had gotten it right in this situation.

Often, we get so caught up in the busyness of doing work for God that we focus on what we're doing and forget who we are doing it for. We wear ourselves thin attempting to make everything perfect and get angry at those who don't seem to appreciate the care we put into things. We forget that God hasn't called us to lives of simply doing. He wants us serving others with His heart, and the only way to do that is to step aside from our to-do lists and sit with Him and learn from Him for a while.

Don't reduce your mission-possible life to busywork. *Do* for God, yes, but *be* with Him too.

Where in your life do you need to stop doing
and start being with Jesus?

Balance for Your Body

✝

Do you not know that your body is a temple of
the Holy Spirit within you, whom you have from God,
and that you are not your own?

1 Corinthians 6:19

If you know me, you know that I am passionate about physical health. I believe it's important to eat well and give our bodies the nutrients they need not only to survive but also to grow stronger. I want to be as healthy and focused as I can be, and what I put into my body plays a huge part of that. I want to make the most of every day that God gives me, today and fifty years from now!

Staying healthy isn't for vanity purposes; we should do it because God created our bodies and, belonging to Christians, they are the homes of the Holy Spirit. We are required to treat them as temples and, therefore, care for them.

A mission-possible life goes only as far as your health allows. Honor God with your body. Get enough sleep, eat well, and exercise. Work within your limitations, but stretch yourself so that one day you will be able to do more. Train your body so you can have strength, endurance, and stamina.

Treat your body with the care God requires, keeping a balanced lifestyle so that you can be ready to go wherever He calls you.

Do you treat your body as God's temple?
How can you care for it better?

Balance for Your Soul

✝

[Jesus] answered and said, "It is written:
'Man shall not live on bread alone, but on every word that
comes out of the mouth of God.'"

Matthew 4:4

Just as it is important to keep your body healthy by putting it in the right environment and treating it the right way, the same goes for your soul. If your spiritual life isn't operating to full potential, you won't be able to pursue the mission-possible life that God has called you to live.

A well-balanced physical life is maintained through proper nourishment, exercise, and rest. The same goes for your spirit. People cannot live on bread alone. They also need the life-giving Word of God. Consistently reading and meditating on Scripture is necessary for hearing the voice of God.

Going through life without spending time in God's presence will make us go hungry. Without the right sustenance, it's easy to become exhausted and weak. In order to keep going, we need to nurture our souls regularly. Although we often would like to believe that having a quick five-minute devotional is enough to keep us fed, we need more. We need to read Scripture regularly to nourish ourselves. We need to actively work out what we take in through the Word and allow for times of rest in which we pray and allow the Lord to speak to us.

Just as physical health is dependent on a balanced lifestyle, so is our spiritual health. Maintain a consistent regiment to grow stronger and more ready and able for whatever the Lord has for you.

*In what area of your spiritual life could you act
to nourish your soul and body?*

Ask People for Help

✝

Bear one another's burdens, and thereby
fulfill the law of Christ.
Galatians 6:2

We live in a culture that prides itself on independence. For many people, the goal is to be able to single-handedly get through life without needing others. We find satisfaction in going our own way, serving ourselves with whatever we wish.

While it is noble to be able to stand on our own two feet, we were not meant to journey through life on our own. It's important that we dwell in community, building relationships, encouraging one another, and praying for others. There are moments when we struggle to maintain balance of everything going on. Between school, work, family, and social calendars, it can sometimes be too much to handle.

We are told to bear one another's burdens. If the body of Christ is functioning properly, this means that you help others out but also accept assistance from your community. When you feel like your load is too heavy and you can't keep up, ask for help. Most people are willing to give freely of their time to meet a need, but usually they do not know of one unless they are told about it. This means it's up to us to approach others for help when we need it. This requires humility, but in that humility, we allow others to come alongside us and make the load we have more manageable to carry.

Do you find it difficult to ask others for help,
even when you desperately need it?
If so, how can you change that?

Ask God for Help

✛

My help comes from the LORD,
Who made heaven and earth.

Psalm 121:2

You know the cliché "God won't give you more than you can handle"? I'm sure Moses would disagree. After the Israelites complained about the miraculous manna (remember that stuff?) they were bored of eating, Moses just about lost it.

He had never signed up for this. It was too much. God had given him too much responsibility, and he wanted to quit—rather, die. He was burned out. Unable to meet the needs of the people God gave him to lead, Moses turned to Him in his frustration and exhaustion. In turn, God responded to Moses's cry for help and mercy. He set up seventy leaders to help Moses carry the burden. (See Numbers 11 to read more.)

If you have been obedient to God and a good steward of all He has given you to work with but feel like you're on the edge of burnout, lay it before Him. Lay the burden of too many burdens at the feet of Jesus. God had compassion on Moses because he turned to Him instead of trying to fix the issue on his own. The point of living a mission-possible life is not to take on more than you can handle and attempt to muster your way through it but rather to live a life dependent on God.

When you feel like you are carrying more than you can handle, go to Jesus. Stay connected to Him. Ask Him for help and depend on Him to give it.

***Take a moment to tell your frustrations to God
and ask Him for help instead of trying to deal
with them on your own.***

Don't Run on Only Momentum

✝

[Look] only at Jesus,
the originator and perfecter of the faith.
Hebrews 12:2

It's tempting when you're on a roll to keep going without seeking the Lord. When everything is going great and you're jumping over all the hurdles that are in your way, you may want to keep going in your own strength.

After forty years of wandering the wilderness, the Israelites were eager to cross the Jordan into the Promised Land. But before they could, Joshua invited them to pause and consider the One who had gotten them to that point. They had been led for decades by God's hand to a land flowing with milk and honey, and before they would step into it, it was important to acknowledge Him in their next move. There, they laid twelve stones to remember God's deliverance and faithfulness, trusting that the same God who got them to that point would be the One to carry them to the next.

When living a mission-possible life, acknowledging God is more important than going on momentum. Even when you're excited, instead of getting caught up in running to the next thing, set your eyes on Jesus and follow where He leads you in His way and in His timing.

Are you constantly thinking about the next thing in
your life? How can you take your focus off your duty
and put it on Jesus?

Light in the Darkness

✝

The light shines in the darkness,
and the darkness has not overcome it.

John 1:5, NIV

Guest devo by Levi Veirs
Relationship to TTF: W15H recipient

Have you ever felt alone or that things are going the exact opposite of the way you want them to go? I have felt like that many times. In those moments, God continues to show up and remind me that just as He spoke light into existence, His light can overcome any darkness.

When I was younger, I had a bunch of surgeries that required intense recovery times. Just when I thought everything was good, something would seemingly happen to require yet *another* surgery. I was in a dark place in my life, and sometimes I had a hard time seeing the good. God knew I was struggling, and He used those moments to show me just how much He loves me.

If you turn a flashlight on and cup your hand over the top, you can still see the light through the creases of your fingers. It's as if the light is fighting to get through. God's love is like that. In those moments when it is difficult to understand why hard things are happening, even though you try to cover it up, God doesn't turn off the light of His love. He uses every one of those opportunities to pursue you. He will use other people to shine love over you through their actions and words. He separated night from day to give you rest and affirm that just as the sun is constant, so is His love for you.

How can you shine God's light on others today?

When You Get Rerouted

✝

I am under obligation both to Greeks and to the uncultured,
both to the wise and to the foolish. So, for my part, I am eager
to preach the gospel to you also who are in Rome.

Romans 1:14–15

As a boy, I dreamed of one day making a million dollars through sports and giving it away to support my dad's ministry and other organizations like it. Over the years, though I'd had a certain image in my head of how I'd earn money and give it away, the picture changed. My desire to make a difference remained the same, but the ways it manifested weren't what I'd had in mind.

Paul knew that feeling. For the longest time, he'd had his heart set on going to Rome to preach the gospel. He'd prayed about it. And it was clearly in the will of God. Paul wasn't going there to tour the Colosseum; he wanted to share the message of Jesus. Despite the apostle's prayers, God had a different plan for him. Eventually, Paul got an opportunity. He was transported to Rome—as a prisoner! He lived under house arrest for two years while his case was being heard. During that time, he wrote four books of the Bible (Ephesians, Philippians, Colossians, and Philemon) and shared the gospel with countless people, including highly ranked officials.

Trust God with your prayers. Understand that the image you create of your future will look different than how it turns out, but God will still carry out His plan.

In your heart of hearts, what do you dream
of accomplishing? Offer up that dream to God
in active prayer. He has a way of carrying out both
His plan and our desires simultaneously.

Take the Risk

✝

*One who watches the wind will not sow
and one who looks at the clouds will not harvest.*

Ecclesiastes 11:4

Living for Jesus might just be the most incredible privilege we have. However, it's not entirely possible to do without taking what we might consider risks. Maybe you're petrified about the possibility of being ridiculed for sharing the gospel, so you don't; or you're not sure bold prayers are the way to go, so you stay safe by maintaining a tepid prayer life. Yet when we scour the Bible and read story after story of imperfect humans pursuing mission-possible lives, there lies a common thread: risk taking.

One could call Abraham a pictorial definition of faith. When God called him to move out of his neighborhood and into a place where God would lead him (see Genesis 12), he trusted God and obeyed. When God told him he would become the father of many generations, Abraham trusted God and believed, even though he was already in his geriatric years.

Are you taking enough leaps of faith in your spiritual life that you've put what you have on the line so God can show up in a big way? I know it can be hard to do, but it's always worth the reward. Often, we live so cautiously that we never give God a chance to come through. Risk what you have for the sake of helping other people and seeing what God can do in your life and in the lives of others.

What's one risk you've been afraid to take?
Tackle it this week.

It's Not Over

✝

The plan of the LORD stands forever,
The plans of His heart from generation to generation.

Psalm 33:11

What are you dealing with that's unexpected and unprovoked and makes you think your best is gone? Did you just lose your job? Are you nursing heartbreak? Devastated over your latest health report? The tough times and the trials we endure are real and painful, but life is not over for you. Wherever you are in life, now can be a beginning.

King Nebuchadnezzar thought throwing Shadrach, Meshach, and Abednego into the fire would kill them. It didn't. Job's wife tried to convince Job to quit believing and to curse God and die. He didn't. The woman with the blood disorder may have gotten discouraged after her twelfth year of physical struggle, but she continued to believe even though she was not healed yet. The stories are different, but the message remains the same: It's not over. (To read these, see Daniel 3:19–27; Job 2:9; and Mark 5:25–34.)

God's love and purposes don't change when unplanned events, circumstances, or people disappoint you. You can still have impact through these things. When you give your pain and heartbreak over to Him, He will always find a way to use those for good.

Don't worry about what you've lost or what lies ahead. Be rooted in God and watch as He unfolds a plan that has more love, more meaning, and more purpose than you could ever imagine.

Write down the self-talk you hear in your mind.
Now sort through it using the list of qualities God gives
us in Philippians 4:8. Identify which of your thoughts fall
under that list and which do not. Every time one of the
thoughts that doesn't align with God's list appears
in your mind, work to reject it.

Remember Whom
You're Trying to Please

+

Am I now seeking the favor of people, or of God? Or am I
striving to please people? If I were still trying to please people,
I would not be a bond-servant of Christ.

Galatians 1:10

Criticism can at times be a bit painful for me to hear because I'm
a people pleaser by nature. I have almost no greater joy than
honoring a coach or a father figure and doing my best to come
through for that person. I want to strive to give my best, my all. I like
bringing people happiness, whether that means making wishes
come true through my foundation or doing something extra-special
for my wife, Demi, for no reason. But I've learned that if I'm motivated only by making others happy, I am left with a hollow feeling.

There is nothing wrong with wanting to be the best, with wanting to succeed, with wanting to land that big deal, score that client,
write that hit song, or dominate that game. It's good to have passion
and work hard. However, it can become a problem when the desire
for praise, success, or a pat on the back becomes everything. Why?
Because those doesn't last! After winning the Heisman Trophy in
2007, I was told I was the best in the world. Then, only three years
later, I was told I couldn't throw.

One goal we should strive to achieve every day is to be the people
God created us to be rather than who those around us think we
should be. While it might make you feel good to please people, it
will make you feel *fulfilled* to please God.

**How can you be sure that your motivations
are in the right place?**

The God of Comfort

✝

Just as we share abundantly in the sufferings of Christ,
so also our comfort abounds through Christ.

2 Corinthians 1:5, NIV

Guest devo by Hollen Frazier
Relationship to TTF: ministry partner, AGCI House of Hope

We all crave comfort. Although there is nothing wrong with seeking comfort in our lives, sometimes it has a clear enemy: challenge. In my decades of serving vulnerable children and families with All God's Children International—an orphan-care ministry dedicated to showing God's love to every child—there have been many times that we've had to leave what feels comfortable in order to follow God's call and challenge.

This pull away from comfort isn't new! When a literal flood was due to fill the earth, God called upon one man to make a difference: He chose Noah to take on the massive challenge of leaving the comfort of life as he knew it. Noah became a shipbuilder and a zookeeper, all for the purpose of keeping life afloat.

Because this is a story only God could write, even the meaning of Noah's name is significant: *Comfort*. Scripture says that "[Noah's father] named him Noah and said, 'He will comfort us in the labor and painful toil of our hands'" (Genesis 5:29, NIV). The very word *comfort* in Hebrew means "to strengthen much."

Comfort is not a destination. It is a restrengthening for the road ahead, a mystery captured in that verse (above) to the church at Corinth.

Where do you need some comfort today?
How does it change your understanding when you see
comfort as a sign of being strengthened?

A Personal Love

✝

I am giving you a new commandment, that you love one another;
just as I have loved you, that you also love one another.

John 13:34

L ove has been described as "the greatest and purest essence of who a person is[,] and its proper expression brings fulfillment."[39] God doesn't choose to love; love is His nature, His essence, His being. "God is love" (1 John 4:16). God was love even before creation, because He has always been a part of an eternal community of love: the Father, the Son, and the Holy Spirit (see 1 John 4:8).

Who am I? Who are you? We are the objects of God's love. That's a big deal. When is the last time you took God's love personally? Doing so is a challenge for many of us. It's easier to reflect on God in an abstract way—to believe He loves us collectively, as a whole. With billions of people populating the planet, taking God's love personally might even seem a bit selfish. Breaking news, however: It's not.

God loves the world, but He also loves each one of us individually. Every single person on earth is the object of His love. In fact, Jesus died for you. You! Did you get that? If you were the only person on this planet, He still would have died for you. That's some powerful stuff!

Knowing we are the object of God's love lays the groundwork for our identities. We are adopted into His family. We are wanted. We belong.

List the ways or reasons you know that you are
the apple of God's eye.

A Prayer of Confession

✝

Be gracious to me, my God, according to Your faithful love and abundant compassion, for I have sinned and fallen short of Your glory. I know I have been made new in Christ, but too often I revert to old sin, old habits, my old way of life. I confess that

- *I worry when I shouldn't.*
- *I get spiritually lazy and go through the motions.*
- *I miss opportunities to show Your love.*
- *I lack patience and self-control.*
- *My pride consumes me at times.*
- *I forget that I'm fighting not against flesh and blood but against the rulers, against the authorities, against the cosmic powers over this present darkness, against the spiritual forces of evil in the heavenly places.*

Forgive me, Lord. You're the One who sees all, and it is You, and You alone, that I have ultimately wronged. Completely wash away my guilt and shame. Give me a fresh start today. Renew my spirit and restore the joy of my salvation! I am glad You don't despise a humble and broken heart. I come before You willing—willing to do whatever You ask. May Your peace, which surpasses all human understanding, guard my heart and mind today in Christ Jesus!

In His name I pray. Amen.

Based on: Psalm 51; Romans 3:23; Ephesians 4:22; Matthew 6:25; Ephesians 6:12; Philippians 4:6–7

Do You Hear the Bombs?

✝

The way of a fool is right in his own eyes,
But a person who listens to advice is wise.

Proverbs 12:15

In August 1982, seventy-one-year-old Mother Teresa marched into the siege of Beirut. As part of the bloody Lebanon War, Israeli planes had bombed the city, leaving more than thirty children with special needs trapped in a mental hospital in the middle of the war zone. A key witness recalls a conversation between Mother Teresa, a religious leader, and an officer:

> PRIEST: "You must understand the circumstances Mother. Two weeks ago, a priest was killed. It's chaos out there. The risk is too great."
>
> MOTHER TERESA: "But Father . . . I believe it is our duty. We must go and take the children one by one. Risking our lives is in the order of things. All for Jesus. All for Jesus . . ."
>
> OFFICER: "But do you hear the bombs?"
>
> MOTHER TERESA: "Yes, I hear them."

The next day, Mother Teresa entered west Beirut and somehow negotiated a cease-fire to extract and rescue the children. Mission accomplished.[40]

In Proverbs 12, Solomon wrote about how a person who listens to advice is wise—which I believe is true. However, it's important to note that not all advice is wise. Mother Teresa had a conviction, but the advice she received was against her clear mission. Do not let the opinions of others distract you from living mission possible.

***Have you ever let the advice of others distract
your living on mission?***

Comparison Trap

✝

Jesus said to him, "If I want him to remain until I come,
what is that to you? You follow Me!"
John 21:22

Comparison is deeply intertwined in our culture. We crave to compare, compare, and compare ourselves to others. One research study concluded that on average, 12 percent of our thoughts each day are comparison-based.[41] I imagine that number increases based on the amount of time we spend on social media. But that's the way our sinful nature is wired. Even those who were closest to Jesus struggled with comparison.

In John 21, after the Resurrection, Peter and some of the boys took a spontaneous fishing trip . . . but it was cut short when Jesus surprised them with breakfast on shore.

When they were done eating, Jesus asked Peter three times if he loved Him. Each time, Peter answered yes. Then Jesus proceeded to tell Peter how he would eventually die—apparently death by crucifixion. When Peter heard this, he turned around, saw his disciple-friend John, and wondered, "What about this man?"

Jesus simply replied, "What is that to you? You follow Me!"

Peter's first thought was comparison. *What about John?* Jesus basically responded, "That's none of your business, Peter." These frank words should serve as encouragement to us.

Jesus doesn't want or ask us to be like anyone else. All He desires is for us to *follow* Him. That means keeping our eyes fixed on who God has called us to be and not on what culture says we should be.

Do you struggle with comparison? Be reminded
that there is freedom and joy in knowing that
Jesus has a plan just for you!

Heart Check

✝

Where your treasure is, there your heart will be also.

Matthew 6:21

I n 2002, Disney released the action-packed intergalactic animated thriller *Treasure Planet*. Based on Robert Louis Stevenson's classic adventure *Treasure Island*, it tells the story of a fifteen-year-old boy, Jim Hawkins, who stumbles upon a treasure map that supposedly leads to the legendary "loot of a thousand worlds"—a planet full of gold. As Jim is working as a cabin boy aboard a spaceship (literally a boat that could fly in outer space), the voyage gets interrupted by greedy pirates who are also looking for the same mythical treasure.

Full of twists and turns, the climax of the movie reveals the heart of the antagonist, Captain John Silver. When forced to choose between the loot and young Jim, Captain Silver gives up the treasure and saves Jim's life just in time as the planet self-destructs.

Though the film is science-fantasy, there are some lessons to be learned from it. Many of us can be, like the pirates, so locked in and distracted by material things, spending our entire lives pursuing them, that we don't realize they are leading us toward destruction.

During His Sermon on the Mount, Jesus reminded us, "Do not store up for yourselves treasures on earth, where moth and rust destroy, and where thieves break in and steal. But store up for yourselves treasures in heaven, where neither moth nor rust destroys, and where thieves do not break in or steal; for where your treasure is, there your heart will be also" (Matthew 6:19-21).

Give yourself a heart check. Where are your treasures stored? Like Captain Silver, when you're forced to decide on what matters most, how would you respond?

There Is No Lion

✝

The lazy one says, "There is a lion outside;
I will be killed in the streets!"

Proverbs 22:13

O n October 18, 2011, fifty exotic animals escaped from a private zoo and roamed the streets of Zanesville, Ohio.[42] Imagine driving home from work that day and seeing a four-hundred-pound lion walking on the side of the road. Odd, right?

Well, this is not the case in Proverbs 22:13.

King Solomon here is using an illustration about making excuses. He says the reason the "lazy" person will not go outside is that he fears he'll be mauled by a lion in the public square. His point is that in our laziness, we can say rather extreme things to avoid work. Think about it: Is it likely a lion would be wandering around the streets of an Israelite city? No! You'd find one in the savanna.

How often do we give excuses that hinder us from carrying out our responsibilities or achieving our goals? Maybe they're not as far-fetched, but I hear excuses like these all the time:

- "I'm too old (or too young)."
- "I'm too busy."
- "It costs too much."

When we say things like this, we don't get better. We can sometimes create lions in our own heads and get stuck in complacency out of fear or insecurity. Excuses won't get you anywhere. This hypothetical king of the jungle pales in comparison to how the King of the universe wants to use you.

God sets us free to run fast toward the things He's called us to. What excuses prevent you from doing this?

Entitlement Mentality

✝

This is the way any person is to regard us: as servants of
Christ and stewards of the mysteries of God. In this case,
moreover, it is required of stewards that one be found trustworthy.

1 Corinthians 4:1–2

One of the greatest distractions in living mission possible is having a "you owe me" attitude, in which we feel like we're entitled or deserving of special treatment and favor. I think if we're honest, we've all been there. But actually we're entitled to *nothing*. In his first letter to Timothy, Paul wrote, "We have brought nothing into the world" (6:7). We have nothing to offer. God created everything and owns everything. And if we are deserving of anything, it's death! But thanks be to God, for He has given us everything through His Son, Jesus Christ (see Romans 6:23). Not only has He given us the gift of eternal life, but He's also entrusted us to be good stewards with what's been provided.

Stewardship is an interesting word. In English, it denotes the idea of handling time, money, and resources. But in biblical Greek, it meant "the management of a household or of household affairs."[43] A steward in ancient Greek culture was not the owner of the house. Instead, a steward was a person employed to manage another's property, especially a large estate.

In the same way, creation (the world and everything in it) is God's "property." He has made us stewards of His "house" on earth. Though it's not ours, we're invited to look after it and enjoy it.

***How can you avoid an entitlement mentality and
steward your blessings today?***

"Making It"

+

One who trusts in his riches will fall,
But the righteous will flourish like the green leaf.

Proverbs 11:28

Have you ever said or heard someone say, "When I _____, I'll have made it"? Maybe it's getting a job promotion, earning a certain income, fulfilling a dream, or gaining a specific number of followers on social media. This idea of *making it* essentially means you've reached a level of success that you find completely satisfying. It's what we all live for, but perhaps our definitions may differ.

In January 2018, a survey of two thousand people was taken to understand how the majority of America defines *making it*. Here's part of the sample. *Making it* in America means

- being married, having two kids and four friends
- obtaining at least a bachelor's degree
- having an annual income of $147,000
- working only thirty-one hours a week
- having a ten-minute commute *or* working from home
- having 5.3 weeks of vacation and traveling
  three times a year
- having a home valued at $461,000
- having a car worth $41,000[44]

How many of the things on this list are you pursuing as your end goal? Money, time, and less responsibility? I can tell you right now, for believers, that's not what it means to make it.

Making it is being in relationship with Jesus Christ. *Making it* is denying self. *Making it* is caring for the lost and broken. *Making it* is being a generous giver. *Making it* is showing up to heaven and hearing, "Well done, good and faithful servant" (Matthew 25:21, ESV).

Don't get distracted by how the world defines *making it*. When you stay focused on God's mission for your life, you've made it!

How would you define making it?

Master the White Belt

✛

The word of the LORD is right,
And all His work is done in faithfulness.

Psalm 33:4

I never took karate or jiujitsu growing up, but I am somewhat familiar with the belt-ranking system. Depending on what martial arts program you're in, there are a certain number of belts with varying colors. Each colored belt represents a level of mastery. White, green, red, brown, black, and so on symbolize the skills one possesses. These belts give students a goal to work toward. Coming to class doesn't necessarily guarantee the rank upgrade, but naturally, the more often students study and practice the art, the faster they're probably going to progress.

The white belt—a student's first belt—signifies *beginner* in most systems. A white-belt student is someone who desires to learn. In the Christian life, when it comes to reading and studying the Bible, the white belt should be our daily mindset.

Some of my biggest faith heroes have studied God's Word all their lives. I can't say they know the Bible like the back of their hands; they know the Bible *better* than the back of their hands! However, they often confess, "The more I learn about Scripture, the more I don't know."

Don't get distracted by thinking you have to know it all. The Bible is a huge book! It's not about the head knowledge; rather, it's about the heart hunger. No matter where you are on your faith journey, together let's always have a white-belt mentality and continue learning.

What have you been studying in God's Word recently?
Be reminded that it's good to be a lifelong
white belt of the Bible.

Set Free from Sin

✝

After being freed from sin,
you became slaves to righteousness.

Romans 6:18

Have you ever felt stuck or trapped in your sin? Have you ever told God you're never going to do *that thing* again but then end up falling soon after?

Sin is serious. It's destructive, deceptive, and distracting. Sin can hinder us from living mission possible. Whether the lust of the flesh, the lust of the eyes, or the pride of life, living in sin is not what God desires for human flourishing (see 1 John 2:16). Unfortunately, we were born into it because of our fallen nature, but the good news is we've been set free. In Christ, sin no longer has any authority, power, or dominion over us!

In Romans 6:6–7, Paul wrote, "Our old self was crucified with Him, in order that our body of sin might be done away with, so that we would no longer be slaves to sin; for the one who has died is freed from sin."

Because of Christ's victory on the cross, His death became our death. His righteousness became our righteousness. Will we still sin? Yes. But by God's grace, we don't have to try to beat it by our own willpower. Jesus defeated sin once and for all; therefore, we don't have to feel stuck. Sure, we may not yet be who we want to be, but we're not who we used to be. When we run toward Jesus—by spending time in His Word, being in community with other believers, and loving people—our old ways start to change as we look more like Him.

What sin do you feel stuck in?
What choices will you make today to walk in freedom?

Know Your War

✝

Put on the full armor of God, so that you will be able to
stand firm against the schemes of the devil. For our struggle is not
against flesh and blood, but against the rulers, against the powers,
against the world forces of this darkness, against the spiritual
forces of wickedness in the heavenly places.

Ephesians 6:11–12

When you're in battle, armor is necessary to keep you defended against an enemy's attacks. In the first century AD, when the apostle Paul wrote his letter to Ephesus, Roman soldiers would adorn themselves in protective gear that involved heavy breastplates, ornate belts, and showy helmets. There were many pieces to their battle gear, and every part had a purpose.

As believers, we fight in a spiritual war. We are in constant battle with forces of darkness. Every time we face fear or shame or question our place in the kingdom of heaven, the Enemy is working against us. When we recognize that we fight against principalities of darkness, not flesh and blood, we recognize our need to protect our minds, hearts, and souls. Just as soldiers wear armor to fight, we, too, have armor to put on every day to thwart the Enemy's attacks.

In Ephesians 6:10–17, Paul laid out this spiritual armor. Just as each piece in the Roman soldiers' gear served a purpose, so do these pieces. We are required to put on all of it because inadequate protection is costly. So equip yourself. Understand the spiritual war you are in. Be on high alert and constantly prepared. Then you can stand firm against the attacks of the Evil One.

What battles are you facing lately?
Acknowledge whose they ultimately are.

Righteousness and Truth

✢

Watch over your heart with all diligence,
For from it flow the springs of life.

Proverbs 4:23

When God created the human body, He did so with intention-ality and attention to detail. Far out in your extremities, you can hold things and move with ease, while tucked into the center of your body are your vital organs. Your heart, lungs, liver, and kidneys all take up space in your core. Because of their importance in your body, you also have a rib cage as a built-in shield to protect them.

When you're in battle, though, your rib cage isn't enough defense for any attack you may face. It's important to put on extra guards to protect the area. That's what the breastplate does. Without a breast-plate, you are left vulnerable in the very places you want to secure most. However, the breastplate is unable to stay anchored on its own. It needs a belt to keep it in place.

God's righteousness is our breastplate. When we follow His stat-utes and walk in the way He paves for us and live rightly according to His Word, we protect the vital areas in our lives. His righteous-ness is our defense. And when we gird ourselves with the belt of truth by remaining in God's Word, we secure our defense.

Your heart is your source of life, and it's important to watch over it diligently. Live rightly and remain steadfast in truth to protect the vital areas of your life from anything that may corrupt them.

Is your heart vulnerable to attack? How can you take steps to defend it with righteousness and truth?

Spread Peace

✝

How delightful on the mountains
Are the feet of one who brings good news,
Who announces peace
And brings good news of happiness,
Who announces salvation,
And says to Zion, "Your God reigns!"

Isaiah 52:7

Different shoes serve different purposes. You wouldn't wear winter boots while training for a marathon, and there are better options than sneakers for a day at the beach. We dress our feet with intentionality, depending on where we're going. As we continue to fight in this spiritual war, it's important to be equipped with the proper footwear for our mission.

To overcome the attacks of the Enemy, we need to put on sandals of peace. It's the feet that God calls beautiful, those that bring good news of peace and salvation to others. So often our instinct is to wage war on our neighbors, but He has not called us to go and declare war. He's called us to go and make disciples by spreading the gospel.

We are called to fight for God, not to fight against the world. Remember that the battle is ultimately His own and that He desires that all should come to repentance. When you bring the good news of peace to the world, you awaken people to their need for Jesus. Only He can rescue our souls from the Enemy, and because of His death and resurrection, salvation is freely available for all. But people need to know that it is available. Spread peace.

***How can you spread peace and good news
to others in your life?***

Shield of Faith

✝

...so that your faith would not rest on the wisdom of mankind,
but on the power of God.

1 Corinthians 2:5

Your adversary is vicious and cruel. He's not out to simply harm you; he wants to destroy you. There is an entire war going on, and the closer you walk with Jesus, the greater threat you will be to the Enemy. He will aim arrows at you to incapacitate you—flaming arrows. He plays hard. But God has not left you defenseless. In this battle, He knows all the tricks of the Enemy and has equipped you with a shield so you can protect yourself. That shield is faith.

Faith is unrestrained belief in God. It does not waver in different environments or situations. Regardless of the breadth of attack, however difficult it may be or long it may last, faith is the assurance that we already know who wins: God! Not only that, but He has promised you in Scripture His everlasting presence. Just as He was with Moses at the Red Sea or with Daniel in the lions' den, He will be with you.

Without a doubt, the more you live a mission-possible life, the more you will face moments when the attack feels especially hard. You may question your ability to keep going, but remember your mission in those times. Keep in mind whose battle this is, and maintain your confidence in the Lord, not in your own wisdom or ability. He will get you through it.

Do you feel as though flaming arrows are hitting you
from all around? Declare your faith in God
and use that truth as a shield.

Helmet of Salvation

✛

The peace of God, which surpasses all comprehension,
will guard your hearts and minds in Christ Jesus.
Philippians 4:7

Have you ever lain awake in bed at night filled with anxious thoughts? You're plagued with memories of past failures, reminding you of your imperfections. Thoughts of the future hit you and you wonder how you'll be able to get through the next day or even the next year. A full-throttle debate erupts in your mind and you want to cave under the pressure.

Satan is a liar and an accuser (see John 8:44; Revelation 12:10). He is after your usefulness and will often infiltrate your thoughts to weaken you. But by the blood of Jesus, you have been given authority over his manipulative tactics. Wear this salvation as a helmet to cover your head and protect your mind from the Enemy's assaults. When your thoughts are bombarded with lies and accusations, put your focus on the Cross and what Jesus has done. Remember whose you are and who you are. You are a child of God, saved by grace by the blood of Jesus, who died on a cross for you and was resurrected three days later.

Continue to go to God with all your anxious thoughts, understanding that it is through the salvation of Christ that you can go freely to Him. He will exchange your anxiety for peace, and that peace will act as a guard against the schemes of the devil.

What anxious thoughts are you fighting today?
Remind yourself of your salvation and bring
your thoughts to God in prayer.

Sword of the Spirit

✝

The word of God is living and active, and sharper than any
two-edged sword, even penetrating as far as the division of soul
and spirit, of both joints and marrow, and able to judge the
thoughts and intentions of the heart.

Hebrews 4:12

S words have been around for thousands of years. Their designs
tend to vary depending on when or where they originated. Some
swords are single edged, much like a long knife. Double-edged
swords—having two sharp edges for cuts in both directions, plus a
thrust—were widely used. A highly effective weapon, this type of
sword also prevented the opponent from grabbing the blade to use
it against the holder.

We have been equipped with one and only one offensive weapon
in our spiritual arsenal: the Word of God. The Bible is more than a
book or history lesson, and reading it is more than a task. When you
neglect doing so, you forfeit your ability to fight back in times of attack. God has spoken through His Word, and He continues to speak
to us through it as we dig more deeply into it.

You don't have to sit back and take every hit the Enemy throws
at you. You get to return the attack. When you are in the Word
regularly, the Holy Spirit works to etch it into your heart so that
when the onslaught comes, you are equipped with biblical truth to
recite back to yourself. Don't take this weapon for granted. Use it
to fight back wherever you may need it in your life.

**Do you treat reading your Bible as a chore or as
battle prep? Intentionally dive into it today.**

The Power of Prayer

+

With every prayer and request, pray at all times in the Spirit,
and with this in view, be alert with all perseverance
and every request for all the saints.

Ephesians 6:18

If you feel alone today, please know that God has not left you. Despite all He has supplied you with for the fights of your life, He has not abandoned you to fight your battles alone. In fact, He wants you in constant relationship with Him. He's opened a line of communication. Use it. Even Jesus, God's own Son, often slipped away from the crowds so He could pray to His Father in heaven.

When we pray, we do more than recite a few words to God. We reach His heart and put our entire focus on Him. Prayer keeps us alert and focused on the mission. Through it, we can witness God's miracles. By setting aside intentional time to talk to and listen to Him, we find that He begins to transform us and work in ways that we never imagined.

But the battle you're fighting is bigger than just you. There are others around you who are also in this spiritual war, and none of us must fight this alone. When you pray, you have the chance to affect not only your own life but also the lives of others. Through intercession, we stand in the gap for them.

Don't neglect or underestimate the power of prayer. When we pray in the Spirit, we can trust God to work behind the scenes in ways that we cannot imagine.

How have you witnessed God work through your prayers?

A Prayer to Stand Firm

✝

Lord, as I make the conscious choice each day to follow You, I am not ignorant to the fact that this world will not always like what I do and what I stand for. As You have promised, I will face trouble, trials, and tribulation. There is an enemy who prowls around like a roaring lion looking for someone to devour. Because You were persecuted, when I stand for You, I too will experience some form of persecution.

But thanks be to God, for in Jesus, I have victory! You have overcome the world, and that is why I can take heart, be courageous, and stand firm. By the power of Your Spirit, I will let nothing move me today. I will live by my convictions and not by my emotions. I will pursue respect and not likes. I will be unashamed of the gospel, for it is by Your power that I have been set free. Sin and death have been defeated. Therefore, I will not be burdened by old sin habits. I will continue to do good works for You, knowing that my labor is not in vain. May I be alert and on guard, ready to do everything in love today.

In Jesus's name. Amen.

Based on: 1 Peter 5:8–9; John 15:18–25; Galatians 5:1; 1 Corinthians 15:57–58; 16:13; John 16:33

Take the Bloody Nose

✛

I am confident of this very thing, that He who began a good work
among you will complete it by the day of Christ Jesus.

Philippians 1:6

When you know God has called you to do something, you do it and keep doing it, no matter what adversity comes your way. That intestinal fortitude is something my dad has modeled for me as a father and missionary.

When he was called by God to go to the Philippines with his family to serve there as a missionary, many people voiced a lot of opinions, most of which were not the most helpful. Still, Dad knew God had called him. It wasn't easy for my parents, that's for sure. Moving a family of four kids to the other side of the world on a limited income (and my mom's eventual pregnancy with me that almost caused her demise) was challenging. But because Dad knew he was supposed to go, and with Mom's and our support every step of the way, he took every blow of adversity and kept loving, serving, and leading millions of people to the Lord.

Dad would always say to me, "Timmy, if you know God has called you to do something and you get punched in the process and get a bloody nose, that's okay. Keep going. But if you don't know you're called to do whatever you are doing, the first time you get a bloody nose, you're going to look for every reason to retreat." If you've gotten a bloody nose on the journey of a mission-possible life, don't use it as an excuse to retreat. Stay in the fight.

What has God called you to that you feel
afraid to try or do?

Source of the Setback

✝

You cannot stand against your enemies until you have removed
the designated things from your midst.

Joshua 7:13

When the Israelites entered the Promised Land after an arduous forty-year journey, they experienced a succession of miraculous victories. First, God parted the Jordan River for their journey. Second, they conquered the first city they encountered, Jericho, when they marched around its walls seven times and it collapsed.

Perhaps some of the people thought they were invincible. After all, they had experienced miracle after miracle. After Jericho, however, they came to a place called Ai and found no reason for celebration.

The Israelites, led by Joshua, were confident they could crush the enemy's small army. In a shocking twist, they were defeated. Joshua 7:5 says, "The hearts of the people melted and became like water." What a picture of hopes dashed! Unfortunately, someone in the camp had been disobedient, and this unchecked disobedience was the source of the terrible defeat.

Setbacks come in all shapes and sizes. Sometimes life happens in a bad way, through no fault of our own, and sometimes consequences are incurred because of the choices we've made. I'm in no way saying that every adversity is a direct result of sin, but I'd like to encourage you to always be in the business of checking yourself. Remain connected to God and ask Him to help you keep your motives in check and for the wisdom to remain obedient.

Sometimes adversity serves as a reminder to tap into our relationship with God. What's going on in your life right now, good or bad? Purposely take time today to talk to God about it.

Beyond All That We Think

✝

Is anything too difficult for the LORD?

Genesis 18:14

A few years back at an event, I was approached by a young woman in her twenties who was holding a baby. With tears streaming down her face, she said, "I just want you to hold a life that you helped save." Then she mentioned the TV commercial my mom and I did in 2010.

The message of the thirty-second clip was simple: "Celebrate family. Celebrate life." Through the website that shared Mom's story, this young woman learned that my mom was very sick when she became pregnant with me. Though she was advised to abort me, what doctors thought was a tumor, Mom refused. She trusted God with the outcome.

Years later, sitting with this young woman in an auditorium, I listened as she said, "A few days after the commercial aired, I was scheduled to have an abortion." Tears streamed down her face as she looked lovingly at her little girl, then added, "But I didn't." What a powerful moment!

A handful of people discouraged me from participating in that commercial, but because I am passionate about celebrating life, I was honored to be a part of it. I believe that every life matters. My conviction and what God holds to be true were bigger than those who tried to dissuade me from doing the commercial.

Whatever is blocking your way—whether opinions, fickle feelings, or an unforeseen setback—trust that God is in control of your mission. He's got a greater purpose in store than you may think.

***Identify the setbacks that have gotten
in the way of your mission.***

Weapons of Worship

✝

Let the word of Christ richly dwell within you, with all wisdom
teaching and admonishing one another with psalms, hymns, and
spiritual songs, singing with thankfulness in your hearts to God.

Colossians 3:16

Paul chose a man by the name of Silas to help him lead a mission
to Syria and Cilicia to minister to the churches there. They continued to other cities and followed a journey through Asia Minor.
On the men's mission-trip tour, many people were saved and
churches planted. When the two arrived in Macedonia, God continued to do a great work, but the opposition picked up strength. After
Paul set a girl free from demon possession, he and Silas were brought
before the city magistrates, where they were beaten and thrown in
jail.

Paul and Silas, a winning team who had brought many to the
Lord and endured trials as well as successes in the ministry, were
fastened in stocks. Debilitated. Stranded. What do you think these
two missionaries did? They may have been disappointed, but they
certainly didn't wallow in pity, start discussing parting ways, or look
for a new gig. They prayed. They sang. They worshipped. Then at
midnight, an earthquake erupted, opening the prison doors. Paul
and Silas were able to minister to the suicidal jailer, who knew he
was going to be in big trouble with his employers, and he came to
know the Lord.

Praise has a powerful place in our pain. When resistance comes,
make a habit of lifting up your heart. It may not come naturally
when you feel defeated or deflated, but worshipping God keeps our
perspective grounded.

*Take a few undistracted minutes to sing your favorite
worship song a couple of times. This could become
your best tool against adversity.*

Wind Is Your Friend

✜

Rejoicing in hope, persevering in tribulation,
devoted to prayer . . .
Romans 12:12

Y ou might think that wind, at least the violent kind, makes for a bad flight. And while that certainly can be true, did you know that pilots *prefer* to take off into the wind? Not with the wind at their backs, pushing them forward, but into what you might call a force of resistance. Common sense may tell us that taking off into the wind will result in slowing the plane down and forcing it to burn more fuel than necessary, yet the opposite is true. When a plane takes off into the wind, it can reach a higher altitude in less time and with less speed. For example, a Boeing 747 that requires 150 miles per hour of airspeed to reach wheels up when taking off into 30 miles per hour of headwind needs 180 miles per hour of airspeed to lift off with no wind. Though wind might seem like resistance, it is really a plane's ally.

When we live saturated with purpose, we ought not be blind-sided when obstacles try to stake their claim on whatever mission we're trying to accomplish. If we flip our perspective, we can try to consider as a friend whatever resistance we are facing. A problem doesn't have to have a negative effect on your outlook, your energy, and your goals. It might help you achieve a greater purpose, such as building your character, opening a door of opportunity on a path you wouldn't have otherwise chosen, or helping you reach the next level of your mission.

Don't waste all your time bemoaning the weight of resistance. Pray and ask God to use it to make you better and bring Him glory.

***What did you learn from a time
when a hardship became an opportunity?***

Wounds Get Used

✝

It is through many tribulations
that we must enter the kingdom of God.
Acts 14:22

There are so many heroes of the Bible who were wounded deeply before they were ever used greatly. Think of the trials that Job wrestled with: losing his loved ones, his business, his health, and the love of his wife. Think of Joseph, who lost the loyalty of his family and his freedom. Think about Paul, who gained a miraculous conversion experience but was persecuted and prosecuted for his faith. In fact, many of the characters in the Bible are well known because of the struggles they endured.

You may be going through a time when you feel like you've been wounded. Maybe it hasn't been your year. It's been tough and the dark tunnel hasn't gotten any brighter. I want to encourage you to hang on to hope just a little tighter. This could be your time for learning. This could be your time for growing. This could be your time for adapting. This could be a season of testing and tomorrow will turn into a testimony.

You never know what God is doing with your life now or what He is preparing you for tomorrow. If the saints who came before us had called it quits on the battlefield, they would have missed out on some of the most impactful times of their lives, and their legacies would have been sheared. Suffering isn't fun or easy, but it always sheds a purpose.

Are you or a friend experiencing a season of difficulty?
Remind yourself or tell your friend that the God
who was at work for Job, Joseph, and Paul
is also at work for you.

See Things Differently

✛

"My thoughts are not your thoughts,
Nor are your ways My ways," declares the LORD.
Isaiah 55:8

E rik Weihenmayer is one of the world's most accomplished adventure junkies, and he "sees" life a little differently.

Fifty-three years old, he has kayaked the raging whitewater through the Grand Canyon, skied black-diamond slopes, and scaled several of the world's tallest mountains and is a certified solo skydiver and paraglider. Erik is also blind. After completely losing his vision at age fourteen, Erik struggled to adjust to his new reality and lived in denial for some time. Eventually accepting his condition, he said, "Once I was able to accept [blindness], I was able to push the perimeters of what I was capable to do."[45]

We don't always get to choose our adversity, but we do get to choose how we want to deal with it. The attitude, the effort, the courage—those are all choices we get to make. I think I've been most inspired by the W15H kids our foundation has been able to serve over the past ten years. They've had to overcome so much in their lives, and they've done so with amazing attitudes. They've made the choice to do things differently—to have faith, hope, and love amid their challenges. Just like Erik, these children didn't get to decide the details of their health, but they did choose a positive perspective despite their discomfort.

If God's perspective is always full of hope,
love, and potential, how can you tweak your
thoughts to coincide with His?

The Dash

✝

We look not at the things which are seen, but at the things
which are not seen; for the things which are seen are temporal,
but the things which are not seen are eternal.

2 Corinthians 4:18

When I was younger, I read a poem written by Linda Ellis called "The Dash," which focuses on the line separating how we write the year of a person's birth and the year of the person's death. This tiny punctuation mark represents what we stand for, what or whom we influence, and ultimately what legacy we leave behind.

Not many of us want to think about our mortality. We prefer to distract ourselves. We watch mindless TV shows and overstuff our calendars. But ignoring the reality that our days are numbered may leave the most important questions in life unconsidered and unanswered.

When we think about our dash, we can live with more passion. We can identify our priorities. We can be intentional in how we live. We can make a difference and do things that matter. I have realized that my one goal in life is to show Jesus in the way I live and the way I love. This doesn't mean I always do it, but it's something I strive for.

The ultimate legacy that your "dash" can leave behind is a life of faith, believing the gospel and living in a way that exemplifies Jesus.

How do you want your life to matter?

Be Eternally Minded

✝

*Our citizenship is in heaven, from which we also eagerly wait
for a Savior, the Lord Jesus Christ.*
Philippians 3:20

O ne of my most valued pieces of biblical wisdom is the recognition that this world is not our home. Heaven is our ultimate home. The fact that life on earth is temporary has been ingrained in my heart ever since I was a little boy. My sense of heaven has shaped my outlook and decisions. It's also one of the hardest things to consistently focus on. It has forced me to ask myself, *Why spend a life building up for a place I'm going to leave when I could spend a life building up for the place I'm going to go to?*

The following four things last forever: God, His Word, people, and heavenly rewards. Choosing to focus on those eternal things is what will make one of the biggest differences in our lives today. Not the number of followers we have. Not making the team. Not which college we attend.

Be honest: How much time have you spent shopping for decor to spruce up your home? I know it can take days or even weeks to find the perfect rug. (Actually, I don't know. Demi has the decorating skills in our relationship, not me.) Are you spending your time and energy building up a home in heaven or your dream one on earth?

Live for what matters most in life.

**Choose and do one thing that can help make
an eternal impact.**

Have a Worthy Endgame

✛

Do not work for the food that perishes, but for the food that
lasts for eternal life, which the Son of Man will give you.

John 6:27

One of my goals is to live my life with a worthy endgame. What
I do on earth has to be worth it in the end. This looks different
for everybody. For some people, it might be to accumulate wealth,
fame, or success. Maybe it's winning a Pulitzer or an Emmy. As believers, people who ought to live and think a bit differently than
everyone else, we live not for material success but to leave legacies
that last.

I ask myself,

- *How can I make a difference in the lives of the next generation?*
- *How can I leave this earth knowing I brought others closer to Jesus?*

Can you imagine getting to the end of your life and realizing that
you spent your precious years climbing the wrong ladder? To keep
that from happening, you must be conscious of making your life
count today! Use that sense of urgency I've talked about to motivate
you to make the necessary changes to live in such a way that what
you leave behind is worth it.

**How can you use a talent God has given you
for a greater purpose?**

It's Not Just Your Own Soul That Counts

✛

If I preach the gospel, I have nothing to boast about,
for I am under compulsion; for woe to me
if I do not preach the gospel.
1 Corinthians 9:16

I remember the first time I heard the Christian artist Ray Boltz singing "People Need the Lord." I was a kid at the time, and the song absolutely wrecked me. Although I was just a boy, I began to understand the magnitude of sharing the gospel with others. But sharing the gospel is a scary thing to do. It can come across as weird. Maybe you're not sure how to communicate the message correctly or effectively. I get that. But the gospel is hope for a dying world, light that can shine in a room of darkness; we can't let our fears stand in the way.

I'm a very intense guy. I give my all in whatever I'm doing, whether I'm training, practicing, learning a new skill, developing leadership skills, or trying to be a better husband. It's not always easy, but I strive to be better at who I am and what I do. Sometimes I wonder how far I'm willing to go to invest in someone's eternity. Do I share the gospel with the same intensity with which I try to live? While I'm not saying it's necessary to give a gospel presentation to every single person who crosses your path, I am challenging myself and all believers to become more intentional about caring for the souls of others.

Name someone you can share the gospel with this week.
Pray for that person, and when the time is right, share!

Is Your Life an Invitation?

✝

Accept one another, just as Christ also accepted us,
for the glory of God.

Romans 15:7

I must admit, there's no way I'm listening to people give me fitness or nutrition advice who don't respect their bodies enough to maintain healthy fitness and nutrition habits themselves. If you don't practice what you preach, your words won't carry much weight. As believers, we invest in things that last forever. People, for one. While Jesus was on this earth, He gave His disciples a command to share the good news, a command that still applies to us today. It is not a suggestion.

We must step out in faith and seek spiritual conversations with people we come across. But it's not only with our words that we welcome those who don't know Jesus to experience a life with Him. We must reflect Him in how we live—what we say, how we act, what we do.

Think about your character for a moment. The way you treat people. What you do when no one is looking. Are you quick to forgive? Do you love and serve only the people who can do something for you in return? As you live each day, may your actions, speech, and character be invitations that welcome others into the arms of Christ.

**How can you live today
in a way that invites others to Jesus?**

A Crown That Lasts Forever

✛

Everyone who competes in the games exercises
self-control in all things. So they do it to obtain a
perishable wreath, but we an imperishable.

1 Corinthians 9:25

When the apostle Paul wrote his first letter to the Corinthians, he knew the Christians reading it would understand his athletic references. Located less than ten miles from Corinth was the city of Isthmia, known for hosting the Isthmian Games.

The Isthmian Games was a prominent ancient athletic event. Historical records tell us that it probably started in the sixth century BC and recurred every two years in the spring. Sporting events included running, boxing, wrestling, and chariot racing.

The Greek word translated "wreath" in the above verse is *stephanos*. It means "a crown of victory, royalty, or honor."[46] In the Isthmian Games, victors would have been awarded a *stephanos*—a crown made of withered pine or celery leaves.[47] Paul described this type of crown as "perishable." And he's right: A crown of celery or pine leaves won't last, just like modern medals, trophies, and other awards won't last either.

Trophies and awards aren't bad things, but they just can't be our ultimate goal. Rather, as Christians, we should work hard, exercising discipline in all we do, so that our efforts affect eternity.

Do a little soul searching.
What are you really chasing after?
Will it eventually wither away, or will it last forever?

One More

✝

Hear, Israel! The LORD is our God, the LORD is one!
And you shall love the LORD your God with all your heart
and with all your soul and with all your strength. These words,
which I am commanding you today, shall be on your heart.

Deuteronomy 6:4–6

In November 2016, the award-winning film *Hacksaw Ridge*, directed by actor Mel Gibson, released in theaters. Based on a true story, this movie documents the life of Desmond T. Doss, a combat medic during WWII who won the Medal of Honor despite refusing to bear arms. Doss, a man who wouldn't touch a weapon or work on the Sabbath for religious purposes, was drafted into the United States Army in April 1942. Though he vowed not to kill, he still believed it was his duty to serve God and country.

As the movie depicts, the Army wanted nothing to do with him. His fellow soldiers called him a coward and made fun of him for carrying around his Bible, and his commanding officer, Captain Jack Glover, even tried to get him transferred out of his battalion.

But all the harassment ceased in spring 1945 when Doss single-handedly saved approximately seventy-five men—including Captain Jack—over a twelve-hour period on the island of Okinawa. Under Japanese fire and unarmed, Doss crawled from wounded soldier to wounded soldier, praying, "Lord, please help me get one more." *One more.* With machine-gun rounds whistling past his head, Doss's prayer represented his true motivation and desire to save the lost and forgotten.

As Christians, this should be our mantra: "Lord, please help me get one more!" Our job is to keep pursing the *one*.

Who's your "one more"?

A Prayer for Perspective

✝

Lord, let me see people like You do. Let me love people like You do. Let me listen to people like You do. Help me step outside myself—my worries, my concerns, my comfort zone, my world—and let me view life from Your perspective, for Your ways are established, far greater than any of my plans. Whatever You do lasts forever. Nothing can be added to it, nor can anything be taken from it. Forgive me for doubting Your purposes, making assumptions, and jumping to conclusions too quickly. I can get so locked in on what I think is important that I miss out on what You're doing in and through my life.

As a citizen of heaven, may I work hard today, whether at home, in the office, at the grocery store—wherever I am—for the glory of God. You are the only audience I should strive to please. Keep me rooted and grounded in Your love. Give me a heavenly perspective as I wage war against the Enemy. Thank You for being constant yesterday, today, and forever.

In Jesus's name. Amen.

Based on: Ecclesiastes 3:14–15; Philippians 3:20; Colossians 3:23; Hebrews 13:8

Do You Have Peace?

✛

The steadfast of mind You will keep in perfect peace,
Because he trusts in You.
Isaiah 26:3

How do you know whether you're on the right path? Have you ever struggled with this question? It would be cool if some sort of multiple-choice quiz existed that alerts us to how much or how little our walks line up with the call of Jesus on our lives. However, I haven't found one yet. Still, there are some checkpoints, which I call mission markers, that we as believers can use to examine our own lives and give us peace about the direction we're headed. Note that what follows in the next set of devotions are *not* the only characteristics by which you can measure the impact you are making with the life you've been given. But these markers have their place in context, and I have found them helpful.

Peace is essential to mission-possible living. This doesn't mean you won't wrestle with making important decisions or that you won't have questions as you journey forward. The sure mark of mission-possible living is trust and dependence on God. Because our own strength and knowledge are limited, we must have faith in a supreme God. Scripture says that the person who trusts the Lord has perfect peace. When we submit to God and surrender control, He freely gives His peace to us. As we focus solely on Him, we are content and at rest. We might still have questions, but we choose to trust in His plan rather than our own.

Where do you lack peace in your life today?
How can you submit those areas to God?

Does Your Life Speak Your Mission?

✝

Prove yourselves doers of the word,
and not just hearers who deceive themselves.

James 1:22

In Matthew 21:18–22, Jesus sees a fig tree on the side of the road. Hungry, He reaches for a fig to eat, but seeing only leaves, He curses the tree so that it withers. The disciples were surprised when they saw what Jesus did, but this was not just a hangry moment that Jesus had. He was showing them the way He condemned hypocrisy.

The issue with this fig tree was that, from afar, it seemed to be flourishing, but a closer look revealed how empty it really was. As Christians, we can learn to play our parts well. If we know the right things to say, attend church often, and memorize a few scriptures to post on our Instagram stories, we may appear to live holy lives. But we are called to live lives based on more than just appearance.

How do you know if you're living out a mission-possible life and not just putting on a show? It's important to examine your heart and determine if your life is in line with Scripture. We are to be *doers* of the Word. Our actions *and* intentions should reflect the way Jesus shows us how to live in every aspect of our lives because mission-possible living means total commitment to God.

***Are you speaking your mission with just your words
or actually with your life?***

Are You Facing Opposition?

✝

Beloved, do not be surprised at the fiery ordeal among you,
which comes upon you for your testing, as though
something strange were happening to you.

1 Peter 4:12

When Moses led the Israelites out of Egypt, they fled to the edge of the Red Sea, with the body of water in front of them and the entire Egyptian army gaining speed and advancing on them from behind. Talk about being stuck between a rock and a hard place! The Israelites were trapped and convinced they were going to die.

Though they were afraid, they were exactly where God had led them. The moment was terrifying and uncertain, but it was by no accident that they came to this place. The dangers surrounding them were real, but so were God and His faithfulness. In a miraculous act, He parted the sea in front of them and made a way where there was no way.

Don't be surprised if you are living a mission-possible life and suddenly find yourself in the middle of difficult trials. The Enemy attacks those who are a threat to him, and he doesn't want you to be free from him. The hardship in your life may be evidence of God's hand leading you if you are obedient to Him, providing a backdrop for Him to work in ways only He can.

**When things are hard, is your tendency to fear
the circumstance or trust God?**

What Do Your Friends Say?

✟

Faithful are the wounds of a friend.

Proverbs 27:6

Have you ever had something stuck in your teeth but not noticed until you saw yourself in the mirror and then wondered how long it was there and why nobody you were with mentioned anything about it? In those moments, we appreciate the friends who tell us the truth, even if it makes us uncomfortable or embarrassed.

It's important to surround yourself with people who know you. Friends who really understand you and encourage you to live out your mission-possible life. When you have people invested in you in such a deep way, they can gauge where your life is. You need people who won't just tell you the things you want to hear. The ones who care more about protecting your feelings by hiding the truth than about you reaching your God-given potential aren't the kind of friends you need walking with you on your journey.

This doesn't mean that you allow people to berate you. Abuse is always wrong and is not in line with the gospel. But sometimes the truth hurts, even if it's spoken in love and with grace. Use those moments as opportunities for course corrections. Trust that the people in your life are there as gifts from God to help you in your walk.

What's some advice you would give yourself that
may be hard to hear but you know you need to hear it?

Are You Using Your Gifts?

✛

*As each one has received a special gift, employ it in serving
one another as good stewards of the multifaceted grace of God.*

1 Peter 4:10

How many times have you woken up on Christmas morning, opened some gifts from loved ones, talked about how much you loved the gifts, and then just left them there in their boxes to collect dust? Hopefully not often. Gifts are given with love and are meant to be enjoyed, even if you didn't ask for them. Now, how often have you tapped into the gifts God has given you, only to put them aside where they would never be used?

God has given each of us special gifts. You may be a talented speaker or a good host. You may have a knack for teaching or be a natural cheerleader to those around you. Whatever the case, even if you're not sure your gifts are worth much, God has given the many members of one body unique gifts to use for the purpose of serving one another.

Are you using your gifts, or are you hiding them? A mission-possible life involves boldness and risk taking. Even if it feels scary, make it a point to showcase the gifts God has given you for the purpose of furthering His kingdom.

What are your gifts? Are you using them,
or are they sitting in a box collecting dust?

What Is Your Motive?

✛

Do nothing from selfishness or empty conceit, but with humility
consider one another as more important than yourselves.

Philippians 2:3

In his book *The Purpose Driven Life*, pastor Rick Warren says that "humility is not thinking less of yourself; it is thinking of yourself less. Humility is thinking more of others."[48]

When Scripture tells us to have humility in the way we work, it does not mean we should put ourselves down; it means we must shift the focus from our own lives to the world around us. It comes down to motive. Why are you doing the things you do?

In mission-possible living, you can still strive to beat your personal best, hustle hard, and have big dreams, but it's about doing that with a willing and obedient spirit.

You use your God-given gifts not for selfish gain but because you know that God has blessed you so that you can bless others. Jesus was always focused on serving others, so to live a life like He did, we need to mirror His actions. If all you are thinking about is yourself and how your plans and actions may affect your personal success, you may achieve it, but you likely won't see God at work. If, on the other hand, you consider others more important than yourself, you will show others the heart of Christ.

What drives you to live a mission-possible life?

Whom Do You Aim to Please?

✛

Subject yourselves to one another in the fear of Christ.

Ephesians 5:21

A mission-possible life is one of service to others. But this doesn't mean that we are indebted to people. Even though Jesus was a servant to others and even washed the feet of His betrayer, everything He did was in obedience to the Father, not to people. Likewise, as we live mission-possible lives, we need to be obedient to Christ.

Whom do you aim to please? While we are called to submit to others, we are to do it out of reverence for Christ. People, even well-meaning friends or pastors, do not get the final say in our mission-possible lives; God does. Often, we may be so caught up in pleasing others that we become doormats, but this isn't the point. Mission-possible living is not about choosing the college you don't want to go to or putting your life on hold because you think you need to do the opposite of what you want. It's about living your life where you are today, entrusting your desires to God, and being obedient to where He calls you.

Put God first. Put His Word, His truth, and His opinion of you first. Seek to do His will and follow wherever He leads you. Let Him show you the way to living a mission-possible life.

Who are you most afraid of letting down, and why?

Burn the Ships

✛

Blessed is a man who perseveres under trial; for once he has been approved, he will receive the crown of life which the Lord has promised to those who love Him.

James 1:12

In 1519, Spanish conquistador Hernán Cortés set sail to the shores of Yucatán, Mexico. His eleven ships were filled with soldiers and sailors. Though they were markedly outnumbered, Cortés was intent on conquering the land from the Aztecs. Once every man was on shore, Cortés had the ships destroyed so his army had one of two options: conquer or die. Retreat wasn't part of the plan. Some historians believe the conquistador had the ships burned; others believe he had them sunk into the water.

While I'm certainly not hailing Cortés as a hero, this illustration speaks to the idea of steadfast commitment. Focusing on our mission, we must teach ourselves that retreat is not an option. Sure, it's normal to get unsettled when we hit a wall. It gets tiring praying for the same thing without seeing any movement. It's difficult when life gets in the way—and it often does. But rather than curling up with our phones in a dark corner, we must press on. Pause, pivot, and find a way to move forward. The worst thing you can do is give up because it's too hard. That's what perseverance in a mission-driven life looks like.

Don't look back; you're not going that way.

What ship do you need to burn to be obedient to what God is prompting you to go and do?

Listen to the Voice of Truth

✝

Take care what you listen to.

Mark 4:24

If there's one thing I learned early on playing football, it was that I couldn't live my life if I was constantly concerned about what other people were saying about me. There have always been people saying that I couldn't do something, along with my own doubting thoughts. But through it all, there's been only one voice that mattered. And I strive each day to try to hear Him loud and clear.

What voices call out to you as you try to live a life of purpose? Do they rehash past mistakes? Dredge up insecurities? Compare you to a teammate or colleague and announce how far you fall short? In those moments, instead of allowing the clamor of negative voices to hold your attention hostage, listen to the voice of truth. Listen to what the Creator says about you.

Sometimes the harder the climb to make your life count, the more tempting it is to tune in to negativity. But what God says about you is what matters most. When you feel less than or unequipped, listen to the voice of truth. I get that we can't hear God audibly, but there's no mistaking His voice in the pages of the Bible. Here are just a few things His Word says about you:

- You are a new creation (see 2 Corinthians 5:17).
- You are forever loved (see Romans 8:38–39).
- You are strong (see Psalm 18:32).
- You are forgiven (see 1 John 2:12).
- You are whole (see Colossians 2:10).
- You are created with purpose (see Esther 4:14).

Write down three more statements the Word of God says about you and speak them over yourself this week.

God's Presence over Fear

✝

Have I not commanded you? Be strong and courageous!
Do not be terrified nor dismayed, for the LORD your God
is with you wherever you go.

Joshua 1:9

When I was a kid, I never dreamed about winning football games 45–0. Boring! I dreamed about being down six points, crushing it in the last few minutes of the game, and then having a crazy celebration with my teammates after our unimaginable win. Because that's what you remember in life—the comebacks when you face unbeatable odds. There's something about pressure, not ease, that drives me, that makes me want to push through.

What's pressure? For some people, pressure is closely related to fear.

Fear is a powerful emotion. It can push or motivate you to do things, sometimes even good things, but it will never take you as far as love can take you. I learned about fear and love from my dad. He taught us a lot of Scripture about fear—many verses that my mom put to song so that we would always remember that God is greater than anything we could possibly be afraid of.

What fears overwhelm you? Are you afraid that living mission possible will require too many sacrifices? That you'll never find your purpose or that you'll spend more time searching than doing? And what are you feeding more: your fears, or your love for a God who has promised to be faithful? Remember, God never promised a life absent of pressure, but He did promise us His presence.

Meditate on how to prioritize love over fear.

Difficulties Produce Endurance

✝

Consider it all joy, my brothers and sisters, when you encounter
various trials, knowing that the testing of your faith produces
endurance. And let endurance have its perfect result, so that
you may be perfect and complete, lacking in nothing.

James 1:2–4

As you live a mission-possible life, don't be surprised when it gets tough. But don't let the resistance keep you from maintaining your momentum, placing one foot forward after another. It's doesn't get hard without a purpose.

Human beings were created with a fight-or-flight response. This is an innate physiological reaction that sets in motion when we're threatened or under attack. So, we're wired to handle stress. Biologically speaking, our bodies' stress response was designed to help us maintain our well-being and meet the demands of survival. Research indicates that stress can affect our well-being in a positive way if we have the right perspective. As Holocaust survivor Viktor Frankl wrote in his book *Man's Search for Meaning*, "In some way, suffering ceases to be suffering at the moment it finds a meaning, such as the meaning of a sacrifice."[49]

When you say yes to what God is pricking your heart about, can you expect to sacrifice and experience trials? More than likely, yes. You will also experience joy, peace, fulfillment, and meaning beyond expectation. Living the purpose God has for you means that the hard stuff has value. And in this case, the difficult times will produce in you maturity, perseverance, and endurance.

How have trials affected the endurance of your faith?

Keep Running

+

May the Lord direct your hearts to the love of God
and to the perseverance of Christ.

2 Thessalonians 3:5

One of the most famous ultramarathons in the world takes place in Greece every year. Since 1983, runners who compete in the Spartathlon must finish the 246-kilometer/153-mile journey between Athens and Sparta within a time limit of 36 hours. The fastest time achieved was 20 hours 25 minutes, and runners have been trying to beat it since 1984.[50] Dean Karnazes, famed ultramarathon runner and one of *Time* magazine's "Top 100 Most Influential People in the World," has said this about the endurance required to run such a race: "I think the first half you run with your legs and the next half you run with your mind. There comes a point in the race where the pain, it owns you."[51]

You can learn a lot about a relationship or organization by looking at how it has dealt with hardship. In fact, when our foundation chooses employees or business partnerships, we look for people who have faced strong resistance and experienced growth through it.

What challenges are you facing today? Don't give up. If you quit, you will never know where that breakthrough was going to be. Yes, it's hard, but know you don't have to deal with it alone. God is with you as you run your race.

*How would you answer if you were asked to tell a story
of something tough you've endured and
how it changed you?*

Endurance Produces the Greatest Highs

✝

In Your presence is fullness of joy;
In Your right hand there are pleasures forever.

Psalm 16:11

You know by now that as you strive to live a mission-possible life, it's not going to be easy. When God moves your heart to do things that will require His partnership and your surrender, you're going to find yourself in a place of resistance. And if you're in that place right now, know that I've prayed for the Lord to encourage your heart, to remind you of His presence and His promise to never leave you, to never forsake you, and to finish what He has started in your life.

There's one more thing I hope to encourage you with: Yes, mission-possible living is accompanied by the hard things, but it also brings with those hard things some of your greatest highs! Joy. Meaning. Fulfillment. Peace. I can think back to every moment God pricked my heart to do something for Him. And though I may not have been sure of how to start or where the idea was going to go, I trusted Him, took a step forward, then another, and kept moving, despite the pain, struggles, and at times doubts. I can say that every one of those pricks have been some of the best parts of my life and have provided me with more fulfillment than anything I could have imagined. Were those some hard moments? Absolutely! But they were always some of my greatest highs!

Keep enduring. With Jesus, you're going to get more out of this life—far beyond anything the world can offer.

Think back to a hard season in your life. What joy also came out of that season?

Keep Pushing the Mission Forward

✛

Not that I have already grasped it all or have already become
perfect, but I press on if I may also take hold of
that for which I was even taken hold of by Christ Jesus.

Philippians 3:12

Every day is a day to push the mission forward. But not every day is game day. What does that mean?

Not every day is a day where you see your mission come to fruition. Not every day is a day that our foundation executes a raid to rescue human-trafficking victims. Not every day is a day we grant a sick child a W15H. But every day is a day we get to push the mission forward. This means that every day, we are doing research, making phone calls, setting up appointments, having meetings, conducting interviews, creating budgets, finding sponsors, making partnerships, and so much more. You know what a lot of this is? The grind. Putting in the hard, necessary, and unglamorous daily work that people on the outside don't see or appreciate. On its surface, the grind can seem to be absent of meaning or reward.

Those moments don't feel like the payoff. But if you don't put in those moments, you'll never get the reward. Whatever God has called you to do, every day is a day to push the mission forward.

Never forget that purpose lies even in what you may consider meaningless or boring. Attack each day with as much purpose and conviction in the preparation as you would the execution.

Write about the ordinary ways you need to press on
in your mission. Why are they necessary?

A Prayer for Endurance

✝

Lord, I pray for relentless energy and focus to keep going today. You have established a path for me to run on. As I look to You, the Author and Perfecter of my faith, help me remain steadfast and on mission through tests and trials.

I pray I can run with endurance and do all that You have entrusted me to do. When temptation hits, help me stand firm. When it is painful, help me remain under Your hand. When everyone else is retreating, help me not budge. This is what love does: It bears all things, believes all things, hopes all things, and endures all things.

Thank You, Jesus, for being the greatest example of love. For the joy set before You, You endured the cross, despised the shame, and sat down at the right hand of the throne of God. It is for this reason I ask that I will not grow weary and lose heart, for Your Word says to consider it all joy whenever I experience hard seasons, because the testing of my faith produces endurance, and endurance produces growth in Christ.

Renew my strength and refresh my spirit today.

In Jesus's name. Amen.

Based on: Hebrews 12:1–3; 1 Corinthians 13:7; James 1:2–4, 12

A Simple Gospel

✝

When I came to you, brothers and sisters,
I did not come as someone superior in speaking ability or wisdom,
as I proclaimed to you the testimony of God.

1 Corinthians 2:1

An article by the Jesus Film Project listed four main reasons people give for not sharing their faith:

- "I'm afraid they'll ask questions I can't answer."
- "I struggle with my own faith."
- "I never learned how."
- "I don't know how to start a conversation."[52]

When it comes to evangelism, we can get ourselves all worked up. Fear, busyness, personality, rejection, and intelligence are all things we claim for not doing what God has called us to do. As Christians, we know that the best thing we can do for someone is introduce them to Jesus!

That's why I love the beginning of 1 Corinthians 2. Paul simply told the church in Corinth that his gospel presentation wasn't perfect. It wasn't eloquent. He was nervous, weak, and fearful. But he said, "I determined to know nothing among you except Jesus Christ, and Him crucified" (verse 2). This is the essence of the gospel.

God the Father loved the world *so* much that He sent His perfect Son to die in our place and pay the penalty for our sin so that by trusting in Him (His death and resurrection), we may be made righteous!

Salvation isn't dependent upon your performance. God is the One at work and invites us to be a part of it (see 3:5–9). Breathe, keep it simple, and let God's power be on display (see 2:4–5).

What keeps you from sharing the simple gospel?
How does Paul's approach give you confidence?

The Great Mission

✛

Jesus came to them and said, "All authority in heaven and on earth
has been given to me. Therefore go and make disciples of all
nations, baptizing them in the name of the Father
and of the Son and of the Holy Spirit."

Matthew 28:18–19, NIV

A t the end of Matthew's gospel, he recorded a charge given by
Jesus to His followers to "go and make disciples." This charge
has become one of the most well-known passages in the Bible and is
often referred to as the Great Commission.

However, I was shocked when I recently read a 2018 report by the
Barna Group, a leading research organization focused on the inter-
section of faith and culture. In *Translating the Great Commission*, they
asked more than a thousand U.S. churchgoers if they had "heard of
the Great Commission." Fifty-one percent said they did not know
the term.[53]

When taking a deeper look, I noticed approximately 82 percent
of people surveyed did not know the "exact meaning" of the Great
Commission! This means that every Sunday, eight out of ten people
who walk through church doors and sit in chairs and pews across
America are missing out on a very important piece of Christianity.

As a church, Matthew 28:18–19 is something we should study
and understand the best we can. It's not just the Great Commission;
it is our *Great Mission*! It's what the church is all about: disciples making disciples.

*Part of our job as Christians is to help each other
know what God has called us to do. What's your part
in fulfilling the Great Mission?*

To the Ends of the Earth

✛

You will receive power when the Holy Spirit has come upon you;
and you shall be My witnesses ... as far as
the remotest part of the earth.

Acts 1:8

On May 8, 1886, a man named Dr. John Pemberton sold the first glass of Coca-Cola for $.05 at a pharmacy in Atlanta, Georgia. Originally serving around nine drinks per day, the Coca-Cola Company is now valued at an estimated $87.6 billion. Coca-Cola, in just 130 years or so, is in more than two hundred countries and territories, making it one of the most powerful brands in the world.[54] No matter where you go—the jungles of the Philippines or the streets of Los Angeles—the Coca-Cola logo is recognized.

So, what's the problem with this?

Simple: More people know about Coca-Cola than about the person of Jesus Christ. In a conversation I had with David Platt, pastor and author of the bestselling book *Radical,* he shared that there are more than three billion people in over seven thousand people groups who currently do not have access to the gospel. So I asked myself, *How is Coca-Cola doing a better job at evangelizing their product than Christians are at evangelizing the gospel?* We have had more time (two thousand years), we have more people, and the good news of Jesus Christ is *free!* You don't have to pay for it.

Now, I understand Coca-Cola isn't a belief system or facing spiritual warfare as believers are. But our job isn't done. We must continue to be witnesses of Christ to the ends of the earth.

You may not always have the chance to travel "to the ends of the earth," but are you taking the gospel to the end of the driveway? To the ends of your school? Your community?

Practice, Practice, Practice

✝

What use is it, my brothers and sisters,
if someone says he has faith, but he has no works?

James 2:14

I remember my first time stepping up to the plate after not playing organized baseball for more than a decade. I had forgotten how fast the ball comes at you from sixty feet away, especially at the professional level!

But fastballs didn't cause as much concern. It was the off-speed pitches that were most challenging for me. Sitting back and waiting for the ball to break demands patience—a patience that I didn't always have—which, if you know the game of baseball, when you lack patience too many times in the batter's box, it doesn't go well for you! *Strike three!*

If I wanted to be a successful hitter in the minor leagues, I had to practice hitting off-speed pitches: curveballs, sliders, knuckleballs, changeups, and so on. Once I felt like I practiced enough, I practiced some more. Though I didn't master the off-speed pitches, I got a lot more comfortable and confident at the plate by the time I retired.

The lesson here is simple: The more you practice something, the better you get. In the Christian life, no matter whether you're a new believer or you've been walking with the Lord for decades, *practice* produces a sense of confidence and comfortability. Right where you are, you can practice sharing your faith, practice memorizing Bible verses, practice being uncomfortable—you name it! It may not be an actual curveball, but when you put yourself in repeated situations, things come more naturally. As James says, if we're not actively practicing and living out our faith with works, what use is it?

What's one thing you can practice so that you're ready when the curveball is thrown?

Take Courage

✝

They brought to Him a paralyzed man lying on a stretcher.
And seeing their faith, Jesus said to the man who was paralyzed,
"Take courage, son; your sins are forgiven."

Matthew 9:2

While studying Scripture one afternoon, I came across an interesting word. It's the Greek verb *tharseó,* and it means to have courage or be of good cheer.[55] It occurs seven times in the New Testament and is typically translated "take heart" or "be courageous."

Jesus specifically used this word four times in His earthly ministry. When looking at each occurrence, I noticed that the first three instances that Jesus said *tharseó* were in the context of a miracle: healing a paralyzed man (see Matthew 9:2), healing the bleeding woman after she touched His robe (9:22), and when He walked on water and calmed the wind (see 14:27; Mark 6:50). But what about the fourth occurrence?

In John 16:33, speaking to His disciples, Jesus said, "These things I have spoken to you so that in Me you may have peace. In the world you have tribulation, but take courage [*tharseó*]; I have overcome the world." It doesn't seem like there's a miracle here.

But think about it: In the context of John 16:33, Jesus was talking about His departure—His upcoming arrest and crucifixion. He told His disciples to "take courage" because He was about to defeat sin and death very soon. By saying *tharseó,* Jesus was looking ahead to another miracle, the greatest miracle in history: His resurrection! In all four instances of Jesus using this word, a supernatural event occurred. How cool is that!

How can you choose to take courage today?

Who's Watching Your Flank?

✝

Encourage one another and build one another up,
just as you also are doing.

1 Thessalonians 5:11

A round the seventh century BC, the ancient Greeks developed a military formation called the phalanx. The phalanx was made up of infantry soldiers who fought in a tight, stacked, shoulder-to-shoulder rectangular position and moved forward as one group. In this formation, their shields would overlap, creating a "shield wall" that made the phalanx nearly impenetrable. When interlocked, the shield would cover not only a soldier's own body but also the flank of his brother next to him.

In head-to-head combat, each soldier trusted one another to do their job—to cover their back. If one man got lazy and let his guard down (a.k.a. his shield), his brother in arms would be exposed to danger. Each man wasn't just fighting for himself; they fought for one another.

The truth is, we all have blind spots. As the psalmist says, "Who can discern his errors?" (19:12). Just like the ancient Greeks, we need people to fight with us. We cannot do life or ministry alone! As the body of Christ, by the power of the Holy Spirit, we were meant to fight the forces of evil together. We need people in our lives who make us stronger, complement our weaknesses, and are willing to go to the hard places. Maybe it's a co-worker, a friend from church, a family member—I don't know. But whoever it may be, our job is to encourage and build one another up in this fight.

Do you feel that you have people in your life who would protect your flank? If so, who are they, and how do they keep you accountable?

Remember Often

✛

Be careful for yourself and watch over your soul diligently,
so that you do not forget the things which your eyes have seen and
they do not depart from your heart all the days of your life;
but make them known to your sons and your grandsons.

Deuteronomy 4:9

Written around 1406 BC according to some scholars, the book of Deuteronomy contains some of Moses's last written messages to the Israelites before he died. After wandering the wilderness for forty years, God's chosen people camped out on the east side of the Jordan River, on the plains of Moab, across from the Promised Land. The children who had left Egypt were now adults, and God wanted to reiterate His law to this new generation before they entered the land. (Deuteronomy means "second law" or "repeated law.")

The book primarily serves as a written covenant between God and His people, but one consistent theme throughout is a call to "remember" and to "not forget," specifically where the Israelites had come from and what God had done for them.

The Hebrew verbs for "remember" and "to forget" appear *twenty-two times* in Deuteronomy! From "not forgetting" how they were once enslaved in Egypt to "remembering" how they were supernaturally led by the Lord in the wilderness to "never forgetting" how they aroused the anger of God by their acts of disobedience.

I think this is a valuable lesson anyone can do right where they are. Moses's emphasis on remembering is to remind us that we were all once foreigners of God but that by His grace He saved us, and now our lives can be symbols of thankfulness in action.

**What has God done in your life that causes you
to remember His love?**

Chosen by Jesus

✝

You did not choose Me but I chose you,
and appointed you that you would go and bear fruit,
and that your fruit would remain, so that whatever you ask
of the Father in My name He may give to you.

John 15:16

There may be moments when you wonder if you are actually called to live a mission-possible life. The Enemy's voice can fill you with doubt and make you feel unworthy and unqualified for the mission God has called you to. You may believe that others are more capable than you and that you have nothing to offer. But you are called to live a mission-possible life. Yes, *you*.

Mission-possible living is not simply for people who are perfect or seem to have it all together. God has a history of choosing the unlikely people to work His miracles through. Even when Jesus walked this earth, He chose imperfect people to follow Him in His ministry.

Jesus's twelve disciples were a team of misfits, rejects, and nobodies. He called fishermen, tax collectors, zealots, and others to come follow Him. He was a rabbi, and they, from all different backgrounds, became His students. Many people, past and present, didn't think there was anything special about them. Some of them didn't even get along. In fact, the only thing these people had in common was that when Jesus told them to follow Him, they went.

The same is true for us today. God is not seeking out special requirements for us to follow Him. He is looking only for our willingness to go wherever He leads. That is what makes us His disciples.

Do you feel equipped to live a mission-possible life?
Why or why not?

A Hesitant Skeptic

✝

Nathanael said to Him, "How do You know me?"
Jesus answered and said to him, "Before Philip called you,
when you were under the fig tree, I saw you."

John 1:48

When Nathanael first heard of Jesus, he was a bit a skeptical. "Can anything good be from Nazareth?" he asked his friend Philip (John 1:46). As far as Nathanael was concerned, Philip's declaration that he had found the long-awaited Messiah was nonsense. There was no way that it could be true.

Despite his skepticism, Nathanael followed Philip to see who this Jesus of Nazareth was. And when Jesus saw Nathanael, He said, "Here is truly an Israelite, in whom there is no deceit!" (verse 47). Nathanael was undoubtedly shocked at this revelation. How did Jesus know who he was? They had never met before! Then Jesus said something even stranger: "Before Philip called you, when you were under the fig tree, I saw you." How was that even possible? Amazed by this, Nathanael devoted himself to following Jesus.

When you first heard of Jesus, did you believe? Or were you a little skeptical too? Did you, like Nathanael, question the goodness of God because it came from a place you didn't expect? Are you hesitant now to accept that the Jesus you've heard of could be a Savior?

Jesus sees you and knows you, even if you aren't really convinced of Him. His power and ability are not dependent on your belief in Him. Even still, He welcomes the hesitant skeptic to join Him and follow Him. And when we, despite our questions, choose to follow Him, we will find that He has always known us.

How has Jesus met you in your skepticism?

All Over the Place

✝

I also say to you that you are Peter, and upon this rock
I will build My church; and the gates of Hades
will not overpower it.

Matthew 16:18

S imon Peter was always putting his foot in his mouth. He was
eager for the things of Jesus but often acted on impulse. On the
Mount of Transfiguration, he blurted out words without thinking
them through (see Luke 9:32–33). When Jesus was washing the disciples' feet, Peter adamantly refused and then hastily begged Jesus to
wash all of him (see John 13:8–9). That same night, he declared his
absolute loyalty to Jesus and swore that he would die for Him, only
to deny Jesus three times (see Matthew 26:31–35, 69–75). He also cut
off someone's ear (see John 18:10).

Peter was . . . all over the place. Jesus was not surprised by any of
this. He knew the man He called to follow Him. He understood all
Peter's weaknesses. Still, He called him Peter, saying he would be the
rock on which the church would be built. Despite being all over the
place, Peter would be called steady and strong, because Jesus knew
that it wasn't about who he was in the moment but about what he
would become the more he walked alongside Him.

Sometimes you may feel all over the place. You may have seen the
glory of Jesus displayed in your life and may be passionate to declare
His name, only to find that you mess up, sometimes in big ways. But
you don't have to be perfect to follow Jesus. Walk with Him and let
His Spirit fill you. He will work inside you to accomplish the purpose that He has for you.

How has the Holy Spirit transformed your weaknesses?

Sons of Thunder

✝

When His disciples James and John saw this, they said,
"Lord, do You want us to command fire to come down
from heaven and consume them?"
Luke 9:54

James and John were brothers and fishermen when Jesus called them to follow Him. They were honored to walk with Jesus—so honored, in fact, that they asked Him a brazen question: Would they one day be able to get the two most special seats in heaven, to the right and left of Jesus (see Mark 10:35–37)? Another time, they made an audacious suggestion to call down fire on a town as punishment for the people refusing to accept Jesus.

Despite these shocking requests, James and John were part of Jesus's inner circle, along with Simon Peter. Jesus called them the Sons of Thunder, presumably for their force-of-nature ways. He saw their passion, even if it was misplaced, and He kept them close to Him so they could watch and learn from Him.

Both James and John followed Jesus wholeheartedly. James eventually was the first of the disciples to be martyred for preaching the gospel. John went on to write five books in the New Testament.

Despite the men's pride and desire for vengeance, time with Jesus softened their hearts. They followed Him at whatever cost, learning how to love others like He did. Jesus did not call them because they knew what it meant to be disciples; He taught them what it looked like as they followed Him. Even if you are not sure you have what it takes to be like Jesus, the more you walk with Him, the more He will teach you what it means to be His follower.

Have you felt Jesus soften your heart? In what way?

A Despised Outcast

✛

As Jesus went on from there, He saw a man called Matthew
sitting in the tax collector's office; and He said to him,
"Follow Me!" And he got up and followed Him.

Matthew 9:9

Matthew didn't really fit in anywhere. As a Jewish tax collector working for the Romans, he would have been viewed as a traitor to other Jews for forsaking his people to serve their enemy. He would, however, have been wealthy. He had a solid career that, even if others hated him for it, would have supported a lavish lifestyle.

Still, when Jesus saw Matthew and invited him to follow Him, the tax collector immediately got up. Despite having riches, he did not hesitate to go where Jesus went, even if it meant traveling with people who would have been his enemies.

Matthew was considered a sinner by the Pharisees, and to be seen with him would be a disgrace. Yet Jesus didn't seem to mind that Matthew had betrayed his own people before He called him. He wasn't concerned with Matthew's past choices; the only choice that mattered was his willingness to leave his life behind and accept Jesus's invitation to a new one.

Matthew ended up writing the first gospel. He had a keen sense of awareness, and God enabled him to use his unique ability for His glory, as a record keeper of the life and miracles of Jesus. No matter what you have done in the past, how others may look at you, or what choices you have made, when you accept the call to follow Jesus, you can have new life and find a new purpose for the gifts God has given you.

How has Jesus accepted you and given you new purpose?

An Adamant Disbeliever

✛

The other disciples were saying to him, "We have seen the Lord!"
But he said to them, "Unless I see in His hands the imprint of
the nails, and put my finger into the place of the nails,
and put my hand into His side, I will not believe."

John 20:25

After Jesus was resurrected from the dead, He appeared in the Upper Room, where all the disciples but Thomas were hiding. He showed them His scars and told them not to be afraid. It was really Him, and the disciples were amazed to see their beloved Jesus, victorious over death, standing in front of them.

When they told Thomas, however, he didn't believe them. Despite walking with Jesus and being told several times by Him during His ministry that He would die and then be resurrected, Thomas doubted the news. In fact, he adamantly refused to believe that Jesus was alive unless he would be able to see it for himself. He wouldn't even believe the other disciples with whom he had traveled for the past three years. He was headstrong.

Eight days later, the disciples were once again in the Upper Room. Out of nowhere, Jesus showed up, in the same way He did for the other ten. He went up to Thomas and instructed him to touch His hands and His side. He fulfilled Thomas's request from the previous week exactly as he had made it.

Jesus was not intimidated by Thomas's doubt, nor is He afraid of your doubt. Offer it to God. Ask Him your questions and expect His response.

What doubts do you have about Jesus?
Present them to Him today.

Suffering to Salvation

✝

*I consider that the sufferings of this present time are not worthy
to be compared with the glory that is to be revealed to us.*

Romans 8:18

Guest devo by Abbey Gideon
Relationship to TTF: on-site director of summer camp
at Rising Light Ridge

I went from being in an abusive relationship to being free of suffering, all because God was doing things in my life that, as a nonbeliever, I didn't see. After leaving my relationship, I needed to find myself again. What better way than to go on a road trip and live out of my car? I was on my own for nineteen days, but I never felt lonely. I constantly met new people and experienced new places. Before leaving on my trip, I knew I didn't want to spend the coming summer in my hometown, as I needed time to heal. God provided an answer to prayer just before I left on my road trip. I received an opportunity to work for Rising Light Ridge, a learning and ministry facility providing a community of belonging to participants of all backgrounds and abilities in Pennsylvania. I had no idea what to expect other than I knew I had to go. After returning from my road trip, I headed to Pennsylvania. I began seeing God work, but I wasn't a believer yet. At Rising Light, God put me in a community in which His presence surrounded me for the first time in my life. Finally, I made the decision to trust and follow Jesus.

Sometimes you can't see God until you endure something that causes you to look up. He always has a plan, even when we cannot see it during times of suffering. There is a greater glory that will be revealed to us.

How has God revealed Himself to you
through your suffering?

Strength Is a Key Ingredient to God's Heart

✝

I can do all things through Him who strengthens me.

Philippians 4:13

Guest devo by Kelly Faughnan
Relationship to TTF: W15H recipient

I think of prayer as the key to getting to better know God and the purpose of life. Through prayer, God gives us strength and guidance to help us through our faith journey in ways we can't even imagine. Prayer reveals unexpected ways to look for exciting blessings in our lives. It strengthens us during good times and bad times. During good times, I use prayer to thank God for my many blessings. When difficult times arise, I pray that God gives me strength to overcome whatever obstacle presents itself.

Not long ago, I was diagnosed with a brain tumor. I prayed, and I prayed some more. Although I was afraid, I believed that God had a plan. I also recognized that He had blessed me with a loving family and amazing friends to support me through this ordeal. He also blessed me with an incredible medical team that was doing His work here on earth. I survived.

Through prayer, God revealed to me that because of my challenge, I was in a position to help others who were experiencing similar challenges. Specifically, God blessed me—with the assistance of numerous generous people He had put in my life—with the ability to help children who had life-threatening illnesses. As a result of the challenge that was presented to me, as well as many prayers, God has led me to a great place where I would not have gotten to alone.

What do you believe God can do through you today?

A New Perspective

✝

In this you greatly rejoice, even though now for a little while,
if necessary, you have been distressed by various trials, so that
the proof of your faith, being more precious than gold which
perishes though tested by fire, may be found to result in praise,
glory, and honor at the revelation of Jesus Christ.

1 Peter 1:6–7

Guest devo by Stacie Mockbee
Relationship to TTF: Night to Shine director

"I can't wait to die." My son, Jacob, spoke these words with such confidence that it emptied my lungs. He continued to talk about how exciting it will be to see Jesus. "I will have a new body in heaven, and I want to race with Him!" Suffering and pain were Jacob's lifelong companions, yet his life was also full of hope and expectation. How? Because he understood God's goodness and focused on that truth rather than his daily battles.

Suffering is inevitable. In these scriptures, Peter wasn't suggesting that we rejoice over our trials and pain; rather, he was reminding us that we have a tried-and-true hope, one that won't fall apart like everything else around us. Our suffering doesn't define our stories; our living hope in Jesus does. Through the resurrection of Jesus Christ, we have an inheritance waiting for us! Understanding the magnitude of this gift can shift our mindsets as we traverse the pain we experience.

Jacob died shortly after our conversation. I can only imagine what it must have been like for him to leave behind his wheelchair, ventilator, and daily suffering and experience the joy of the inheritance kept in heaven for him. And I'm sure he ran a few footraces with Jesus.

As you face trials or suffering today, how can you change your focus from them to God and His goodness?

A Prayer for Faithfulness

✝

Lord, with You all things are possible! Help me today to walk with conviction, even when things are uncertain.

Give me faith like Noah, who spent many years preparing for what was to come. Give me faith like Abraham, who was willing to go wherever You led him. Give me faith like Moses, who trusted Your power and provision. Give me faith like David, who honored Your anointed even when treated harshly. Give me faith like Shadrach, Meshach, and Abednego, who didn't give in to peer pressure. Give me faith like Daniel, who stood firm in chaos. Give me faith like Esther, who put everything on the line to save her people. Give me faith like the disciples, who simply obeyed Your command "Follow Me." Give me faith like Paul, who was unashamed to share the gospel, even when faced with opposition.

Lord, all throughout Your Word, I'm encouraged by the belief of those who have gone before me. Like those men and women, may I walk by faith and not by sight. May I surrender my plans, wants, desires, and dreams and trust what You're doing in and through me. Thank You for always being faithful!

In Jesus's name. Amen.

Based on: Matthew 19:26; Hebrews 11; Matthew 4:19; 2 Corinthians 5:7; Ecclesiastes 3:1–11

Respect Divine Timing

✛

His anger is but for a moment,
His favor is for a lifetime;
Weeping may last for the night,
But a shout of joy comes in the morning.

Psalm 30:5

After defeating the Philistine giant, Goliath, David saw his popularity grow throughout the land of Israel. King Saul (David's father-in-law) feared him, saw him as a threat to the throne, and attempted to kill him multiple times. As a result, David fled for his life and spent many years on the run.

Utilizing friends and family, David built a small army of his own. When presented with opportunities to kill King Saul, he did not take them: first, in a cave where he was so close to Saul that he cut off a piece of his robe, and second, while Saul was sleeping at his camp. Instead of putting a spear through Saul's heart, David let his king live. In both instances, David honored God's chosen leader, saying, "As the LORD is my witness, I would never do such a thing to my lord [Saul], the LORD's anointed. I will never lift my hand against him, since he is the LORD's anointed" (1 Samuel 24:6, CSB).

David respected divine timing. Was he confused by how God was working? I'm sure. He had a bounty on his head for no reason! But in all the chaos, not knowing if he would survive long enough to be king, David remained obedient. He didn't try to take things into his own hands. He let God be God and did his best to walk in faith.

Obedience is hard, and we don't always like it.
How does this snapshot of David's life encourage you
to trust what God is doing?

Your Will, Not Mine

✝

Father, if You are willing, remove this cup from Me;
yet not My will, but Yours be done.

Luke 22:42

Guest devo by Irene and Alfredo Salazar
Relationship to TTF: pastors of Vida Church in Guatemala
and founders of Tebow Down Guatemala

In August 2005, our son, Alfredo, entered the operating room. He had five heart defects, and open-heart surgery was the only way to correct them. We asked the doctor if he could guarantee that our son would live. He couldn't promise that outcome.

The doctor's words were harsh, but it was the truth. It was time to put our trust in the only Giver of life, Jesus. Minutes later, the nurse took Alfredo to the operating room and told us, "It's time."

We asked the nurse to give us a moment to say goodbye to our son and pray for him. Our prayer was, "Father, You gave us Alfredo, a beautiful baby with Down syndrome. If Your will is for him to return to heaven, we will accept it, but our desire is for him to stay with us on this earth and for us to be able to take care of him and watch him grow. Yet not our will, but Yours be done."

Twenty-four hours after the surgery, Alfredo left the intensive care unit. A week after his surgery, he was leaving the hospital ready to continue with his life. The doctor told us, "I don't understand how he can be so well. You can take him back home."

We knew that the Lord's will was to bless many lives through Alfredo's life, and we have done so throughout all these years. We learned that the Lord's will is always the best for our lives, even as we go through very difficult times.

How have you been able to leverage
difficult times for God's glory?

Suffering in Faith

✝

To this you were called, because Christ suffered for you,
leaving you an example, that you should follow in his steps.

1 Peter 2:21, NIV

Guest devo by Tracy Umezu
Relationship to TTF: adoption-grant recipient

I never thought life would be easy or perfect, but the loss of two of our daughters broke my heart. In the days and years following my losses, I turned to the church. As my faith deepened, I was drawn to the suffering Jesus experienced for us (and to the visceral pain Mary must have felt watching her son suffer).

Thinking about the physical and mental pain Jesus felt for me made my heart ache. I wanted to do all I could to ease His pain and help carry His cross. I felt as if His cross was also my cross to carry. Living in faith while simultaneously grieving my daughters began to feel like the least I could do for all the suffering Jesus endured for me.

God never promised a life free of suffering, but He has promised that He is with us always if we open our hearts and let Him in. The resurrection of Christ was God's faithful promise to us that through all the suffering we will experience, at the end of our journeys heaven waits for us and we will be completely healed. By allowing God in at our darkest hours and holding on to the faithful promises He gives us, we are drawn into a closer and more intimate relationship with Him. This allows us to physically feel closer to eternal life and hope for what is to come.

How might remaining faithful to God in your darkest hour
be an example to others of the strength faith gives
during hard times?

Lord, First Let Me . . .

✝

He said to another man, "Follow me." But he replied,
"Lord, first let me go and bury my father." Jesus said to him,
"Let the dead bury their own dead, but you go and
proclaim the kingdom of God."

Luke 9:59–60, NIV

Guest devo by Hope Kim Pranza
Relationship to TTF: storyteller at the Tebow CURE Hospital
in the Philippines

Let the dead bury their own dead? That seems harsh, or so I thought. My father had been confined at a hospital in Florida for months, when a ministry opportunity in the Philippines came up. I had many questions about God's timing. I thought the same as the man in the in the verse above: *Lord, first let me . . .*

Just like mine, it's likely the man's father wasn't dead. He wanted to follow Jesus, but his request was to let him wait a little while. By "let[ting] the dead bury their own dead," Jesus reminds us that following Him should be our priority.

Convicted in my response, I wholeheartedly surrendered my decision—and my dad—to God. During my first week of serving, he had six cardiac arrests, leading him to his final rest. Thanks to the internet, even as I served at the Tebow CURE Hospital, I was able to attend my father's funeral through video call. Answering God's invite, I witnessed life-changing surgeries leading to faith in Jesus. "Let the dead bury their own dead" doesn't mean leaving your responsibilities to your family; it means stepping in faith to obey Him as He invites you to a most incredible opportunity in making His name known.

What do you need to surrender
so you can go and proclaim the kingdom of God?

Don't Underestimate the Small Steps

✟

Come and see the works of God,
Who is awesome in His deeds toward the sons of mankind.

Psalm 66:5

In 1855, Edward Kimball, an ordinary man who taught Sunday school at his church in Boston, had a goal to share the gospel with every teenage boy in his class. Concerned about one of his students, Kimball showed up at the shoe store where this seventeen-year-old worked. There, Kimball shared God's love with the boy, and shortly after, the boy received Christ. His name was Dwight L. Moody.

Moody went on to become one of the greatest evangelists of the nineteenth century, leading millions of people to Christ. But the story doesn't stop there. In one of Moody's evangelistic meetings, he befriended a college student named J. Wilbur Chapman. Chapman eventually became a famous evangelist as well! But the story is still not over . . .

During Chapman's ministry, he hired a former pro baseball player to be his assistant. His name was Billy Sunday. Sunday went on to become a dynamic evangelist himself, particularly influencing a group of Christian men in Charlotte, North Carolina.

Then, in 1934, this same group of men invited Dr. Mordecai Ham to hold a tent revival in their city. It was there where a teenage boy surrendered his life to the lordship of Jesus Christ. This young boy's name was Billy Graham. And throughout his life, he shared the gospel with more than two billion people.[56]

Here's the point: Don't underestimate your small steps of obedience. Just like with Mr. Kimball, God will use your faithfulness too!

What small step in obedience is God asking you to take?

I Will Not Be Overwhelmed

+

When he falls, he will not be hurled down,
Because the LORD is the One who holds his hand.

Psalm 37:24

Failure is inevitable. It's a given. It's going to happen. And that's okay! Let me be honest: I've had my fair share of highs and lows. I've been blessed to win a Heisman Trophy and a couple of national championships. But I've also been cut four times and traded once, so basically I've not been wanted by five teams. It didn't feel good. But the simple fact is that life isn't easy. Nowhere in the Bible does it say it is. In our pursuit of obedience, there are going to be giants that get in our way and knock us down.

Whether we bring it on ourselves or it's caused by some external factor, failure is a part of our sin nature. But from failure, we learn important lessons. It's what shapes a lot of who we become, probably even more than success does. Only from screwing up and making mistakes do we find out what works and what doesn't.

I believe our *response* to failure is what's most important. It's what you do with failure that makes all the difference. That's why I love the psalmist's attitude here. He acknowledged the fact that we *will* fall. Period. But when we fall, we will not stay down. We will not be overwhelmed. Why?

"Because the LORD is the *One* who holds [our] hand."

Let this be your anthem. Human nature will fail us at times, but God never does. No matter what happens to you today, remind yourself that God is the One who supports you.

***Fill in the blank: I will not be overwhelmed by
_____ today!***

Closer Than a Gun

✛

One who dwells in the shelter of the Most High
Will lodge in the shadow of the Almighty.

Psalm 91:1

Guest devo by Michele Potgieter
Relationship to TTF: Night to Shine host, Reni, Ukraine

My husband, Ockert, was locked in a cellar. One of the robbers held his gun to my head. He ordered me to give him all the money that we had or he would shoot me.

We sold all we had in South Africa when we came to Ukraine to be missionaries. In those years, just after the fall of communism, there were no ATMs in Ukraine. So I took the backpack with money out of our baby's stroller and handed it over. The five robbers with masks, guns, and hand grenades told me to go down in the cellar. Each step I took with the baby, I was expecting a gunshot from behind. They locked us in the cellar with these words: "We put a hand grenade on the door. If you do not leave Ukraine within twenty-four hours, we will come back and kill all of you!"

In that moment, fear came into my life. It controlled my every decision for the next five years. One day I broke down and asked God why He allowed the robbery to happen. "Where were You that night?" He answered me: *Michele, thousands of nights I had been with you, and that night I was even closer. I held you in My hand and covered you and your family under My wings. Not a hair fell from your heads, because I was with you; I protected you. It will never happen again—I am with you.* In a moment, all my fear was gone.

Twenty-five years later, though we were robbed, persecuted, falsely accused, and threatened, we are still here in the Ukraine. We may have wanted to give up, but all glory to God, for He is faithful and gives us strength every day.

How is God your shelter?

Seek and Find

✝

From there you will seek the LORD your God, and you will find Him if you search for Him with all your heart and all your soul.

Deuteronomy 4:29

Think back to when you were a kid. I'm sure you have some memory of playing hide-and-seek. You would close your eyes and count to twenty as fast as possible while everyone else ran to find cover. While counting, you would listen closely, hoping to get a mental idea of which direction people headed. Once you reached twenty, you would scream, "Ready or not, here I come!"

As silly as it may seem, in hide-and-seek, everyone knows the object of the game: Try not to get found. In our relationship with God, He's not playing a childish game. At times, you may feel like He's hiding from you or trying to avoid your presence. But that's not the truth. God is not playing hard to get or hide-and-seek. In Deuteronomy 4:7, Moses wrote, "For what great nation is there that has a god so near to it as is the LORD our God whenever we call on Him?" *Whenever we call on Him,* God is near.

Jesus reassures us of this fact during His Sermon on the Mount: "Ask, and it will be given to you; seek, and you will find; knock, and it will be opened to you. For everyone who asks receives, and the one who seeks finds, and to the one who knocks it will be opened" (Matthew 7:7–8). God promises to be with us. Period. He also promises that when we seek and search for Him, we will find Him.

As we come close to God, He is close to us (see James 4:8).
Take some time to seek His presence today.

You're on His Team

+

God is faithful, through whom you were called into fellowship
with His Son, Jesus Christ our Lord.

1 Corinthians 1:9

On March 28, 1990, the Chicago Bulls played the Cleveland Cavaliers. Michael Jordan dominated. In overtime, he led his team to a hard-fought victory, 117–113. Scoring a career high of sixty-nine points in that game, Jordan was unstoppable. It was probably one of his most legendary performances.

That night there was a lesser-known player for the Bulls, rookie Stacey King. King took four shots and missed each one. But on the fourth, he got fouled. King took two foul shots. He missed the first, but the second shot brought the familiar swish of the ball through the net, and grumbling Cavs fans to the exits. After the game, the press bombarded Michael Jordan in the locker room. As reporters crammed around the guy, trying to get a quote, someone started talking to Stacey King. At one point in the postgame commentary, King quipped, "I'll always remember this as the night that Michael Jordan and I combined to score 70 points."[57]

Really? The guy scored only one point. But in the big picture, who cares? The win was a combined effort. Michael Jordan was an extraordinary teammate to have. What would it be like to have him on your basketball team? Pretty awesome, right? When you make the decision to trust in Jesus, you've partnered with Someone greater than a stellar athlete. You're on the team of the King of the universe, who makes all things possible.

If you ever start to think your "point" doesn't matter, remember that with Jesus, it always does.

Comfort in Trials

✛

Blessed be the God and Father of our Lord Jesus Christ,
the Father of mercies and God of all comfort, who comforts us
in all our affliction so that we will be able to comfort
those who are in any affliction.

2 Corinthians 1:3–4

The apostle Paul began his second letter to the church in Corinth by stating that God is the "God of all comfort." For us, the word *comfort* may recall feelings of ease, relief, freedom, and relaxation. In America, comfort is an ideal. We worship its benefits and work hard to obtain it. But this cultural comfort never fully satisfies. In his *New American Commentary*, Dr. David E. Garland noted that

> the word "comfort ... has gone soft" in modern English. In the time of [John] Wycliffe the word was "closely connected with its root, the Latin *fortis*, which means brave, strong, courageous." The comfort that Paul has in mind has nothing to do with a languorous feeling of contentment. It is not some tranquilizing dose of grace that only dulls pains but a stiffening agent that fortifies one in heart, mind, and soul.... God's comfort strengthens weak knees and sustains sagging spirits so that one faces the troubles of life with unbending resolve and unending assurance.[58]

In God's economy, comfort is strength. It's a peace of mind in uncertainty. It's confidence despite the unknown. It's a promise that fuels endurance. In this sense, comfort means stepping into the fight, accepting the trials, and saying, "God's got this!"

**How have you experienced God's comfort
amid suffering?**

He Supplies Our Needs

✝

Look at the birds of the sky, that they do not sow, nor reap,
nor gather crops into barns, and yet your heavenly Father
feeds them. Are you not much more important than they?

Matthew 6:26

I remember on two separate occasions, while I was growing up as a missionary kid, my dad looked my mom in the eyes and told her we had no food and barely any money. In both circumstances, my parents decided to give what they had away and trust that the Lord would provide.

Both times, some family friend randomly showed up on our doorstep. One brought food because she had leftovers, and the other because she just felt that God was wanting her to bring our family a meal.

In Matthew 6:25–26, Jesus tells the crowds,

> Do not be worried about your life, as to what you will eat or what you will drink; nor for your body, as to what you will put on. Is life not more than food, and the body more than clothing? Look at the birds of the sky, that they do not sow, nor reap, nor gather crops into barns, and yet your heavenly Father feeds them. Are you not much more important than they?

Jesus's words here resonate with me. *Are we not much more important than the birds in the sky?* The answer to His rhetorical question is a resounding yes! God promises His children provision. It may not be what we have in mind, but the Lord does provide all our "needs according to His riches in glory in Christ Jesus" (Philippians 4:19).

**How does knowing God's promise of provision
give you peace today?**

Eternal Life

✛

Truly, truly, I say to you, the one who hears My word, and believes Him who sent Me, has eternal life, and does not come into judgment, but has passed out of death into life.

John 5:24

While studying for ministry, young J. Wilbur Chapman attended an event in Chicago to hear the popular evangelist Dwight L. Moody preach. As he recalls, after the event, Chapman found himself in a room, and to his great surprise, Moody came and sat beside him.

Moody asked Chapman if he was a Christian, and Chapman replied, "Mr. Moody, I am not sure whether I am a Christian or not."

Without hesitation, Moody took out his Bible and flipped to John 5:24.

Moody asked, "Do you believe it?" Chapman replied, "Yes." Moody responded with, "Are you a Christian?" Chapman said, "Mr. Moody, I sometimes think I am, and sometimes I am afraid I am not."

Very kindly, Moody stated, "Read it again." So Chapman read John 5:24 again. Then Moody repeated his two questions. Chapman's answers remained the same, which caused Moody to ask, "Whom are you doubting? Read it again."

After reading John 5:24 for the third time, tears rolled down his cheeks. Chapman finally realized he was doubting God's Word. When asked again if he was a Christian, Chapman answered, "Yes, Mr. Moody, I am."[59] On that day, J. Wilbur Chapman stopped questioning his acceptance by God. He finally believed that his salvation was secure in Christ.

Have you ever doubted your salvation like young Chapman? Be encouraged today that God does promise eternal life in heaven for those who believe.

He Will Go Before You

✝

The LORD is the one who is going ahead of you; He will be
with you. He will not desert you or abandon you.
Do not fear and do not be dismayed.

Deuteronomy 31:8

When Moses was 120 years old, he was no longer able to act as Israel's leader. God appointed Joshua to take over his position. As a consequence for Moses's unbelief, Moses was forbidden to enter the land of Canaan (see Numbers 20:1–13). However, God's plan for His people was not dependent on any one person; it was dependent upon His perfect power to fulfill His promises.

Back in Genesis 15, God made a covenant with Abram to give his offspring a specific piece of land (see verses 18–21). This land is what we often refer to as the Promised Land. Fast-forward several hundred years, and the Israelites now stood along the border of this Promised Land. The problem, however, was that the land was currently occupied by their enemies.

Despite this, in one of Moses's last public speeches, he charged Israel to be fearless and obedient because the Lord was with them (see Deuteronomy 31:6). He reminded the nation that God would destroy the Canaanite armies under Joshua's leadership and that the Israelites would enter the land as promised (see verses 3–5).

After meeting with all of Israel, Moses then gave Joshua a pep talk, part of verse 8. As daunting as the task was, Joshua could take comfort in the fact that God was going before him.

This is the same God that goes before us today.
Ask the Lord to give you comfort in this truth.

An Inheritance in Heaven

✛

Blessed be the God and Father of our Lord Jesus Christ, who
according to His great mercy has caused us to be born again to
a living hope through the resurrection of Jesus Christ from the
dead, to obtain an inheritance which is imperishable, undefiled,
and will not fade away, reserved in heaven for you.

1 Peter 1:3–4

There are two major ways we understand the word *inheritance:*

1. any money, land, or property you receive typically after
   the death of a loved one
2. a genetic trait that is passed from parent to child

In 1 Peter 1:3-4, Peter wasn't talking directly about either of those.
He was using the word *inheritance* to describe a believer's future
home in heaven. In the *Holman New Testament Commentary,* David
Walls and Max Anders noted that "Peter used a triple word picture
to describe this inheritance. Our inheritance can never perish, spoil,
or fade. These three verbal adjectives indicate that the inheritance is
untouched by death, unstained by evil, and unimpaired by time.
Our inheritance is death-proof, sin-proof, and time-proof."[60]

Aren't you glad that, according to God's great mercy, our "living
hope" is guarded, reserved, and waiting for us? No matter what happens on this side of heaven, I'm filled with joy knowing that in
Christ, nothing can undermine my and your coming inheritance.
May this promise motivate us today to continue to live out the good
works God has prepared for us.

***As we think about the glory that awaits us, let's do things
on this earth that we will talk about in heaven!***

Coming Back

✛

In My Father's house are many rooms; if that were not so, I would
have told you, because I am going there to prepare a place for you.
And if I go and prepare a place for you, I am coming again and will
take you to Myself, so that where I am, there you also will be.

John 14:2–3

While in the Upper Room during the Last Supper, Jesus informed His disciples that He was going away but made a
promise: He will come again. Although this passage has some interpretive debate among scholarly circles, the traditional understanding is that Jesus's "coming again" refers to His second coming at the
end of the age.

Now, pastors, scholars, and nearly everyone under the sun have
theories about how and when Jesus will return. But that's not what
He was talking about here. In context, as Jesus readied Himself for
His upcoming arrest, death, resurrection, and ascension, He sought
to strengthen His friends by letting them know He wasn't going to
forget about His people! In just these two verses, Jesus used "I" five
times! Count them!

This was personal for Him. He wasn't just going away and staying
away. No, Jesus's preparation was for our sake. Though the disciples
didn't understand it at the time, more than two thousand years later,
you and I get to anticipate Jesus's return and our future home.

Sure, no one except the Father knows the day or hour of Jesus's
second coming, "not even the angels of heaven," but in the meantime, may we "encourage one another and build one another up,"
just as Paul instructed (Matthew 24:36; 1 Thessalonians 5:11).

*Jesus's impending return should create a sense of urgency
in your life. How are you living in a way that makes you
ready for when He comes back?*

A Prayer of Praise

✝

Father, praise can be a churchy word, but it simply means to express admiration—feelings of wonder, respect, gratitude, and approval. You are deserving of all these things! From the rising of the sun to its setting, Your name is to be praised above all others. There is no one like You. Blessed be the name of the Lord forever and ever!

In Your name, Your character is revealed. You are my helper and comforter in times of distress. You are Abba, Father, the Creator of all. You are the Christ, Jesus, the Son of the living God, and the Savior of the world. You are El Shaddai, the Lord God Almighty. You are Jehovah Jireh, my provider. You are El Roi, the God who sees me. You are Jehovah Shalom, the very source of my peace. You are the Alpha and Omega, the Beginning and the End, the King of kings, who will reign with love from everlasting to everlasting! I bow my knees before You today. According to the riches of Your glory, strengthen me by the power of Your Spirit. May my life bring You praise.

In Jesus's name. Amen.

Based on: Psalm 47; 113; 118; Ephesians 3:14–21

Unshakable Confidence in God

✝

Rejoice in the Lord always; again I will say, rejoice!
Philippians 4:4

O ver the years, I've learned it's easy to trust when you're winning championships and everyone loves you. But when your
reality isn't worthy of a social media highlight reel, it's harder to believe that God has it all under control.

Someone I admire who always had a healthy confidence in God,
especially during the worst of times, is Paul from the Bible. He
teaches us that we can find joy and purpose in even the darkest
places. That's not only something the apostle Paul wrote about; it's
what he lived. Paul wrote the book of Philippians, a pretty cheery
book, to a group of people he loved—people he considered family.
Ironically, he was writing these encouraging words from prison.
Even more surprising, according to some scholars, he was actually
holed up in the basement sewage system of the prison.

I love how Paul launched the fourth chapter: "Rejoice in the Lord
always." I don't know how rejoiceful I would be waking up in a dun-
geon that smelled like an open garbage truck. While spending time
in my *NIV Study Bible*, I came across a footnote that substituted "ex-
pressing confidence in" for "rejoice in."[61] While imprisoned and facing the possibility of being killed for his faith at any moment, Paul
could have written about how anxious, worried, and afraid he felt.
Instead, he chose to record an expression of his unshakable confidence in God. That's a goal we all ought to strive for!

***When's the last time you put your confidence in
something other than Jesus? What was the outcome?***

J.O.Y.—Jesus Over You

✝

Rejoice always.

1 Thessalonians 5:16

Happiness and *joy* are two distinct words with different meanings. Happiness stems from an external source. It's a state of being "delighted, pleased, or glad, as over a particular thing."[62] We're happy when the sun is shining, when we get in a good workout before the workday, or if the dentist says, "No cavities," at our six-month checkup. Joy, on the other hand, is deeper. It's birthed in an internal source rather than tied to a specific situation or event. Joy is actually one of the gifts of the Holy Spirit and is found in God (see Galatians 5:22).

It's no wonder Paul told us to rejoice always. He didn't want a believer reliant on only external circumstances for joy to show up. It'd be impossible this side of heaven. I like to think of the word *joy* as an acronym that stands for Jesus Over You. When I think of joy in the context of my Lord and Savior reigning supreme over me, over the cares of this world, over my failings and shortcomings, over the scenes in my life that spur disappointment and rejection, I feel more capable of choosing it. Joy isn't something you feel. It doesn't give you goose bumps or make the little hairs on your arms stand up. The only way to choose joy—and keep choosing it—is to seek it in Jesus. He is unlike the fickle emotions we juggle or the shifting circumstances of life. He never changes. He is the same yesterday, today, and forever.

How can reading the Bible bolster your confidence in Jesus and ignite joy in your life?

Beloved, Take Heart!

+

*These things I have spoken to you so that in Me
you may have peace. In the world you have tribulation,
but take courage; I have overcome the world.*

John 16:33

Guest devo by Janice Tucker
Relationship to TTF: national legal advocate, victim advocate,
survivor leader for Her Song

When God saved me, I believed that my life would all of a sudden be problem-free. I have found myself so many times wondering where He was because things did not end up going the way I wanted them to. I began asking myself, *Am I looking for comfort and strength in the things of this world?* and *Is my joy based on my circumstances?*

I am not guaranteed a life that is without trouble on this side of heaven, but I am guaranteed the Comforter and the Helper in my time of need. I am guaranteed that Christ has conquered death and is interceding to the Father on my behalf. I am guaranteed that nothing happens outside the will of my Father in heaven. My joy is found in Christ, regardless of my circumstances or happenings. For forever, Christ is enough, and how He overcame the world is enough too.

The joy we have as believers comes from belonging to Christ, and because He has already won the ultimate victory, nothing in this world can change that. The peace that Christ provides is not of this world, nor can it be obtained void of Him. We are called to hold fast to this hope as an anchor for our souls (see Hebrews 6:19). Rest easy and trust in the sovereignty of God.

***How can you be intentional about trusting God
in all circumstances?***

God Will Do This!

✝

Commit your way to the LORD,
Trust also in Him, and He will do it.
He will bring out your righteousness as the light,
And your judgment as the noonday.

Psalm 37:5–6

Guest devo by Ken and Amy Ashley
Relationship to TTF: adoption-grant family
through Lifesong for Orphans

Have you ever started to do something that you felt God was calling you to do and then fear and anxiety set in as you began to wonder, *What if I can't do this? What if the obstacles ahead are impossible? What if this just doesn't work out?* We were in the early stages of our first adoption from China when all these questions began to keep me up at night, especially when the government briefly shut down and we needed our fingerprints to come back from the FBI for our home study.

During that first adoption, we came across the passage above, which we began to memorize and use to stamp out those fearful thoughts. It truly reminded us to trust God to act on our behalf and bring justice to our cause.

We are still clinging to these verses as we are currently in the process of our third adoption from China, temporarily on hold due to Covid-19. The waiting is hard, to say the least, but through our experiences, we have realized that when God calls us to do something, He doesn't expect for us to do it alone. We are called to commit our ways to Him, then wait on the Lord and trust Him to accomplish His purposes through us in His power and in His time, even when it seems impossible.

What is it that you need to commit to the Lord today?

It's Not Too Hard for God

✛

Behold, I am the LORD, the God of all flesh;
is anything too difficult for Me?
Jeremiah 32:27

God said the above words to the prophet Jeremiah while he was in prison. The king of Judah at the time, Zedekiah, didn't like something Jeremiah had to say, so he threw him in jail. It had to do with Jeremiah's prophecies over the nation and the king—that both would be captured and defeated by the Chaldeans. You can imagine how the devastating news bruised the king's ego.

While Jeremiah was imprisoned, the prophecy unfolded in real time. Israel was under captivity. But just as God knew what was going to happen and revealed it to Jeremiah, He also knew that one day Israel would be free and return home. God wasn't going to leave Israel captive to another army and left for dead. He had a plan. He had a purpose. And though the atmosphere was fraught with disaster and calamity, it wasn't going to stay like that forever.

What prayer have you repeated for the past few months? What question has been running through your mind and in your dreams? I don't know what your outcome will be, but I can tell you that God loves to perform the impossible. It's part of who He is. It doesn't mean He will always answer our prayers in alignment with our desires; it means He is able to do what we think is too hard. That could mean that you will get your *yes,* or it could mean that He will give you the strength you need to handle the *no* or *not now.*

**What do you need to surrender to God
and allow Him to do instead?**

He Forgives You

✛

He rescued us from the domain of darkness, and
transferred us to the kingdom of His beloved Son, in whom
we have redemption, the forgiveness of sins.

Colossians 1:13–14

Regret. *Guilt. Shame.* Those are some heavy words that make us cringe or remind us of something we know we shouldn't have done or said or watched or listened to. Those three feelings usually come about as a result of sin or falling short of where God wants us to be.

Often, we use our sin as our own reason why we can't live mission-possible lives. We've done too much of one thing or not enough of another thing, and carrying the weight of regret on our shoulders impedes forward movement. Some of the greatest blessings of choosing to trust in Jesus is what Paul wrote about in the above verse: God rescued us from darkness, and He forgives our sins.

When you repent before God, He forgives and cleanses you. And yes, it is now your responsibility to change your mind and turn away from that sin, but the fact remains that you are forgiven. When Jesus forgives you, He views you as righteous. Not that you are perfect or have finally arrived at your best life, but He looks at you through the lens of the price He paid: His death.

Don't allow leftover guilt from sin to keep you stuck or cause you to stop dreaming or believing that God can use you to do impossible (by your own standard) things. Instead, accept what He has given you so you have the confidence to share His story with others.

Is there a past relationship or event that might be keeping you from experiencing God's forgiveness?

Don't Get Rid of It

+

Do not throw away your confidence,
which has a great reward.

Hebrews 10:35

When the author of Hebrews wrote this verse, he was referring to a particular group of Christians who were throwing away their faith in Jesus and returning to their Jewish faith because Christians were being persecuted. He was begging the people of the church not to give up their faith.

We live in a consumer society. When something isn't working, has faded, or has been knocked off its first-prize pedestal for "latest and greatest," most of us get rid of it. We throw it out or maybe put it in a pile of goods we can donate if we're feeling philanthropic. If the diet hasn't worked in three days, it's on to the next one. If the relationship loses the warm fuzzies, it's time to part ways. For the early Christians addressed in Hebrews, the persecution of believers was on the rise. Some of them, in order to be more accepted into society, watered down their beliefs to conform with culture. It was easier that way. But the author of Hebrews warned them not to.

"Do not throw away your confidence," he wrote. He was talking about a vertical confidence in who Jesus is—that He is the Son of God and that He died for our sins to reconcile us back to God. If you feel like the pressure is getting too hot, don't cut bait and run. There's a reward for maintaining your confidence in Jesus: You get to live with Him and see Him face to face for eternity.

How can you feed your confidence in Christ so you hold fast to your faith and not give up?

He Is the God of Hope

✝

Hope does not disappoint, because the love of God
has been poured out within our hearts through the
Holy Spirit who was given to us.

Romans 5:5

Guest devo by Vadim Martinyuk
Relationship to TTF: Night to Shine honored guest,
Reni, Ukraine

In my childhood, I did not see and did not feel love from my parents. They traded their family for alcohol. After I was taken away to live in a boarding school, I was alone and scared, not knowing what the future held. Later, I learned that after graduating from a boarding school, since I was an orphan, I would be sent to live on a permanent basis in a nursing home. I lost hope for a happy future and took comfort in drawing and painting.

One day Jesus Christ knocked on my heart and I let Him into my life. He began to work on me. He gave me love to forgive my parents. My faith grew that my life would not be the same. I asked God in faith for a new family. Time passed and the Lord blessed me with a new family, so I didn't have to go to a nursing home. In my new home, I developed as an artist and was loved and cared for by new parents.

When I turned twenty, I hoped to get married. After several years passed, despite no one believing that anyone would fall in love with someone like me, a young man in a wheelchair, God blessed me with a loving wife and two wonderful children. Only in Him is my help! I am so grateful to God. His love and grace are with me forever.

In light of this testimony, write about a miracle
God worked in your life.

Your Best

✝

Since we have gifts that differ according to the grace given to us,
each of us is to use them properly.

Romans 12:6

Spend five minutes scrolling on your social media feed.

Look at those straight white teeth. Sigh.
That family goes on way better vacations than we do.
Another new car? Really?

Studies prove that we spend so much of our lives wishing we had what others had and disappointing ourselves in the process. When jealousy or envy or bitterness snake their way into our hearts, they can negatively control our actions, our days, and even our outlooks on life.

The science is in: Comparison makes us unhappy. A 2019 study determined that the happier people are, the less they compare themselves and their lives to others.[63] Do we really need a study to tell us that?

All your life, you've probably been told, "Be the best." I'm going to give you different advice: "Be *your* best." Stop comparing your skill, talent, job, and platform to anyone else's. Work on your gifts and talents in a way that challenges you. It's okay to desire to be the best, but it's more important to want to be *your* best. When you feel the urge to compare and contrast who you are with others, stop. Instead, practice positive self-talk. Be grateful for who God made you to be and the gifts He has equipped you with. Work on your weaknesses, and focus on your strengths.

In what areas do you need to cease striving to be the best
and focus on being your best?

Boot the Bitterness

✝

See to it that no one comes short of the grace of God;
that no root of bitterness springing up causes trouble,
and by it many become defiled.

Hebrews 12:15

Somewhere along in your life, someone you loved, someone close to you, said something hurtful to you.

- "You suck at this!"
- "Why do you keep screwing up?"
- "Can't you ever get anything right?"
- "You're just not qualified/pretty/talented/good enough."

Those words may have been uttered years ago, but they still echo in your ears today, sometimes with the same hiss of disgust as when they were said the first time. I know many athletes who have just stopped trying because someone told them they weren't good enough. Instead of honing their skill or improving areas of weakness, they shut down. Some even quit.

Are you nursing or rehearsing past commentary that served to demean or belittle you? If so, I'm sorry it happened. But I wonder if those words slipped through the gatekeeper of your heart. Maybe you're holding back on starting that new thing because someone keeps pointing out your previous failures. Maybe something your parents or an old boyfriend said keeps you from trying.

If disappointment is not processed in a healthy way, it can morph into bitterness. When we cradle the disappointment and keep feeding it, talking about it, and reminding others about it, bitterness sinks into our souls. Mission-possible living isn't possible because we've cemented ourselves in that circumstance. Instead of reciting the negativity, it might be time to let it go. Start listening instead to the God who has engraved you on the palm of His hand.

What words of disappointment are you holding on to?
What words would God say to you instead?

A Pathway for Change

✝

Was it not You who dried up the sea,
The waters of the great deep;
Who made the depths of the sea a pathway
For the redeemed to cross over?

Isaiah 51:10

Sometimes disappointment serves as an unexpected pathway that leads us toward change. Just ask Vinny.

When Vinny was twenty-six, he wanted to follow in his father's and grandfather's footsteps by becoming a minister in the Dutch Reformed Church. He became a student of theology and eventually was called to a Belgian village to serve coal miners. But Vinny was a little undignified in his approach, at least according to his superiors. He believed the best way to minister was to live as the coal miners did: poor. He sold all his possessions and slept on floors. A self-sacrificing man, Vinny served with abandon, feeding the hungry and helping whoever needed it. The dignified leaders of his denomination, however, were uncomfortable with such selfless sacrifice. In fact, they fired him. The rejection afforded him a way to work on his art. He'd been sketching local miners while he was in the ministry, and he decided to nurture the artistic ability God had blessed him with.

We know Vinny today as Vincent van Gogh, a celebrated artist whose name is revered throughout the world, though he died before being able to celebrate his success. Had this famed artist rejected the path to make art and instead buried himself under the soil of disappointment, there would be no *Starry Night* or *Irises*. God can use any closed door to open your eyes to a change of direction.

Name a disappointment in your life, past or present.
Then spend time praying over it, imagining what
pathways God had or has for you instead.

Persevere

✝

Here is the perseverance of the saints who keep
the commandments of God and their faith in Jesus.

Revelation 14:12

I am inspired by Winston Churchill, the political icon most recognized for his stellar leadership during World War II. The man is known as a wartime legend who gave rousing speeches. A lesser-known fact is the disastrous military campaign he led earlier in his career: the battle of Gallipoli. The plan was to seize control of the Dardanelles Strait and give the Allies an advantage for them to attack Constantinople and force the Ottoman Empire out of the war. But the campaign failed. Tens of thousands of Allied lives were lost. Churchill was blamed and thus demoted to the lowest seat in the cabinet. To say Churchill was disappointed would be an understatement. His wife, Clementine, lamented of her husband's failure, "I thought he would never get over the Dardanelles; I thought he would die of grief."[64]

Of course, Churchill *didn't* die from his disappointment. He persevered. Six months after his demotion, Churchill resigned from his cabinet position and joined the war in France as an infantry officer. He took time to reflect and think of his disappointment as a learning opportunity, all while serving his country and others.

Disappointment has a way of following us around. When our expectations, of ourselves and of God, don't match reality, the disconnect is, well, disappointing. It's not always easy to get over an unmet expectation or a sucker punch we never imagined would swing our way. But we do have the choice, like Churchill, to reframe the experience as an opportunity to grow and persevere.

***What is a choice you can make this week
about responding to an unmet expectation in your life?***

Don't Let It Define You

✝

Certainly there is a future,
And your hope will not be cut off.

Proverbs 23:18

Lewis and Clark weren't the first explorers to cross America from east to west. Fourteen years earlier, in 1789, a Scottish fur trader named Alexander Mackenzie achieved this mission in search of the Northwest Passage. He hoped this elusive waterway would flow into the Pacific Ocean via an inlet in southern Alaska. If so, it would open up a new trade route to China and make him a ton of money. Traveling on the river for 1,200 miles, he never found the Northwest Passage. He did, however, reach the Arctic Ocean by a river he named Disappointment River for obvious reasons. Later renamed the Mackenzie River, it's the second-longest river in North America, as well as a major trade route.

Mackenzie didn't find what he was looking for, but he discovered something else. And he labeled that new thing by what he assumed was a past failure.

Think about your own life. As you navigate through your own exploration and create a life that counts, are you allowing previous disappointments to affect your present? Are you so attached to that failure that you are letting it define what may lie ahead?

Yes, it hurt. It was hard. It was unfair. But you don't have to let what happened impose its shadow on what could be.

**What failures in your past are you still allowing
to define your present?**

Why Me? Why *Not* Me?

✝

The LORD is my light and my salvation;
Whom shall I fear?
The LORD is the strength of my life;
Of whom shall I be afraid?

Psalm 27:1, NKJV

Guest devo by Jana Watts
Relationship to TTF: mother of W15H recipient who is with Jesus

When our daughter Chelsie was diagnosed with appendix cancer at the age of seventeen, many asked the question *Why?* But Chelsie asked a different question: *Why not me?* Watching our daughter battle this disease for four years was agonizing. But seeing her faith unfold through much pain and suffering, seeing others find Jesus, was what this journey was all about, even if our prayers were not answered the way we wanted.

Sometimes we envision how we expect things to turn out but that's not how they go. Sometimes we make well-intentioned plans, only to have them fall apart.

Know that even in these times, God is working things out on your behalf with His best for you in mind. He sees the big picture, and He knows what's right and what's wrong for you in certain seasons of your life.

If today you find yourself in a place you never expected to be, don't get discouraged. This is where God wants you to be. He chose you! You don't have to understand it. You don't have to know the answer. You just need to trust Him in it. He will never let you down.

Reach out and up and hold on to God, and when you do, you'll discover that He has been holding you all along.

How has your journey unfolded in unexpected ways?
Thank God for what He has chosen for you,
and pray for trust in His plan.

A Prayer for Contentment
✝

Lord, it's easy to always want the next best thing or what someone else has. The new phone, the new shoes, new clothing, the cool car, the big house, more likes, and so on. Everyone could make a list of things they want, whether physical, mental, spiritual, or emotional. I confess, I have been feeling discontent about _____.

Forgive me, God. Teach me to be like Paul, who said, "I have learned to be content in whatever circumstances I am." Eliminate my desire to compare. Help me focus on who You've made me to be and what I do have. I don't want to chase happiness; I want to run after You, the God who brings peace and never breaks His promises.

I understand that contentment does not equal complacency or laziness. It means to be truly satisfied because I have everything I need. God, You are all I need.

Thank You for Your continuous provision. Thank You for never failing or abandoning Your children. I pray that fame, greed, money, and possessions never become idols in my life. You are enough. You owe me nothing, yet You've given me everything! May I be motivated by the gospel today.

In Jesus's precious name. Amen.

Based on: Philippians 4:11–13; 1 Corinthians 2:2; Hebrews 13:5; 1 Timothy 6:6–7

The Measure of Excellence

✝

You are a chosen people, a royal priesthood, a holy nation,
a people for God's own possession, so that you may proclaim
the excellencies of Him who has called you out of
darkness into His marvelous light.

1 Peter 2:9

What is excellence to you? Many people equate excellence with success. They look at themselves in terms of their achievements and goals. They rely on accomplishments and the things they have done to tell them how good they are.

As Christians, though, our worth is not in what we have done but in what Christ has done for us. Through His sacrifice on the cross and our belief in Him, we are set aside as God's own possession. We have achieved the greatness of eternal life not through our work but through His. In this, now, we ought to pursue excellence.

Excellence has far more to do with your character than with your accomplishments. Coming from the Greek word *arete*, which means "moral goodness or virtue,"[65] excellence is about the way you act, not the things you do. This means that excellence must encompass your whole life.

We live with excellence not to show how wonderful we are but to proclaim the goodness of God. Our aim as Christians is to make the name of Jesus known, not our own name. Remember the measure of excellence as you pursue it. You have already been called worthy by God. Now go and live in a way that reflects His character.

In what areas of your life do you want to
pursue excellence?

Faithful Stewardship

✛

*If the willingness is present, it is acceptable according to what
a person has, not according to what he does not have.*

2 Corinthians 8:12

R emember that parable Jesus told about three servants in Matthew 25? The first was given ten talents to manage, the second,
five talents, and the third, one talent. Each servant was given exactly
what he could handle. When their master asked to see what became
of their original portions, the first two servants reportedly doubled
the investment. However, the third, though he had the smallest
portion and therefore the least risk, only hid his share, in the name
of keeping it safe. His master, angry with the servant, declared him
unfaithful with his portion.

What has God given you to work with? It may be tempting to
look at what others have and neglect to care for what He has given
you to manage, especially if it seems that others have more. Excellence is being and doing your personal best. It's working with what
you have, as the servants were required to do. We are all in different
situations in life. We have different limitations and are expected to
work within them. The goal is not to do everything perfectly but
to give of what we have.

If you have time, give it. If you have a talent, offer it. If all you can
do is offer genuine prayers, then offer those. Don't look around you
to the other people. God works through our obedience, not our
abundance.

**How can you be a faithful steward of
whatever you have today?**

Whatever You Do

✝

Whatever your hand finds to do, do it with all your might.

Ecclesiastes 9:10

Sometimes people believe that the only things worth excelling at are the things that others can see. You can't save excellence for the big game. Although nobody can see the training or the practice, if you don't give your all in the things you don't think matter, it won't have the same effect at the big event.

Whatever you do—on the field or off the field—do it for the glory of God. When you study for an exam, do it for the glory of God. When you practice your instrument, do it for the glory of God. Even in the things so mundane as eating or drinking, do it all for the glory of God.

Sometimes we get so caught up in proving our excellence to others and showing off what we can do that we forget that God sees everything. The hard work that we put into training and practice isn't what others notice, but He sees it all. Don't disregard the small stuff while waiting for big events in life in which to pursue excellence. Make it a life habit, knowing that the everyday, routine moments of life matter just as much as the major ones.

Are you pursuing excellence in the mundane
areas of life? How can you work on that?

Keep Your Standards High

✝

Be diligent to present yourself approved to God
as a worker who does not need to be ashamed,
accurately handling the word of truth.

2 Timothy 2:15

King Darius's high officials had a vendetta against Daniel, who was placed in a position of authority by the king (see Daniel 6). In order to have him removed, they tried so hard to find something wrong with him, but they could not. He was responsible and faithful even though he did not believe the same things as the king he worked for.

What others did around him mattered less to Daniel than how he would act. He held himself up to a greater standard—a God standard. Though others hated him, they had to find a loophole to condemn him because, aside from their opinion, he was so respectable that they could not find any fault with him. Eventually, Daniel was thrown in the lions' den for his faith, but while he was there, God protected him.

Even when it's not popular, be the best you God has called you to be. Set your standards high. Worry less about what others are doing or what they think of you, and focus more on pursuing your mission-possible life with excellence. It may be hard, but your character will speak for itself, and no matter what happens, God will be with you as you remain obedient to Him, just as He was with Daniel.

**Daniel was unique because he was willing to be.
Would others say that you are different?**

Keep Showing Up

✟

My beloved brothers and sisters, be firm, immovable,
always excelling in the work of the Lord, knowing that
your labor is not in vain in the Lord.

1 Corinthians 15:58

Hard days will come. People will try your patience. What you work for won't happen the way you hoped it would. Your character will inevitably be tested at some point. When that day comes and you want to give up and stop pursuing excellence, just keep showing up.

Life happens and you're human. You may grow weary and depleted, drained of all your natural resources, unsure of what you may be able to give anymore, but remember why you are running. Remember your purpose. God has called you to bring glory not to yourself but to Him. To keep showing up means going to Jesus exactly as you are, allowing His spirit to continually transform you.

Having grit is more than just pressing through in our strength; it's relying on the strength that God gives us when we have no more. We are instructed to be firm and immovable in what we do. Instead of succumbing to the circumstances around you, remain steady in Jesus. Show up even when it's the last thing you feel like doing. Allow Him to work through you to do what He has called you to do. In time, you will see that none of this labor was in vain.

How will you show up today?

No Overnight Successes

✝

The soul of the lazy one craves and gets nothing,
But the soul of the diligent is made prosperous.

Proverbs 13:4

Doctors spend eight or more years studying for their degrees. Athletes spend all year training to get ready for the sports season. The world never sees the time and energy people devote to their crafts. Long before I won the Heisman Trophy, I practiced in the middle of the night while nobody was watching. I didn't get to the point of winning without all the hard work that came before it. It takes work to achieve excellence.

In a culture driven by instant gratification and the desire for sudden success, it is often lost on many people that to achieve greatness, you must work hard first. It takes months and years of training, practice, learning, and growing to become an "overnight" success. The road contains twists and turns and some potholes you can't just swerve over to avoid.

Pursuing excellence costs something. You can't just desire to be excellent and expect it to happen. You must work for it. You must work toward it. Laziness gets you nowhere.

If hard work is required to achieve success in most areas of life, how much more would it take for your character to develop into the one God intends for you? Waking up and deciding to be morally good or virtuous is challenging at best. You need the Holy Spirit to dwell inside you if you ever dream of getting to that point.

**Are you working toward your goals or
simply hoping everything will fall into place?**

Pace Yourself

✝

Those who wait for the LORD
Will gain new strength; . . .
They will run and not get tired.

Isaiah 40:31

When you start living a mission-possible life, it's easy to get caught up in the excitement of living out your God-given purpose. At first, you run on momentum, but soon it begins to dwindle and you wonder if you are well trained for this pursuit. That's when the exhaustion kicks in. Tired and out of breath, you may just want to slow down or even quit.

In your pursuit of excellence, it's not about starting strong but about keeping a manageable pace. If you were going to start a sprint, momentum is great for getting you to the end. But in a marathon, it's important to keep a steady speed. Too much sprinting in the first mile will affect how you run in the next twenty-five miles.

Marathoners train diligently for their races and teach their bodies to manage the distance with longevity and speed. We can also train ourselves. Isaiah tells us that the ones who run without growing weary are the ones who wait on the Lord. When you pursue excellence, you don't crawl at a snail's pace either, but you chase it steady until it is yours. If you are getting tired of running, it may be time to readjust your focus. Look to the Lord and wait on Him to renew your strength. He will refresh you and replenish you so that you can continue doing what He has called you to do.

***Are you out of momentum? What does
waiting for the Lord look like for you today?***

The Blessing of the Sabbath

✝

In six days the LORD made the heavens and the earth,
the sea and everything that is in them, and He rested on the
seventh day; for that reason the LORD blessed the
Sabbath day and made it holy.

Exodus 20:11

When the Israelites were commanded to remember the Sabbath, they were given a picture of the creation account. God rested on the seventh day after creating the world in six days, and they were to follow that model. Rest is a command, but it must follow work. Work first; rest next.

Have you ever tried relaxing when you know that you have work that you should be doing? You sit back and try to enjoy yourself, but something constantly nags at you. The whole time, you try to suppress it and avoid the things you know you have going on, and it leaves you sluggish instead of replenished. Rest without work is laziness, and it is difficult to come out of it. Work must come before rest because there needs to be a reason to rest.

This isn't about earning the right to rest. Rest is a command, not a privilege. It's not about completing a job before resting, because some jobs never end. It's about realizing that there is an order we need to follow. God rested on the seventh day after doing work; therefore, we should rest after doing the work that's in front of us.

Work with purpose. If today is a day for work, do your work. Go at it with all your might until your time for rest comes again.

***In what ways do you struggle with
balancing work and rest?***

Rest Is a Command

✛

Remember the Sabbath day, to keep it holy.

Exodus 20:8

The Israelites were enslaved in Egypt for more than four hundred years. They had to labor for others, toiling according to those people's schedules and commands. They didn't get overtime pay or vacation days. There was no time for a break, let alone a steady weekend. Work had to be done, quotas had to be met, and it was up to them to do it.

But when God led the Israelites out of Egypt and through the Red Sea, He had a different idea for them. In the fourth of the Ten Commandments He gave them at Mount Sinai, the Israelites were commanded to set aside a regular day of rest: the Sabbath. This was an intentional time to get away from the busyness of life and focus on God, dedicating the day to worshipping Him.

Rest is a command. It's necessary. I struggle with resting. Sometimes to me, resting means *missing out* on the mission, but recently I've come to realize that resting *fuels* me for the mission. We live in a hectic world of hurrying and hustling, trying to get everything done that we possibly can, but God called us to live a different way. We're not meant to treat rest as a convenience to get around to. It's a command, just the same as "You shall not lie." By honoring a time of rest from our normal day-to-day routine and keeping the time holy, we bring glory to God.

Rest isn't for the weak; it's for the obedient. Make it a point to set aside intentional time this week to focus on God and simply enjoy the good things He has given you.

What does rest look like for you today?

Know When to Take a Break

✛

[Jesus] said to them, "Come away by yourselves to a secluded place
and rest a little while." (For there were many people coming
and going, and they did not even have time to eat.)

Mark 6:31

Have you ever felt overwhelmed by the load you carry? You work hard, do a lot, and begin to sacrifice sleep. Your mood shows it. Your body knows it. You get edgy or cranky and you're suddenly exhausted. You're physically run-down from overexerting yourself.

Even when you're living a mission-possible life and going after what God has called you to do, taking a rest is necessary. Jesus told the disciples to find a secluded place and restore their energy after they had received hard news. There was a moment when they couldn't go on, and to have new strength, they had to replenish their vitality.

If all I do is go to the gym every single day to work out for hours, I haven't gained any muscle. To reap any benefit from my work, I need to allow for proper rest days. Those are the days when the microtears in muscles heal so that they can become stronger than they were before. The rest days are just as important as the workdays.

Living a mission-possible life is impossible without purposeful rest. Don't be a hamster running on a wheel. Know when to take a break. After a brief respite, you give yourself the opportunity to wake up refreshed, prepared for a new set of tasks and whatever God has for you that day.

Take an inward look at your attitudes and actions.
Where would a break be helpful?

Stop Striving to Do
What Only God Can

✛

Stop striving and know that I am God;
I will be exalted among the nations, I will be exalted on the earth.

Psalm 46:10

Throughout my life, I've tried to work hard at whatever I'm doing—not only for the sake of working hard but for the sake of doing my best and being my best. See, I believe that when you care so much about something, you'll do whatever it takes to accomplish it. Call it what you will—drive, passion, self-motivation—but there's never been a day in my life when I've wanted to settle for mediocrity. However, there's another side of this coin.

Trainers have told me that my body has lived in a state of fatigue, which is what I thought was my normal. This worked against me at times. Overtraining without rest can be detrimental. With every training session I put in without adequate rest, I placed more strain on my body. While I don't mind the hustle and grind, what I've come to realize is that without rest, there is no recovery.

If we are pumped to live a mission-possible life and then decide to do all the heavy lifting ourselves, we'll end up taking on too much of a load and it may crush us.

In this verse, the Bible tells us to stop striving and to recognize that God is God. We are not Him. We are not as strong, capable, or knowledgeable as He is. Wherever you might be striving to do things only He can, take a step back and allow God to step in. Trust Him to do what only He can.

**What areas in your life do you need to step back
from and let God control?**

Don't Miss the Point

✦

Jesus said to them, "The Sabbath was made for man,
and not man for the Sabbath."

Mark 2:27

There was a man who was blind from birth. He would sit outside the temple and beg for money. One day Jesus walked by and His disciples asked Him why this man was blind. He declared that it was so the glory of God could be revealed. After Jesus spit on the ground to make mud, rubbed it on the man's eyes, and had him wash in the pool of Siloam, he could see! Everyone was amazed. Well, almost everyone. (See John 9:1–3, 6–7.)

The Pharisees had one issue about this healing. It happened on the Sabbath. According to Jewish tradition, to honor the fact that God himself rested on the seventh day of the creation, Jews abstained from every kind of labor from sunset Friday to sunset Saturday. This included lifting, plowing, hunting, and tying knots. Even writing more than one letter on the Sabbath was forbidden![66]

So, when Jesus healed this man, the Pharisees considered it unlawful work. But they missed the point. In their attempt to honor and worship God, they began to worship man's rules. The point of biblical rest is to be attentive to God—to use the time to spiritually recover and be ready to go at it again.

Whatever your rest looks like, be sensitive to the Lord and whatever He wants to show you.

***How do you best rest with the Lord to keep you
moving forward in your mission?***

Rest While You Work

✝

Take My yoke upon you and learn from Me, for I am gentle
and humble in heart, and you will find rest for your souls.

Matthew 11:29

When we bring our burdens to Jesus, He invites us into rest. However, at the same time, He tells us to take His yoke upon us.

A yoke is a device that connects two animals together at their shoulders and is attached to a plow. In a field, two oxen are paired together to work—usually a stronger one to do the heavy lifting, and a weaker one to learn the trade. Jesus invites us to take His yoke upon us, and He makes the burden light. He calls us to do His work, but He does the heavy lifting. He remains next to us, continually guiding us and enabling us to go forward and further in our mission.

There is work because we are called to do whatever God asks of us. But there is also rest because Jesus takes the heaviness of the burden away from us as we follow His lead. When we allow Him to lead, He does so with compassion and sensitivity to our humanity.

When we work from our own strength, we are at risk of overdoing it or burning out. But when we lay down all our burdens before Jesus, He gives us work according to our abilities and does the rest in *His* ability. Rest with Jesus has a unique relationship, but since He is with us, we are able to accomplish it.

What burdens do you need to lay before Jesus today?

True Rest

✝

There remains a Sabbath rest for the people of God.

Hebrews 4:9

When we talk about rest, we don't mean vegging out on the couch and binging Netflix. Rest can be sitting outside for ten minutes. It can be a getaway weekend with your spouse or reading a book you like before you go to bed. Although it can sometimes mean mindless entertainment, there's more to rest than that. Rest should replenish, restore, and ready us for what's next. It is a sweet gift given to us by God, and it should feel that way. But rest is not limited to our physical nature.

The author of Hebrews tells us that there is a deeper rest that awaits us as people of God. When we invite Jesus to come into our lives and become our Lord and Savior, we receive rest for our souls. We don't have to work to earn the favor of God, because He gives us grace, favor that we could never earn.

When we accept the true rest that the Lord offers us, we become secure in Him and can live from the overflow of His love. With no need to earn His grace, we are free to live out our calling without shame and without bondage. Invite Jesus into your day and ask Him for His grace where you need it most. Rest is available, and He freely gives to all who ask.

**In what areas of your life
do you need true spiritual rest today?**

A Prayer for Rest

✝

Lord, help me rest as I should. Life seems to never slow down and I just try to keep up! Rushing from one thing to the next, it's hard to stop and be still. My to-do list is never-ending. My attention is being pulled in various directions. I confess, I get caught up in the busyness of my day and neglect our time together.

I come before You, weak and burdened. Lead me beside quiet waters and let me lie down in Your green pasture. Restore my soul, God, and guide me down the path of righteousness, for You are my shepherd, who takes care of me. It is You who breathes life into my nostrils. It is You who gives me eternal hope. You alone are my rock, my salvation, and my fortress. When my heart is empty, my mind overwhelmed, and my muscles sore, remind me of Your gentle and humble Spirit. Thank You for loving me! May I rest in Your peace today.

In Jesus's name. Amen.

Based on: Psalm 46:10; Matthew 11:28–30; Psalm 23:1–3; 62:5–6; John 5:24

What Do You Want to Leave Behind?

✦

*Do not store up for yourselves treasures on earth, where moth
and rust destroy, and where thieves break in and steal.*

Matthew 6:19

Having the opportunity to be an ambassador of the Heisman Trophy, as well as becoming a part of the Heisman family, has been a great honor of my life. Still, this achievement did not define my life.

Everybody has their own definition of legacy. For some people, it could mean racking up a certain amount and kind of possessions, having a wing of a hospital or renowned building named after them, or crossing off items on an ambitious bucket list. For me, a legacy well lived is about leaving a big impact on as many people as I am able to come in contact with before I'm called to heaven. That is my goal.

What about you? Talking about your legacy may seem a bit morbid, as it touches on the end of a lifetime, but that fact is something that must be faced. It's never too late, or too early, to start thinking about what you want to leave behind when you exit this world. A legacy is not something that is created by accident; it is built on purpose.

*Think of someone who has left a precious legacy for you
through their character, actions, or commitment to God.
What has that meant for you, and why?*

A Legacy of Love

✛

If anyone loves Me, he will follow My word;
and My Father will love him, and We will come to him
and make Our dwelling with him.

John 14:23

When we think of leaving behind a legacy, it is often measured in material ways. A significant amount of money. A trophy or medal. What if instead of drawing from an impressive list of shoulds, we approached each day by emulating the character of God? And if in each day, as we intentionally walked in love, in who God is, we began to leave lasting footprints simply because of whose we are?

One of the best pieces of advice I can give in how to leave a legacy of a mission-possible life is to love what God loves. What are some of the things He loves?

- the world (see John 3:16)
- "justice" (Psalm 37:28)
- "a cheerful giver" (2 Corinthians 9:7)
- "sinners" (Romans 5:8)
- those who love Him (see Proverbs 8:17)

At times, we complicate life to the point that it paralyzes us from making any forward movement. We seem to think that only the grandest of gestures matter, that bigger is always better, and that our efforts are worthy only if they affect a thousand people as opposed to the one. Don't believe these lies. Stick with the basics. Love what God loves.

*How does what you just read change your vision
of what a mission-possible life looks like?*

Giving Always Wins

+

There is one who scatters, and yet increases all the more,
And there is one who withholds what is justly due, and yet
it results only in poverty.

Proverbs 11:24

The idea that giving is better than receiving is a widely held belief, even by many who do not follow Christ. Giving brings the giver joy—a sense of loving, honoring, or serving another well. Still, for the Christian, it is even more than this. When we consider the One who sacrificed Himself so we could have life eternal, we begin to view generosity in a wholly different light.

The gift offered to us in Jesus's death and resurrection guarantees our freedom and our place with Him in heaven for all eternity. Because He gave His life, we have freedom from lasting punishment, freedom from an eternal death, and freedom from hell itself. We have an opportunity to leave a lasting legacy because Jesus was willing to face that which only He could defeat.

It is from this place of assuredness that we can freely give our time, our treasures, and our hearts to others because He first gave us His. As we do, we will find both a purpose and a joy we could not have otherwise known. And this purpose and joy can live on longer than our act itself, as an example of the greatest Giver Himself.

Ask the Holy Spirit to put someone in your path who needs something you can give. Who knows how the Lord will speak to another person today through your generosity!

Who in your life needs a helping hand, a listening ear,
or maybe just a few words of encouragement?
Make it happen!

Weigh Your Dailies

✦

Teach us to number our days,
That we may present to You a heart of wisdom.
Psalm 90:12

When you live mission possible, you are investing in eternity. That means the choices you make today will have an impact tomorrow. One of the biggest ways we see this in action is how we spend our time.

Personally, I don't do things that I don't care about. I don't endorse brands that I don't believe in or binge-watch TV shows every time I have a break. I'm highlighting the big picture of what we do with the time we have. You don't have to be a genius to discover that our time on earth is limited. As a result, I choose my priorities based on the convictions that God has put on my heart. I want to be the person who follows through on those convictions with my conscious decisions.

We all live no more and no less than twenty-four hours daily, yet how we use those hours is contingent on our conscious decisions. Are you willing to sacrifice a few nights of socializing or a season of your favorite show to reach your next goal? Start thinking about the legacy you want your life to manifest, and then make it happen.

How can you better measure and influence
your daily affairs so they have more of
a positive impact on eternity?

Pass It On

+

We will not conceal them from their children,
But we will tell the generation to come the praises of the LORD,
And His power and His wondrous works that He has done.

Psalm 78:4

Psalm 78, written by Asaph, is known as a wisdom psalm. He opened this song by begging the people to listen to his words. He began by sharing the story of Israel's exodus from Egypt—how God cared for them while they circled the desert for forty years and then finally entered the Promised Land, as well as how they repeatedly put God to the test and misused His grace. In this psalm, the writer encouraged the reader to share these stories with future generations.

In this age of instant communication, we can exchange information within seconds, whether we are endorsing our favorite product, highlighting a photo from our vacation, or videoconferencing with a client. In ancient Israel, there were no memes or Bible verses posted on social media. Stories were not read from books but told orally. While I'm a huge fan of technology and the advances that have been made through the years, I can't help but feel we've lost some of the art of conversation—of intimate connection.

One of the best ways to share your legacy is simply to tell your story one on one, face to face. Sure, you can reach many people by doing so on social media, but don't forget about the value of sharing your story in person. You may find it encourages not just the person you're sharing with but also yourself.

How have the faith stories of others influenced your life?

What's Your Story?

✛

Always [be] ready to make a defense to everyone who asks you
to give an account for the hope that is in you.
1 Peter 3:15

A person's story is a powerful and effective evangelism tool. You might think that yours is boring or irrelevant. God disagrees. You are one of a kind. Out of the almost eight billion people living on this earth, your experiences are unique to only you. No one— past, present, or future—has lived or will ever live your life. That's pretty significant!

Today's verse reminds us that we must have a reason for the hope that's within us. An excellent way to prepare yourself is to write down your story. If you've never done that before, I'm here to help you. I've listed a few questions below to give you a head start. Instead of reflecting on one question at the end of the devotional, I'd like you to grab a pen and paper and then use the following prompts to help you write your story of going to and living for Jesus.

- What was your life like before Christ? Describe your attitude, habits, relationships, and so on.
- How and when did you choose to follow Him? Or if you have not made that decision yet, what keeps you from following Him?
- How has your life changed since making that decision?
- How do you see God using you now and in the future?

Don't get hung up on the details of your story. One thing and one thing alone matters most: Jesus. It's His power in you that makes the difference, not the scenes in your story or your storytelling skills.

Character Fruits

✛

The fruit of the Spirit is love, joy, peace, patience, kindness,
goodness, faithfulness, gentleness, self-control;
against such things there is no law.

Galatians 5:22–23

It's said that our character is best defined by what we do when no one is looking. True, but the Bible defines it as much more. It is a life that overflows with love, joy, peace, patience, kindness, goodness, faithfulness, gentleness, and self-control. It is exemplified in its most full and perfect form only in the person of Jesus Christ. We begin to shape our character for good when we offer our lives in full surrender to Him. It is found in denying ourselves and picking up our cross and in saying no daily to the things that are not of Him and yes to His plans and purpose for us.

In Galatians, the apostle Paul teaches us that living in the Spirit of God will result in our seeing the fruit of that relationship in our lives. This doesn't happen the instant we make the decision to trust in Jesus; it happens over time as we continue to serve, love, and trust Him.

One of the best channels through which character is formed is trials. When we accept hardships and go through them powered by God's strength instead of our willpower, abilities, or unhealthy dependencies that numb the pain, we give God access and permission to mold us as we aim to become more and more like Jesus. A mission-possible life is evidenced not only by what you do for God but also by who you are becoming in Him.

*Describe a season of your life that
has been very fruitful.*

One-Up Each Other with Love

✝

Let love be genuine. Abhor what is evil; hold fast to
what is good. Love one another with brotherly affection.
Outdo one another in showing honor.

Romans 12:9–10, ESV

Guest devo by Kris and Aundrea Whitmire
Relationship to TTF: adoption-aid recipients

While growing up, did you ever have a brother, sister, friend, or even childhood nemesis you always competed with? Regardless of what you did, they were always trying to one-up you, and likewise you one-up them?

The Bible commands us to do something that sparks competition: "Outdo one another in showing honor." Here, Paul was telling the church in Rome that they should not just simply honor or respect each other but rather that they should go so far as to try to one-up each other in doing so. This isn't to be a competition for competition's sake, though. The previous verse states, "Let love be genuine." This tells us that if we genuinely love one another, we'll eagerly and intentionally look for opportunities to honor one another more.

This can come in a variety of ways. We can give up our seats at Sunday-morning service. We can provide a meal to a family (without being asked). We can watch a young couple's children so they can have an evening alone. We can disciple a new Christian who may not have much of a support system. These are just a few of the myriad ways we can honor and love one another. We just need to choose to do so. We must be intentional.

How can you choose to be intentional in honoring
someone else this week in a way that truly
demonstrates your love for them?

Forgive Because God Forgave You

✛

Do not be grieved or angry with yourselves because you
sold me here, for God sent me ahead of you to save lives.

Genesis 45:5

J oseph's story in the Bible is an apt illustration of forgiveness. Tossed
into a pit by his own brothers, sold into slavery, and falsely imprisoned, he had a long history of facing what seemed like impossible
situations. After God had restored him to a place of prominence and
honor, Joseph found himself in an interesting position. When nearly
all of Egypt faced a severe famine, his very brothers who had abandoned him and left him for dead were in danger of starvation. The
tables had turned.

We can only imagine the internal struggle Joseph may have felt
knowing that he was able to save those who had hurt him most. But
because he had continually trusted in God, he chose to extend the
grace that God had already extended to him. Knowing that God had
caused all things (even the terrible ones) to somehow come together
for good, he was able to not only forgive those who had hurt him
but also provide for them in their time of need.

When we strive to live like Jesus, we can do the hard things, like
forgive. However, just to be clear, while forgiveness is a command,
not every situation demands reconciliation as it was appropriate to
do in Joseph's case. If you are in a situation where the poison of bitterness is beginning to seep into your spirit, stop and take a breath.
Forgive, but don't do it for the offender; do it for yourself and because God has forgiven you.

***Is there someone in your life who needs
not only your forgiveness but also your help?***

Honor What God Honors

✝

Everyone who exalts himself will be humbled,
and the one who humbles himself will be exalted.

Luke 14:11

In Luke 14, we read about Jesus being at a dinner with friends. In classic observant fashion, He noticed how quickly the guests, including His beloved disciples, picked out their seats. They were strategic in this, purposely choosing to sit in the best places—the places of honor. In those days, where you sat reflected your degree of importance. The guests at the dinner that day were consciously trying to exalt themselves over the other guests.

Jesus suggested a better alternative; in fact, He offered two suggestions. First, He recommended, if you're at a wedding, not taking the seat of honor in case the host has the seat reserved for someone else. If you do and must be booted out, you will be embarrassed. "So, take the last place," he said, "and the host might offer you a better seat" (see verse 10). Then he delivered the timeless wisdom that humility brings exaltation and not the other way around.

Often, we're quick to honor what we think is important. Many times, that's ourselves. We decide what we deserve, when we need a promotion, when it's time to level up, and who belongs in our circle. Self-centeredness is damaging to a mission-possible life. Jesus, divine in flesh, showed us how to live with humility. Let us emulate His example and allow our Father in heaven to exalt us how and when He chooses.

***What is the difference between a false sense
of humility and the sincere kind that
Jesus is referring to in this passage?***

Know You and Trust God

+

One who trusts in his own heart is a fool.

Proverbs 28:26

I'll never forget one time I was scheduled to give a talk that I wasn't *totally* prepared for. I knew the gist of what I wanted to say, but I didn't have the time I needed to get a feel for the audience.

Fifteen minutes into my speech, I began to feel disappointed in myself. I didn't think what I was saying was coming across powerfully. I remember staring into the crowd of ten thousand people—young, old, male, female, some who had physical disabilities or suffered from serious medical conditions. I wanted so desperately to give them hope through my message but felt I was failing miserably. Then, at that fifteen-minute mark, God took over my babble. I felt Him saying, "Timmy, remember why you are here. It's not about how or what you say; it's about having a heart for these people like I do." In other words, I had to step aside.

When we think we have power in our words alone, they will fall flat. If God's power is in and speaks through us, however, the words we speak will never fail. I ended the talk by giving an invitation to whoever wanted to trust in Jesus. Hundreds came forward and were prayed for and encouraged by volunteers.

I stepped into this event knowing God but trusting me instead of knowing me and trusting God. When I remembered that the message wasn't about me, He took my average and my pride and still brought many people to Him. We serve a big God who will use what we give Him that stands in our way and turn it around for His glory.

Where do you need to step aside and let God take over?

Go Back to the Well

✝

Seek the LORD and His strength;
Seek His face continually.
1 Chronicles 16:11

G oing back to the well, or remembering who you are in Christ, is important to do when distractions run wild or when we get caught up in what Charles Hummel has termed the "tyranny of the urgent." We become so intertwined in what we need to get done or what is consuming our emotions that our internal charge falls flat. No matter how solid our character, we all need spiritual renewal.

Our faith in what God says about us seeps into everything we do. So, when we're feeling down, stressed, tired, or unmotivated, we can trust that God has us where we are for a reason, even when things seem dull or crazed.

When we've lost our motivation, we need to look back and remember what created our motivation in the first place. This is a spiritual practice. Instead of reminding yourself of your own highlight reels—like your accomplishments, your successes, or the awesome things others have said about you—there's a better way to ignite your momentum.

Look back and remember. Remember how God was faithful then, and remind yourself that He will continue to be. Looking back and remembering is not about living in the past; it's about using our past experiences to drive us forward.

Tell yourself to take a break from thinking about the possibilities of what might happen or how things could turn out. Instead, focus on a past moment of your life where you know you saw God show up. Then remind yourself that He is the God who never changes.

Bring Out the Best in Others

✝

Imitate me, just as I imitate Christ.

1 Corinthians 11:1, NLT

We develop our character over time, usually through the process of making wise choices when no one is looking. A sign of godly character is when your public face matches your private face.

Do you know what I love about how humanity is designed? In everything we do, we have a chance to influence. In fact, one of the greatest things we can do in life is influence other people for the better. Like Paul, who wrote the above verse, I want to bring out the best in others, from those who are closest to me to those I meet for the first time. I want people's lives to be better because they know me.

I believe that every time we meet someone, it very rarely ends in neutral. Their experience of us is either positive or negative. Think about the people you encounter in your own life. Reflect on some of the most encouraging or inspiring connections you have made, whether they've lasted a few days or a few years. What was it that the person said or did that sparked growth, made you aware of a bad habit you've been trying to conceal, or gave you the leverage you needed to persevere in your faith?

What we say and what we do is attached to purpose and value. Just as we follow in the footsteps of Christ, may we live in such a way that we can brighten another person's darkest day.

Tell someone they have made
a difference in your life.

Putting It All on the Line

+

After we had already suffered and been treated abusively
in Philippi, as you know, we had the boldness in our God to speak
to you the gospel of God amid much opposition.

1 Thessalonians 2:2

Tied 7–7 at halftime, I knew that to win the 2009 BCS National Championship game against the number one Oklahoma Sooners, we had to play better football. Busting through the locker room huddle, I told my Florida teammates,

> We got thirty minutes for the rest of our lives. Thirty minutes for the rest of our lives. That's our bad in the first half. It ain't happening. We get the ball, I promise you one thing: We're going to hit somebody, and we're taking it down the field for a touchdown. I guarantee you that. Let's go!

We had trained all season for this game. We believed we were the better team, but our play was not showing it. My challenge to the guys before we stepped back out onto the field was essentially, "For thirty more minutes, let's *put it all on the line!* Let's give it all we got!"

As I think about that game—and my sports career in general—I realize there have been so many times when I've sacrificed, worked harder, or had to dig a little deeper for the sake of sports. But how many times have I been willing to put it all on the line for Jesus? To do what's necessary for the advancement of the gospel? That's what really matters . . . way more than a silly game!

Jesus put it all on the line for us. Are we willing to do it for Him?

**What are you willing to give up or sacrifice—to put
on the line—for the sake of impact?**

Righteous and Devout

✝

There was a man in Jerusalem whose name was Simeon; and
this man was righteous and devout, looking forward to the
consolation of Israel; and the Holy Spirit was upon him.

Luke 2:25

Near the beginning of Luke's gospel, when baby Jesus was being presented to the temple in Jerusalem according to religious customs, we're briefly introduced to a man named Simeon.

We're not told much about his life, but what we *are* told is that Simeon was "righteous and devout." Now, if you've grown up in the church, I'm sure you've heard those two words before. They're words that we don't typically use in everyday conversation. After looking at the Greek, I've formed a new appreciation not only for these two words but also for the type of man Simeon must have been.

The Greek adjective translated "righteous" is *dikaios*. It means correct or just. One study resource I read defined it as being "approved by God."[67] Simeon lived in a way that his life was approved by God. The Greek adjective translated "devout" is *eulabés*. It means "taking hold of what is good"—to carefully pursue something that you feel is truly worthwhile.[68]

The problem, however, is that we often can be "devout" toward all the wrong things. We can feel as though something is worthwhile but, when the dust settles, realize that it really wasn't. What I love about this passage is that these two words appear together. Simeon was both devout *and* righteous. He must have been careful in what he pursued, making sure it aligned with what God wants. May my life, and yours, be marked by these two adjectives.

How would people describe you?

A Prayer to Be Different

✛

Lord, I don't want to be like everyone else. I want to be different—not for the sake of being different but for the sake of obedience. When You ask me to do something, even if it might be uncomfortable or against the grain, I want to be willing to do it.

As Your beloved and chosen child, I am called to imitate You—in word, in thought, and in action. This means doing nothing out of selfish ambition but instead showing humility, considering the best interests of others ahead of my own. Today, as I clothe myself with compassion, kindness, gentleness, and patience, may I . . . deny self and pick up my cross . . . be quick to listen, slow to speak, and slow to anger . . . do all things without complaining or arguing . . . treat everyone as an image bearer . . . choose character over popularity . . . and boldly proclaim the praises of the One who called me out of darkness into His marvelous light!

When people ask me why I am different, may I say with confidence, "Because Jesus has made me different!" for I have been crucified with Christ. It is no longer I who live but rather Christ who now lives in me.

In Your name. Amen.

Based on: Ephesians 5:1–2; 2 Timothy 1:9; Philippians 2:3–5; Colossians 3:12; James 1:19; Philippians 2:14; 1 Peter 2:9; Galatians 2:20

Our Entire Selves

✤

*Love the LORD your God and walk in all His ways,
and keep His commandments and cling to Him, and serve
Him with all your heart and with all your soul.*

Joshua 22:5

O ur mission for this world is simple: to love God and love others. To love others, we must love God first, and the Bible instructs us how to do that.

We are multifaceted beings. We are more than our genetic makeup or career or passions. We are more than our physical bodies, our minds, or even our spirits. We are comprised of different parts, all equally important in our service to God. To love Him fully, we must love with all those parts. That means that every aspect of our lives, whether spiritual or mundane, is an opportunity to show our devotion to Him.

We can honor Him by keeping these different areas healthy, including our finances and physical bodies, so that we can, in our love for Him, present ourselves as offerings acceptable to God, presenting our best before Him.

We are humans, not robots, and we need to take care of ourselves. When we keep every part of our lives in check, we will be in better shape to run the race set before us—to pursue the mission that God has called us to.

*If you were to rank the aspects of your life, which would
be healthiest? Which would be the least healthy?*

Finances

✝

Honor the LORD from your wealth,
And from the first of all your produce.

Proverbs 3:9

When you get your paycheck, what is the first thing you do with your money? Do you set some aside into savings or pay off bills? Do you use it as an excuse to treat yourself? Do you tithe a percentage to the Lord? The way you handle your money can say a lot about your financial health.

You may not feel like you have any wealth to manage. When you are living paycheck to paycheck, it's difficult to imagine how you could honor God with the little that you have. I don't want to undermine the financial struggle that many people face. Growing up in a missionary family, I witnessed my parents support our family on next to nothing and continue to trust God with their finances. They gave even when they had too little left to afford a meal.

I learned a lot from my parents' faith in those moments. When they didn't have much, they gave to God first, trusting that He would provide for their needs. In every season, He remained faithful to our family. Mom and Dad lived with open hands and taught me, through their example, how to live that way too. Instead of holding on to what I own or spending frivolously, I believe in giving and investing.

No matter how much money you make, you can be wise with it and learn to manage it. Stewardship has to do with your ability to handle what you are given, regardless of how much it is. Whatever your financial situation, no matter how much or how little you have, you can trust God and glorify Him through that.

Assess your financial health.
In what ways can you grow?

Strength and Vitality

✛

I am still as strong today as I was on the day Moses sent me;
as my strength was then, so my strength is now, for war and
for going out and coming in.

Joshua 14:11

C aleb was ready to fight for the Promised Land, both when he
spied it out the first time (see Numbers 13–14) and when he approached Joshua about it again over forty years later (see Joshua
14:6–15). Though Caleb was more than eighty years old when he
would finally take possession of the land, he insisted he was just as
strong as he was when he was younger. He was ready for the mission
because he was in good health.

One way to have a better chance at being like Caleb—growing
old and still maintaining stamina and strength—is to take care of
your body now. You have to get in the habit of caring for it if you
want to continue to be healthy. Just like anything in life, it won't
guarantee you'll tackle and defeat an enemy army, but it will give
you a better chance at a healthy life.

I am a big believer in nourishing my body with whole foods that
will give it optimal energy to do what I need to do. Junk food will
satisfy a craving, but it won't make you stronger. To get stronger, you
need to work your muscles, even when it's uncomfortable. This
often means starting small, but it's the small choices that add up.
You have only one body. Making healthy choices today could mean
that, like Caleb, you can continue to do what God is calling you to do
decades from now.

**What healthy choices
can you make for your body today?**

Emotional Check-in

✛

The news about Him was spreading even farther, and large crowds
were gathering to hear Him and to be healed of their sicknesses.
But Jesus Himself would often slip away
to the wilderness and pray.

Luke 5:15–16

Do you ever feel like you get so caught up in meeting everyone else's needs that you don't take any time for yourself? This can lead to overwhelming stress and eventual burnout. Although we are called to love others, we are not called to be their Savior. Even Jesus, who was fully God, needed to tend to His humanity and basic needs. When large crowds followed Him, He would care for them but then find a secluded place to be alone with the Father.

Do you follow Jesus's example and make room for moments alone with the Father? Instead of getting caught up in everything that needs to be done, it's important to step aside. Often, it's impossible to find a moment in your hectic life to step away from the noise and get alone with God, so it's important to *make* those moments instead. Use those times to check in on your own emotional needs. Assess your joy and stress, your energy and restlessness. While you can't build a mission-possible life on laziness and a refusal to go, you also cannot pursue it if you are burned out.

It bears repeating: *You are human.* You don't have to be God—you can leave that part to Him. Tune in to your emotional needs by turning to Jesus. By being aware of your own limitations, you will understand how to help other people in theirs.

How would you assess your emotional health
over the past few weeks?

A Clear Mind

✝

Let's not sleep as others do, but let's be alert and sober.

1 Thessalonians 5:6

Your mind is a precious gift. It is so remarkable, in fact, that every time you think, you are sending information through billions of neurons in your brain at an astounding 268 miles per hour.[69] In an age when we have access to tons of information at our fingertips, our minds can work overtime. It is difficult to concentrate when there is so much going on, and it can be tempting to shut our brains off to quiet the noise.

However, the Bible tells us not to sleep but be alert and sober, or to have a clear mind. God has placed us here with a purpose, and we can't allow our minds to lose focus. In a world so clouded with skepticism, doubt, and half-truths, we need to keep our eyes open and our minds sharp so we do not lose sight of the bigger mission.

To strengthen our intellectual minds, we need to exercise them. Critical thinking is a muscle that we need to work out. Read your Bible, first and foremost, but also take advantage of other resources. Read books, listen to podcasts, and watch sermons. Familiarize yourself with ideologies that align with the gospel but feel new to you. Join Bible studies and discussion groups so you can work through ideas with others, bouncing off one another's thoughts.

In doing so, you will develop deeper conviction. You will not be swayed by the world but remain resolute, able to think clearly in your mission even when everything else seems hazy.

What can you do to exercise your intellect over the next week?

Step Away

✝

*Do not merely look out for your own personal interests, but also
for the interests of others.*

Philippians 2:4

I've dug myself into a mental funk more times than I'd like to admit. Maybe you have too, thinking things like,

- *The world is so unfair.*
- *Why is life so hard?*
- *Why does it seem I'm the only one going through a rough time?*

Sometimes we can get so caught up in our own mental funk that we forget that those around us are going through hard times too. Sometimes we just need to step outside ourselves, pay attention to the world around us, and do something, no matter how small, to lighten someone's load.

Think simple. Send an encouraging text to a friend. Take time to listen, really listen, to another. Make some chicken soup for someone who is sick. Instead of constantly purging your problems, find out what another person is going through. Pray for someone instead of always asking that person to pray for you.

Forbes featured an article about how helping others reduces our own stress levels.[70] Emily Ansell of the Yale School of Medicine offered, "Our research shows that when we help others we can also help ourselves. . . . Stressful days usually lead us to have a worse mood and poorer mental health, but our findings suggest that if we do small things for others, . . . we won't feel as poorly on stressful days."[71]

A mission-possible life aims to put others before ourselves.

***Who are the people around you right now who could use
your love, service, encouragement, and prayer?***

Perspective Shift

✛

God is not unjust so as to forget your work and the love
which you have shown toward His name, by having served
and by still serving the saints.

Hebrews 6:10

I was blessed to bring Kelly Faughnan, a young girl I had met, to the College Football Awards ceremony in my senior year. We had just lost to Alabama the week before, and I had been feeling bummed about football. But when I met Kelly, my attitude changed.

Kelly had multiple brain tumors that affected how her entire body worked. She was fighting so hard to just walk. For the first time in a long time, I wasn't focused on me. I was thinking about someone else.

The awards show started and they announced the first award. I lost. *It's okay. Tonight's about Kelly.* Next award, I lost. *That stings a little bit, but it's all right.* Third award, fourth, fifth, sixth—I lost them all. I started to go right back to that place where it's all about me. It's about my legacy. It's about how people are going to look at me.

My mom was sitting behind me and could tell I was struggling. She leaned up and whispered in my ear, "You've already won tonight. You just don't get your reward until heaven." Mom was right.

When we shift our perspective from focusing on ourselves to what really matters, everything changes. When we aim to live mission possible, what will make our lives count is the impact we have on others. One of the greatest questions you can ask yourself is, *Does my life change other people's lives for the better?*

Serving others is central to our mission.

**How should you redefine
what winning looks like in your life?**

Turning an Inward Gospel Out

✛

Proclaim the good news of His salvation from day to day.
Tell of His glory among the nations,
His wonderful deeds among all the peoples.

Psalm 96:2–3

I have found that reaching out to others is important for staying grounded. It's part of the DNA of a believer in Jesus Christ. It's who we are and what we are meant to do. As the pandemic closed in-person gathering at churches, we as Christians had to learn that the church is not just a four-walled structure where you sit for an hour or two every Sunday. The church is more than a building, more than a label.

The church is a living and moving body of believers, a body that reaches out to the community as an extension of Jesus. We cannot love God without loving and caring for others.

We cannot just sit in our pews and wait for people to show up at our doors asking for help. We must leave our nests and meet people where they are. We must be ready to step into the gap when called or when faced with an unmet need. The greatest need any individual has is to be reconciled with God. Begin by sharing your faith with others. Be an example. Share the good news. Be the difference maker who can show others that a life lived for Jesus is a life that counts.

*What are two ways in your Christian life
you can shift your focus from getting to giving?*

Get a Helper's High

✝

Give, and it will be given to you.

Luke 6:38

An ancient proverb goes something like this: "If you want happiness for an hour, take a nap. If you want happiness for a day, go fishing. If you want happiness for a year, inherit a fortune. If you want happiness for a lifetime, help somebody." There are so many ways our culture promises us happiness: feeling better about ourselves by buying the newest gadget, trying a popular self-care treatment, changing something about our physical appearance. Sure, those actions might elevate our emotions, but they do so temporarily and superficially. One of the best ways to bring permanent joy into our lives is to help others.

The term *helper's high* was coined in the late 1980s, when reports confirmed that positive emotions follow selfless service to others. Studies kept coming. Research in neuroscience and psychology continues to support the theory that helping others brings happiness our way.

When we feel depressed, lonely, sad, or disappointed, our impulse is to wallow in those feelings. But when we shift our focus onto others and selflessly do something for someone else, our own spirits get lifted in the process. This feeds our souls. I'm not saying that donating money or helping a stranger is going to forever eliminate all negative feelings. But when those negative feelings arrive, fight the funk by helping another person. Helping others fosters a spirit of gratitude. It pushes you outside your bubble and into the dynamic tapestry of humanity. It increases positivity and boosts your own well-being. Truly, it's a beautiful thing.

Write about your own experiences of the helper's high.
What did it feel like? Or if you haven't experienced it,
imagine what it might be like!

Love Your Neighbor

✤

You shall love the Lord your God with all your heart,
and with all your soul, and with all your strength, and with
all your mind; and your neighbor as yourself.

Luke 10:27

I believe God puts distinct callings into our hearts that He uses to meet needs in the world, whether through our time, money, or resources. But that doesn't mean we approach each day only considering that particular need or cause. You might have a heart to help orphans or the elderly struggling with dementia. While these are wonderful ways to serve, we have to keep our eyes open to other needs too. Jesus was clear that we ought to look out for the needs of our neighbors, and that is not limited to who lives next door to us or on the same floor.

A lawyer once peppered Jesus with questions. In response to His commandment to love our neighbor, the lawyer asked Jesus, "Who is my neighbor?" Jesus responded by telling him the story about the good Samaritan: A Jewish traveler was beaten and left for dead on the side of the road. A Jewish priest came by and did nothing. A second man, a Levite, passed the dying man and he, too, walked right by. Finally, a Samaritan man came by. Although, culturally, tensions ran high between Samaritans and Jews, the Samaritan man helped the injured Jewish man (see Luke 10:25–37).

To whom are you supposed to show neighborly love? *Everyone.*

**Spend time brainstorming who your neighbor might be,
praying for eyes to see even the people
you don't want to see.**

Selfless for
the Wrong Reasons

✝

Freely you received, freely give.
Matthew 10:8

I often talk about how feelings can lure us away from doing what we need to do. If we're tired, cranky, or festering from a hard conversation, it's tempting not to even attempt to battle against those strong-willed emotions. When it comes to looking out for the good of others, sometimes it's a different kind of battle at play: a fight to do the right thing for the right reasons.

Jesus made it clear that doing the right thing for the wrong reason is unacceptable. In Matthew 6:5, He admonished people who made a show out of praying "so that they will be seen by people." He audaciously called them hypocrites.

I want to encourage you today to posture your heart in a humble way. Instead of reaching out because it might make you look good, because you want others to notice your good deeds, because you expect a certain payment for your efforts, or because you believe it will make God love you more, remember what Jesus has done for you.

Raising awareness for a cause is a great thing to do; I do it! Just consider your ultimate goal. Is it to get accolades for your effort, or to make a difference? Model the same selfless humility as Jesus to freely give as you have freely received.

What would it look like to serve for the right reasons?

It's Always the Right Time

✝

[Make] the most of your time,
because the days are evil.

Ephesians 5:16

Night to Shine is an unforgettable prom night experience, centered on God's love, for people with special needs. Our foundation has been partnering with churches all over the world to honor these kings and queens since 2014. It's my favorite night of the year. But our commitment to serve people with special needs doesn't start and stop with Night to Shine. We serve people with special needs on a regular basis through other initiatives, partnerships, and prayer.

Having a heart for other people means more than showing up once or twice a year in a soup kitchen or helping build a home for a family in need. I love the mission statement our foundation's president, Steve Biondi, subscribes to: "Wake up. Serve. Repeat."

Do it once, do it twice, and keep doing it.

Our giving to others will look different in different seasons. We will be able to give more or less of ourselves at various points in our lives, depending on responsibilities and even physical limitations. That said, there will never be a perfect time to give, serve, lead, guide, or love. We should always strive to look out for others in every season we are in, in big or small ways. Rarely, however, is it the right time to do nothing. Don't wait for a special opportunity to put your needs aside and care for someone else. It's always the right time to do what's right for others.

What are you using as an excuse for not serving others?
How can you move toward making the most of your time?

Thanks in the Loss

+

Do not be anxious about anything, but in everything by prayer
and pleading with thanksgiving let your requests
be made known to God.

Philippians 4:6

W hen I was younger, my mom would always tell me, "Thank the Lord. Give it to Him." She wouldn't necessarily tell me this when things were going well; it was when I was bummed, like when I lost a game. It feels unnatural to thank the Lord when you feel low, especially after the loss of an important game. Still, her words have stuck with me to this day. I make it a point, even now in my low moments, to say thank You to God and give my loss to Him.

When we thank God in whatever we are going through, we remind ourselves that life isn't about what we can control; it's about giving up our control to Him. When things don't go as planned, we can trade our disappointment for hearts of thanksgiving, and God can do something with our willingness that we couldn't do otherwise. We never know how He may turn the situation around. Sometimes, though our circumstances may stay the same, our hearts will change because God is working on the circumstances.

The very things that don't go your way may be the very things pointing you back to Jesus. Whatever you're going through today, instead of getting worried or anxious, thank the Lord for it. Give it to Him. The Bible tells us that when we present our prayers to God with thanksgiving, He gives us peace that we can't understand. That's a pretty good trade up.

When was the last time you thanked God after a loss?
How did that affect your spirit?

What's (or Rather *Who's*) Your Edge?

✛

I am the LORD your God who takes hold of your right hand,
Who says to you, "Do not fear, I will help you."

Isaiah 41:13

Typically, when you the hear the word *edge* in sports, you think of the *thing* that gives you a leg up on your competition. Maybe it's the fact that your team is naturally more gifted than the other or you have home-field advantage, or maybe the edge is that motivating factor you've been holding on to (for example, that loss from last year).

I know that in my life, I've had so many things that pushed me to be the best I could be. Whether it was wanting to beat our college rivals (Florida State and Georgia) or working as hard as I could to gain the respect of my teammates, there's always been something I keep in my mind to give me an edge.

But far greater than any possible chip on my shoulder or simple inspirational tactic, having a personal relationship with the God of the universe is the ultimate edge! As Moses was handing over the reins to his successor, Joshua, as the new leader of the Israelites, he said to him, "The LORD is the one who is going ahead of you; He will be with you" (Deuteronomy 31:8). This is a much-needed reminder that God is our definitive source of help, strength, and guidance. There's nothing wrong with being motivated by lesser things, but when you know Jesus, your confidence is ultimately rooted in His presence and power (see Psalm 23:4).

Identify your edge. What or who is motivating you?

A Different Kind of Edge

✛

The LORD is my strength and my shield;
My heart trusts in Him, and I am helped;
Therefore my heart triumphs,
And with my song I shall thank Him.

Psalm 28:7

R emember the concept of the edge? It's that motivational driver that gives players or teams confidence. However, a different way to think about an edge is as a barrier—a hypothetical wall that hinders you from becoming your best.

An edge is that line you don't want to cross because it's hard or intimidating. It's an obstacle that requires you to stretch, push, and move past your comfort zone. It's what's standing in your way between who you are now and who you want to become.

Most people refuse to find their edge because they don't want to experience pain, vulnerability, or potential failure. They shut down when they get pressed. But the reality is, there are edges all over your life: in marriage, in school, in sports, in the workplace. Maybe the edge is selfishness. Maybe it's a lack of faith. Maybe it's a skill you need but don't have.

I don't know what your edge is, but what I love about the concept is that it's a key personal-decision point. If you've reached the end of your natural ability or if growth has come to a standstill, you can *choose* to do whatever it takes to get better.

Remember today that real breakthrough is possible. Paul wasn't lying when he said, "He who began a good work in you will carry it on to completion" (Philippians 1:6, NIV). When obstacles come, choose to put in your work and let God take care of the results.

***What's holding you back from maximizing
your God-given potential?***

Understand the Gift of Salvation

✝

God demonstrates His own love toward us,
in that while we were still sinners, Christ died for us.

Romans 5:8

I n Luke 7, a woman with a bad reputation, who was a guest at someone's house, was anointing Jesus's feet with an expensive bottle of perfume. The host, a Pharisee named Simon, was indignant. He knew this woman's all-too-public list of sins and assumed that if Jesus knew them, too, He would be repulsed at who was touching Him. To respond to Simon, Jesus told a parable about two men. One, He explains, was forgiven a debt of fifty coins, while the other was forgiven a debt of five hundred coins. The more grateful one, He explained, would be the one forgiven of the larger debt. This woman knew the gift of forgiveness and lavished all she had on Jesus because of her gratitude.

How large is your debt? I'm not talking about your credit cards; I'm referring to your sins. Thankfully, we as believers are not in sin debt. While we were still sinners, Christ willingly died because our salvation was that important to Him. Jesus restored our relationship with our Father, and if we believe in Him, we get to dwell with Him forever. No list of debts, however long, can get in the way of that eternity.

As we begin to discuss gratitude, there's no better place to start than with that concept. Christianity is not a religion that offers course correction. When we choose to trust in Jesus, we're not going from worse to better; we are becoming new creations. Let this sink in. It truly is good news.

**Write God a love letter, thanking Him for your salvation
and for making the greatest trade in history.**

Perspective Is Everything

✝

As you have received Christ Jesus the Lord, so walk in Him,
having been firmly rooted and now being built up in Him and
established in your faith . . . and overflowing with gratitude.

Colossians 2:6–7

Have you ever played a mystery photo game? Observing only the visible details of a picture that has been zoomed in on to the nth degree, you must attempt to decipher the image in the photo. For example, you might be examining a black-and-white photo of a surface containing a bunch of holes that could be a sponge . . . or a slice of bread. Only when you zoom out and view the picture as a whole can you be sure of exactly what it is.

In the details of your life, there may not be much that you feel like you should be grateful for. Maybe you're struggling to find a job that enables you to pay your bills, or maybe you're walking through the heartbreak and grief that follows a loss. Yet if you zoomed out far enough and saw the big picture of your life, what would you see?

Gratitude is about perspective. If you look at the particulars of your life today, *grateful* may not be the first word that comes to mind. However, if you look at your life and recount the ways in which God has redeemed you, starting with salvation through Jesus's death on the cross and His resurrection, how might your perspective change?

Sometimes you need to take a distanced view of your life to see all the goodness that has already seeped through it. Keep zooming out until you can clearly see it.

***Looking at the big picture of your life, what has God
done that you are thankful for?***

The Source of Contentment

✝

I have learned to be content
in whatever circumstances I am.

Philippians 4:11

When I was fifteen years old, I went on my first international mission trip. Although we didn't have a lot growing up, we definitely didn't have to take a bucket shower or use a toilet that a ton of kids have stood on or, worse, take a potty break in the great outdoors without . . . coverage. I'll never forget visiting an orphanage filled with children who had been abandoned or whose parents had died. There was no doubt that these kids—some of whom were my age—encountered more tragedy than most people have in their lifetimes. Still, there was something special about them. They lit up. They had *joy*.

Noticing the obvious differences between their lives and mine, I realized how much I really had at home. If they could be happy with what I considered so little, how could I not be content with what I had?

Do you know the secret to being content? Paul said that he *learned* how to be content in all circumstances. He went on to say that because of Christ, he could get by with a little or a lot. Paul said this from a dirty old prison cell in which he was locked up for having shared the gospel. He knew that true joy did not come from his situation but from Jesus alone.

Whatever you're going through today, thank Jesus that He is with you. Let Him teach you what it means to be content, as well as remind you that joy is found in Him alone.

**In what area of your life do you feel
the most content? Why?**

All Your Needs

+

My God will supply all your needs according to
His riches in glory in Christ Jesus.
Philippians 4:19

When the Israelites were wandering in the desert before arriving in the Promised Land, God provided their every need. Even food. He gave them manna. Now, manna wasn't a typical food in those days. You couldn't grow it in your vegetable garden or buy it at your local supermarket. The fact that manna was there at all was proof of God's provision. The Bible tells us that every morning, manna would appear with the dew. There would always be exactly enough food per household, according to their precise needs. If anyone tried to hoard some for the next day, it would spoil.

But the Israelites got tired of manna. They wanted meat and fish and cucumbers and leeks and garlic (see Numbers 11:4–6). They wanted the foods they had eaten while they were slaves in Egypt. Though well fed and safe in the presence of God, they could only think about the meals they did *not* have.

Are you getting caught up in wishing for things you lack? If so, you're missing out. When you set your mind on what you don't have, you miss what God has for you now. He is always aware of your present needs, and He promises to always care for them. Instead of whining about the manna, be thankful for the provision God has already blessed you with. Thank Him for what He has given you and continues to give you.

*How can you shift an attitude of complaint to
one of gratitude today?*

Gratitude:
A Posture of the Heart

✛

*In everything give thanks; for this is
the will of God for you in Christ Jesus.*

1 Thessalonians 5:18

People who practice gratitude are overall happier and healthier than their more doomsday-oriented counterparts. According to a study by the University of Southern California, people who make a habit out of thankfulness are generally less stressed, less tense, and better attuned to their relationships.[72] The benefits of mindful gratitude are many, and practicing it can be as simple as saying thank you.

As Christians, we have so much to thank God for. We can thank Him for giving us His Son to die in our place, for salvation, and for eternal life. We can thank Him for giving us purpose and for calling us to go into the world and proclaim the good news of the salvation He offers. We are secure in His love, and our lives have meaning because of Him. Still, that's just the starting point. We can add more to that list.

By taking a moment every day to name just three things you're grateful for, you can shift your perspective to the good happening in your life. It could be as simple as hearing the birds outside or as huge as winning that championship game.

By practicing daily gratitude, we do more than just say thank you. We become healthier and more joyful, leading to even more abundant mission-possible lives. Start living with that intentional mindset today.

Name three things you are grateful for today.

A Prayer of Gratitude

✝

I will give thanks to the Lord with all my heart;
I will tell of all Your wonders.

Psalm 9:1

As we reach the end of this devotional, list specific things you would like to thank God for. When you're finished, lift them up in prayer, for it is because of Christ, and Christ alone, that we may live in peace with humility, joy, and gratitude.

- _____

- _____

- _____

- _____

- _____

- _____

- _____

- _____

Let the peace of Christ rule in your hearts, since as members of one body you were called to peace. And be thankful. Let the message of Christ dwell among you richly as you teach and admonish one another with all wisdom through psalms, hymns, and songs from the Spirit, singing to God with gratitude in your hearts. And whatever you do, whether in word or deed, do it all in the name of the Lord Jesus, giving thanks to God the Father through him. (Colossians 3:15–17, NIV)

A Final Word

I am so thrilled to have walked this past year with you. We spent time with God, learning about what He has called you to and what it means to live a life that counts. This isn't the end, of course; this is just the beginning. Our time together is only a glimpse into the limitless potential of opportunity that awaits when you surrender to God and begin to live mission possible.

Don't stop now—you got this!

Notes

1. Robert L. Thomas, *New American Standard Exhaustive Concordance of the Bible: Hebrew-Aramaic and Greek Dictionaries*, rev. ed. (Anaheim, CA: Lockman Foundation, 1998), www.biblestudytools.com/lexicons/greek/nas/poiema.html.
2. *Dictionary*, s.v. "purpose," www.dictionary.com/browse/purpose#.
3. Anne Craig, "Discovery of 'Thought Worms' Opens Window to the Mind," *Queen's Gazette*, July 13, 2020, www.queensu.ca/gazette/stories/discovery-thought-worms-opens-window-mind.
4. *The Britannica Dictionary*, s.v. "mission," www.learnersdictionary.com/definition/mission.
5. *Oxford Learner's Dictionaries*, s.v. "mission," www.oxfordlearnersdictionaries.com/us/definition/english/mission.
6. In my research, I've seen the Latin origin of *passion* get attributed to both the twelfth and thirteenth centuries. I don't think we know the exact dating. *Online Etymology Dictionary*, s.v. "passion," www.etymonline.com/word/passion.
7. Thomas, *New American Standard*, https://biblehub.com/greek/3958.htm.
8. Martin Luther King, Jr., The Martin Luther King, Jr. Research and Education Institute, "'Facing the Challenge of a New Age,' Address Delivered at the First Annual Institute on Nonviolence and Social Change," Stanford University (Montgomery, AL: Montgomery Improvement Association, 1956), https://kinginstitute.stanford.edu/king-papers/documents/facing-challenge-new-age-address-delivered-first-annual-institute-nonviolence.
9. Thomas, *New American Standard*, https://biblehub.com/greek/5056.htm.
10. Neuroscience News, "How the Brain Forms Habits," *Neuroscience News*, February 27, 2020, https://neurosciencenews.com/habits-brain-15805.
11. Rodd Wagner, "Have We Learned the Alcoa 'Keystone Habit' Lesson?," *Forbes*, January 22, 2019, www.forbes.com/sites/roddwagner/2019/01/22/have-we-learned-the-alcoa-keystone-habit-lesson/?sh=660fe15458ba.
12. James Clear, "How Long Does It Actually Take to Form a New Habit? (Backed by Science)," *James Clear*, https://jamesclear.com/new-habit.

13. Healthline, "How Long Does It Take for a New Behavior to Become Automatic?," www.healthline.com/health/how-long-does-it-take-to-form-a-habit#takeaway.

14. David Jeremiah, "Believe: Get Your Mind Right," *Sermons.love,* 2022, https://sermons.love/david-jeremiah/6972-david-jeremiah-believe-get-your-mind-right.html.

15. John D. Barry et al., *Faithlife Study Bible* (Bellingham, WA: Lexham Press, 2012, 2016), 17:9.

16. *Dictionary,* s.v. "ambassador," www.dictionary.com/browse/ambassador.

17. *Dictionary,* s.v. "rescue," www.dictionary.com/browse/rescue.

18. Chaim and Laura, "Word Study- Rescue Me,ינצלח," *Chaim Bentorah,* March 12, 2016, https://www.chaimbentorah.com/2016/03/word-study-rescue-me-%D7%97%D7%9C%D7%A6%D7%A0%D7%99.

19. *Britannica,* "carpe diem," May 7, 2021, www.britannica.com/topic/carpe-diem.

20. SnowBrains, "Brain Post: How Far Does the Average Human Walk in a Lifetime?," May 18, 2020, https://snowbrains.com/brain-post-how-far-does-the-average-human-walk-in-a-lifetime.

21. Douglas R. Satterfield, "The Fog of War and Other Things," *The Leader Maker,* September 30, 2020, www.theleadermaker.com/the-fog-of-war-and-other-things.

22. Indrani Basu, "Meet Nischal Narayanam, India's Youngest Chartered Accountant," *Huffpost,* July 23, 2015, www.huffpost.com/archive/in/entry/nischal-narayanam-ca_n_7855452.

23. The Tertullian Project, BookV, chapXIV, Greek Plagiarism from the Hebrews, www.tertullian.org/fathers2/ANF-02/anf02-65.htm#P7631_2301192.

24. A. T. Robertson, *Word Pictures in the New Testament* (Nashville: Broadman Press, 1933), Hebrews 1:3.

25. Josh McDowell and Sean McDowell, *More Than a Carpenter* (Wheaton, IL: Tyndale, 2011), 155–56.

26. Thomas, *New American Standard,* https://biblehub.com/greek/40.htm.

27. Billy Graham, *The Journey: Living by Faith in an Uncertain World* (Nashville: Thomas Nelson, 2007), 21.

28. Harold W. Hoehner, "Ephesians," *The Bible Knowledge Commentary: An Exposition of the Scriptures,* ed. J. F. Walvoord and R. B. Zuck, vol. 2 (Wheaton, IL: Victor, 1985), 623.

29. Thomas, *New American Standard,* https://biblehub.com/greek/4274.htm.

30. Kris Gunnars, "Intermittent Fasting 101—The Ultimate Beginner's Guide," *Healthline,* April 20, 2020, www.healthline.com/nutrition/intermittent-fasting-guide.

31. James Clear, "40 Years of Stanford Research Found That People with This One Quality Are More Likely to Succeed," *James Clear,* https://jamesclear.com/delayed-gratification.

32. *Merriam-Webster*, s.v. "intercede," www.merriam-webster.com/dictionary/intercede.

33. Thomas, *New American Standard*, https://biblehub.com/greek/4697.htm.

34. *Online Etymology Dictionary*, s.v. "compassion," www.etymonline.com/word/compassion.

35. Matthew Williams, "The Prodigal Son's Father Shouldn't Have Run!," *Bioloa Magazine*, May 31, 2010, www.biola.edu/blogs/biola-magazine/2010/the-prodigal-sons-father-shouldnt-have-run.

36. Helen Riess et al., "Empathy Training for Resident Physicians: A Randomized Controlled Trial of a Neuroscience-Informed Curriculum," National Center for Biotechnology Information, May 2, 2012, www.ncbi.nlm.nih.gov/pmc/articles/PMC3445669.

37. Stephen Trzeciak and Anthony Mazzarelli, *Compassionomics: The Revolutionary Scientific Evidence That Caring Makes a Difference* (Pensacola, FL: Studer Group, 2019).

38. Wharton Business Daily, "Can 40 Seconds of Compassion Make a Difference in Health Care?" Knowledge at Wharton, August 6, 2018, https://knowledge.wharton.upenn.edu/article/the-compassion-crisis-one-doctors-crusade-for-caring.

39. R. Keith Whitt, "What Does It Mean That God's Love Is Unconditional?," Biblestudytools.com, September 21, 2019, www.biblestudytools.com/bible-study/topical-studies/the-unconditional-love-of-god.html.

40. Fady Noun, "Mother Teresa, the War in Lebanon and the Rescue of 100 Orphans and Children with Disabilities," *PIME Asia News*, September 2, 2016, www.asianews.it/news-en/Mother-Teresa,-the-war-in-Lebanon-and-the-rescue-of-100-orphans-and-children-with-disabilities-38470.html.

41. Amy Summerville and Neal J. Roese, "Dare to Compare: Fact-Based Versus Simulation-Based Comparison in Daily Life," National Center for Biotechnology Information, May 1, 2009, www.ncbi.nlm.nih.gov/pmc/articles/PMC2597832.

42. Chris Heath, "18 Tigers, 17 Lions, 8 Bears, 3 Cougars, 2 Wolves, 1 Baboon, 1 Macaque, and 1 Man Dead in Ohio," *GQ*, February 6, 2012, www.gq.com/story/terry-thompson-ohio-zoo-massacre-chris-heath-gq-february-2012.

43. Thomas, *New American Standard*, https://biblehub.com/greek/3622.htm.

44. ThermoSoft, "Making It in America," www.thermosoft.com/en-US/blog/making-it-in-america.

45. Lewis Howes, "Erik Weihenmayer: Success Without Seeing: Climbed Everest and Kayaked the Grand Canyon Blind," May 22, 2017, in *School of Greatness*, episode 487, podcast, video, 53:56, https://lewishowes.com/podcast/i-erik-weihenmayer.

46. Thomas, *New American Standard*, https://biblehub.com/greek/4735.htm.

47. Oscar Broneer, "The Apostle Paul and the Isthmian Games," *Biblical Archaeologist*, vol. 25, no. 1 (1962): 2–31, https://doi.org/10.2307/3211017.

48. Rick Warren, *The Purpose Driven Life: What on Earth Am I Here For?* (Grand Rapids, MI: Zondervan, 2012), 149.

49. Viktor Frankl, *Man's Search for Meaning* (Boston: Beacon Press, 2006), 113.

50. Derek Gatopoulos, "Distance Runners Track Ancient Legend in Punishing Race," World Athletics, September 23, 1999, www.worldathletics.org/news/news/distance-runners-track-ancient-legend-in-puni.

51. Dean Karnazes, quoted in Sarah Keating, "The Secrets of Endurance Athletes," *BBC Future*, November 6, 2018, www.bbc.com/future/article/20181106-the-secrets-of-endurance-athletes.

52. "4 Reasons People Give for Not Sharing the Gospel," Jesus Film Project, www.jesusfilm.org/blog-and-stories/4-reason-not-sharing.html.

53. Barna defined churchgoers as those who have attended church within the past six months. See "51% of Churchgoers Don't Know of the Great Commission," Barna, March 27, 2018, www.barna.com/research/half-churchgoers-not-heard-great-commission.

54. "Coca-Cola History," Coca-Cola Company, www.coca-colacompany.com/company/history.

55. Thomas, *New American Standard*, https://biblehub.com/greek/2293.htm.

56. "Billy Graham Resources," Wheaton College, www.wheaton.edu/about-wheaton/museum-and-collections/buswell-library-archives-and-special-collections/research/billy-graham-resources; Laura Bailey, "The Night Billy Graham Was Born Again," Billy Graham Evangelistic Association, November 6, 2017, https://billygraham.org/story/the-night-billy-graham-was-born-again.

57. Stacey King, quoted in "Among Jordan's Great Games, This Was It," *Los Angeles Times*, March 29, 1990, www.latimes.com/archives/la-xpm-1990-03-29-sp-582-story.html.

58. David E. Garland, *The New American Commentary: 2 Corinthians*, vol. 29 (Nashville: Broadman, Holman, 1999), 60, with quotes from N. Watson, *The Second Epistle to the Corinthians*, Epworth Commentaries (London: Epworth, 1993), 3.

59. "Are You a Christian?," Grace Evangelical Society, January 1, 2016, https://faithalone.org/grace-in-focus-articles/are-you-a-christian.

60. David Walls and Max Anders, *Holman New Testament Commentary: I & II Peter, I, II & III John, Jude*, vol. 11 (Nashville: Broadman, Holman, 1999), 8.

61. *NIV Cultural Backgrounds Study Bible: Bringing to Life the Ancient World of Scripture* (Grand Rapids, MI: Zondervan, 2016), 2078.

62. *Dictionary.com*, s.v. "happy," www.dictionary.com/browse/happy.

63. Kyoungmi Kim, "Happy People Does Not Compare: Difference in

Social Comparison Between Happy and Unhappy People," *Asia-pacific Journal of Convergent Research Interchange*, vol. 5, no. 3 (September 30), 2019, http://fucos.or.kr/journal/APJCRI/Articles/v5n3/3.pdf.

64. John Lee, "Winston Churchill and the First World War," International Churchill Society, September 21, 2017, https://winstonchurchill.org/publications/finest-hour-extras/churchill-first-world-war.

65. Thomas, *New American Standard*, https://biblehub.com/greek/703.htm.

66. Later in rabbinic traditions, the Jewish religious leaders created thirty-nine categories of Sabbath work prohibited by the Law; see James R. Edwards, *The Pillar New Testament Commentary: The Gospel According to Mark* (Grand Rapids, MI; Leicester, England: Eerdmans; Apollos, 2002), 93–96.

67. Thomas, *New American Standard*, https://biblehub.com/greek/1342.htm.

68. Thomas, *New American Standard*, https://biblehub.com/greek/2126.htm.

69. Valerie Ross, "Numbers: The Nervous System, from 268-MPH Signals to Trillions of Synapses," *Discover Magazine*, May 14, 2011, www.discovermagazine.com/health/numbers-the-nervous-system-from-268-mph-signals-to-trillions-of-synapses.

70. David DiSalvo, "Study: Helping Others Even in Small Ways Takes the Edge off Daily Stress," *Forbes*, December 21, 2015, www.forbes.com/sites/daviddisalvo/2015/12/21/helping-others-even-in-small-ways-takes-the-edge-off-daily-stress/#2a0b9aa35136.

71. DiSalvo, "Helping Others."

72. Eric Lindberg, "Practicing Gratitude Can Have Profound Health Benefits, USC Experts Say," *USC News*, November 25, 2019, https://news.usc.edu/163123/gratitude-health-research-thanksgiving-usc-experts.

Check Out
Tim's Children's Books!

Also From Tim Tebow!

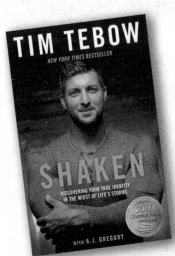

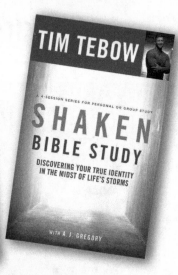

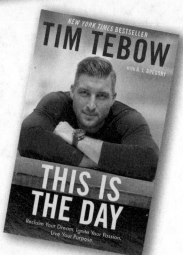

TIM TEBOW is a two-time national champion, Heisman Trophy winner, first-round NFL draft pick, and former professional baseball player. Tebow currently serves as a speaker, is a college football analyst with ESPN and the SEC Network, and is the author of five *New York Times* bestsellers, including *Shaken, Mission Possible, This Is the Day,* and the children's book *Bronco and Friends: A Party to Remember.* He is the founder and leader of the Tim Tebow Foundation (TTF), whose mission is to bring faith, hope, and love to those needing a brighter day in their darkest hour of need. Tim is married to Demi-Leigh Tebow (née Nel-Peters), a speaker, influencer, entrepreneur, and Miss Universe 2017. Tim and Demi live in Jacksonville, Florida, with their three dogs, Chunk, Kobe, and Paris.

www.timtebow.com
Facebook, Instagram, Twitter: @timtebow
LinkedIn: www.linkedin.com/in/timtebow15
TikTok: @timtebow_15

Go Deeper in Your Mission!

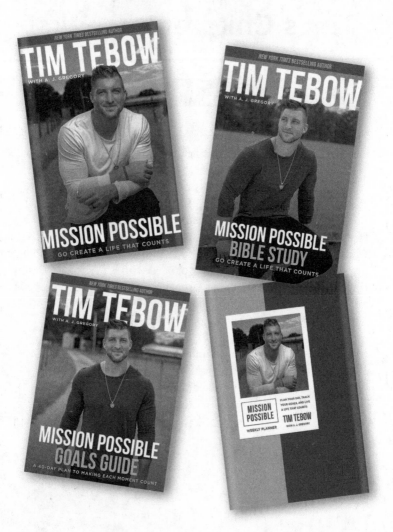